D1557008

INVESTING
WITH A
SOCIAL
CONSCIENCE

INVESTING WITH A SOCIAL CONSCIENCE

ELIZABETH JUDD

PHAROS BOOKS
A SCRIPPS HOWARD COMPANY
NEW YORK

First published in 1990.

Library of Congress Cataloging-in-Publication Data

Judd, Elizabeth.
    Investing with a social conscience / by Elizabeth Judd.
       p.   cm.
    ISBN 0-88687-471-8 : $17.95
      1. Investments—Social aspects—United States.   2. Corporations—United States—Evaluation.   3. Industry—Social aspects—United States. I. Title.
    HG4910.J84   1990
    332.6'78—dc20   89-78436
                                                        CIP

Jacket and book design by Bea Jackson

Printed in the United States of America

Pharos Books
A Scripps Howard Company
200 Park Avenue
New York, N.Y. 10166

10 9 8 7 6 5 4 3 2 1

To my family with love: my parents, Donald and Dianne; my sister, Kathy; and my grandmothers, Annette Bauman and Virginia Judd.

■ CONTENTS ■

Many people offered suggestions, observations, and encouragement during the writing of this book, and I am grateful to all of them. I would like to thank both Eileen Schlesinger and Bert Holtje, who helped shape this project from the start; Herb Kirk, who did a thoughtful and thorough job copy-editing this manuscript; the socially responsible investment experts who offered their ideas and research along the way; and those corporate officials who took this task seriously, lending their perspective to the project.

What strengths this book has I owe to friends and colleagues sending news clippings, making recommendations, and offering their own views on social responsibility issues. For this I would like to thank Donna Minkowitz, Sharon Harvey, Leon and Tanya Pein, Yunah Kim, Susan Wilder, Douglas Pinsky, Pamela Morris, Scott Schrader, and Richard Chimberg. I am particularly indebted to Todd Hollister, who did some of the initial library research for me and taught me to do the rest.

I am grateful to my mother and father in many ways, but particularly for doing an excellent job editing an early draft and for encouraging me throughout this project.

Finally, I wish to thank Michael Wilder, who edited, took phone messages, offered needed moral support, and lived every line of this book by my side.

INVESTING WITH A SOCIAL CONSCIENCE

INTRODUCTION

I n the West African savanna, a biblical-sounding scourge, river blindness, has claimed the sight of more than 300,000 inhabitants. The disease is spread by tiny black flies that breed in fast-moving water; people bitten by these flies are infected with a parasite the offspring of which causes severe itching and frequently causes blindness. "Here," the chief [of a Mali village] says, "before you have white hair it is normal to become blind."[1]

In early 1980 Merck researchers proposed treating people infected with these parasites with Ivermectin, the Merck drug used successfully in battling livestock parasites. Management agreed to the experiment even though its prospects were not attractive from a commercial standpoint given that those suffering from river blindness could not afford the treatment. Merck found that the drug killed the microworms that cause the most serious symptoms of river blindness. The company made a decision, both compassionate and rare: It would provide Ivermectin, free of charge, for as long as it is needed to combat river blindness.

EVANS ISLAND, PRINCE WILLIAM SOUND—Once a sanctuary for loons and kayackers, the rocky coves here are swarming with a noisy, mechanized army in yellow rain suits. One squad, 100 strong and armed with fire hoses, fans out across a 100-yard stretch of cobbled shore, attacking with plumes of water and jets of steam. Others do battle from barges, using huge nozzles mounted on booms to blast cascades of water at the cliffs. [from "Stuck in Alaska," *The Wall Street Journal*, July 27, 1989]

Back in the mainland U.S., nearly 20,000 angry Exxon customers returned their credit cards, cut in two, to the company they hold responsible for the *Valdez* catastrophe. Others snatched up T-shirts emblazoned with TANKER FROM HELL and WE DON'T CARE. WE DON'T HAVE TO CARE. WE'RE EXXON.

Both of these scenarios illustrate how investing in a company can involve people, emotions, and ethical principles. Socially responsible investors acknowledge this and factor these responses into the investment equation. Wall Street's approach to the stock market has historically been pseudo-scientific—some analysts draw graphs, others plug complex equations into their computers; this money manager buys companies selling at half book value and that money manager invests in companies insiders are abandoning. And yet investing is not a science like physics or chemistry. If it were, one approach to investing would be proven right and all others discarded!

The social investment movement encompassed nearly $500 billion worth of assets invested according to some type of ethical screen as of the fall of 1989, according to the Interfaith Center on Corporate Responsibility (ICCR), a coalition of religious institutional investors, which monitors ethical investment issues. One reason that the movement has gained respect is that the returns of some ethical funds have far surpassed that of the Standard & Poor's 500, an index of the 500 stocks with the largest capitalization at a given time.

In 1988 two socially screened mutual funds, the Parnassus Fund (+42.8%) and the Ariel Growth Fund (+39.9%) ranked third and fifth, respectively, among the 1550 mutual funds Lipper Analytical Services tracks each year. This compares very favorably to a 16.5% gain for the S&P 500 that year. The strong performance of these funds has quieted skeptics and attracted new investors to the socially responsible investing movement.

If there's one thing Wall Street doesn't argue with, it's results!

How This Book Was Written

This book will primarily focus on the stock market, perhaps the most complicated and bewildering area for the ethical investor given the diverse characters of the thousands of companies listed on the stock exchanges, and the thousands more traded over-the-counter. And yet what makes the task difficult also makes it exciting. In this book ethical issues will be examined and discussed, standards will be offered against which behavior can be measured and, most importantly, 200 companies will be profiled to show how these principles are upheld through corporate practices.

One corporate spokesman complained that his company had erroneously been placed on a list of companies with South African operations. Like the child's game of telephone, these operations grew a little larger with each retelling and the company found itself on a growing number of boycott lists despite the fact that it had never maintained operations in South Africa. It took years, he said, for the company to stanch the flow of rumors, and he suggested that investor responsibility be addressed as well as corporate responsibility. In response the steps taken in researching this book are outlined below.

Each company profiled in this book was sent a general questionnaire on social responsibility as well as a letter addressing specific issues, news items or questions about its business. Responses varied greatly; some companies sent detailed answers and cartons full of supporting materials, while others did not respond at all. Those companies that did not reply were telephoned and either re-sent the questionnaire or interviewed over the phone—unless, as happened in a few cases, the company declined to respond altogether. All were asked to send materials that pertained to the questionnaire and invited to provide further information to back up their responses.

Because social disclosure is one aspect of a company's overall make-up, the *type* of response each corporation made is noted in the *Fast Facts* section of each profile. "Responded to questionnaire" and "Did not respond" are self-explanatory; however, "Responded with information" indicates that the company either supplied detailed written or oral information for most of the questions asked. "Responded with limited information" means that the company declined to respond to several key questions, and "Responded with annual report/printed material" indicates that the company did not answer specific questions, but did send some form of corporate literature.

The write-ups are a combination of news files on each company and the company's response to inquiries. Whenever news stories and corporate comments conflict, both sides are presented, even though in a few cases these sides directly contradict each other. Every company profiled was mailed a copy of its write-up so it could correct any inaccuracies before the book went to press. What follows has been filtered through this process.

These profiles are brief looks at complicated organizations. In some cases, this is as it should be—the company's essence can be grasped by a few representative policies or facts. In other instances, intricate histories are boiled down to a few telling activities, policies or events. Since the same method was used in profiling each company, the profiles should be consistent. Each profile discusses all the issues in the following chapters for which information could be located, and any unusual or noteworthy extras. However, routine benefits are not listed, nor are typical charitable contributions that could characterize any number of companies. Lengthy descriptions of corporate operations have been left out unless what the company does is of social or environmental interest.

Other omissions and gaps arise from having made inquiries to which companies are unaccustomed to responding. For example, corporations with South African operations are generally quite willing to supply a well written and extensive information sheet on what steps they have taken to help non-whites in that country. And yet companies rarely give out affirmative action information beyond EEO figures for women and minority groups, and many refused to provide these statistics. Frequently, information is supplied for blacks and not for other minority groups; that is because organizations and publications like the NAACP and *Black Enterprise* magazine have begun to investigate corporate policies, while this information is unavailable for other minorities. Similarly, discrimination based on age, sexual preference, religion, or against the handicapped or individuals with AIDS is rarely being addressed at this time, and is regrettably absent from most entries.

Sometimes, deciding what details to include in a profile was extremely difficult. An anonymous tip from an employee at a company with an excellent reputation said the glowing reports were undeserved. The letter likened the situation to incest, where bad acts aren't seen by the neighbors. These ethical dimensions do affect employees; this individual was clearly suffering because of his or her situation. After several conversations with the company, it became clear that the points the letter-writer raised were sometimes true, but generally minor. The company *is* a good one, although not perfect, and within the spectrum of corporations it is much better than most. Socially responsible investing merges the ideal with the attainable; against what companies ought to be, investors must measure what corporations are.

How To Gather Information

Anything that can clue you into the nature and personality of a company is an important evaluation tool. Companies publish information about themselves in their annual reports and 10-K Forms, which all publicly listed companies are required to file with the Securities and Exchange Commission and can be obtained through the corporation's investor relations department. Although financial data must be disclosed in detail, corporations are not currently under any obligation to publish descriptions of, or statistics on, their social initiatives. Still, there are several places in an annual report where valuable social information is often tucked away: a short section on legal proceedings following the financial tables and charts; the composition of the board of directors; and occasionally a mission statement. Some companies are beginning to acknowledge that the social dimensions of their activities are important, too, and these companies might include information on community projects or the environmental impact of their work either in their annual reports or in separate publications addressing these issues. A much smaller number of companies publish equal employment numbers. Most companies that do take the time to write about their social and community projects will gladly send would-be investors these materials; inquiries should be made through the investor relations department.

While all of this is valuable information about a company, it is one-sided. Companies practically never write of the more disturbing aspects of their businesses unless the controversy is so well-known that they cannot escape addressing it. However, news sources *do* write about corporate negatives. While *The Wall Street Journal* is not specifically reporting on issues of corporate responsibility, many of its stories will have some bearing on your decisions. Magazines, television news, and daily papers are all valuable sources of information.

Many of the agencies, organizations, and publications listed in Chapter 10 can help you explore a specific issue in greater depth than general news sources can. Some of these track corporate responses to specific social issues or can direct you to that information. The ethical investing newsletters and services also monitor these issues, although many focus on companies in their own portfolios and may not cover all the companies you wish to follow. Maintaining an ongoing news file of all companies you are considering investing in will give you a solid body of information from which to decide. This file should include the company's own publications, news and magazine clippings, and any information you have gathered from books, various "watchdog" organizations, television, and friends.

■ 1 ■
SOCIALLY RESPONSIBLE INVESTING

No man is an island, entire of itself...
—John Donne

Socially responsible investing encompasses a wide range of complicated issues, but the principle is simple: investors make statements by the investments they choose, and these statements should reflect the investor's beliefs.

If money talks, ethical investors want their dollars to speak out in favor of corporations that demonstrate positive social, political, and ethical positions by the policies they adopt. From hiring practices to business guidelines to the disposal of waste, companies take stands on issues as diverse as affirmative action, military spending and the environment. The challenge for investors is to untangle the various threads in a corporation's story, weigh the good against the bad, and reach an investment decision.

Most people who have rated corporate practices agree that policies trickle down from the top. It is often the chairman, chief executive officer, or even the company's founder who sets the ethical tone for the business and determines what positions a company will take. For example, in the 1940s Johnson & Johnson adopted a social and ethical creed that its current chairman, James Burke, has upheld in recent corporate conflicts. When seven people died in 1982 from taking J&J's Extra-Strength Tylenol that had been laced with cyanide, the company opted for an expensive countrywide recall even though it was not responsible for the tampering, which took place after the medication had been shipped from the company's plant. In a separate but equally admirable decision, Johnson & Johnson underscored its commitment to the deteriorating community of New Brunswick, N.J., by approving a $50-million plan to build its new headquarters complex there. Other companies in similar situations have bailed out of economically hard-hit areas, shifting their operations to the suburbs and allowing their former neighborhoods to become even more depressed. J&J has distinguished itself through these gutsy decisions.

Another strong leader who has put his stamp on corporate policy is George Harvey, CEO of Pitney Bowes. Unlike many other companies, Pitney Bowes took an unequivocal position on affirmative action: in the 1980s Harvey mandated that 35% of new hires and promotions on the professional staff would go to women and 15% to minority members. Pitney Bowes not only holds an annual shareholder meeting; it sponsors a yearly jobholder meeting as well, giving employees an opportunity to ask questions, register complaints, and air their opinions. These examples show how investing with a social conscience entails considering a company's record on a broad range of issues rather than glancing over a column of figures and focusing solely on the bottom line.

Perhaps the most difficult part of the investor's task in sorting through corporate practices is deciding how heavily to weight each element of a company's story. In the Johnson & Johnson example the case is complicated. Although the company was profiled in *The 100 Best Companies to Work for in America*, another book chronicling the experiences of women in corporations, *The Best Companies for Women*, excluded Johnson & Johnson from its 52 top companies because the number of women reaching upper management at the firm remained small. Here's the problem: Is Johnson & Johnson a socially responsible company if a segment of its workers isn't being promoted to upper management? Fortunately, J&J simplified this Ethics 101 dilemma by initiating new programs to meet the needs of women in the workplace. After completing a task-force study, the company adopted several work/family options, including a nationwide child- and elder-care referral service and extended unpaid personal leave. The company planned to open an on-site day care center in its New Brunswick headquarters in 1990 and was encouraging other branches to do the same.

In this book issues are discussed and the positions of professional ethical investment advisers explained, but no absolute answers are offered. Socially responsible investing is necessarily flexible: It's up to the individual to decide which activities are ethical and which aren't, which issues matter and which don't, and even which areas are gray and which are black or white. This book will provide the information necessary for making these decisions.

How Does Socially Responsible Investing Work?

There are three basic approaches to socially responsible investing: avoiding the bad, buying the good, and changing the bad into the good. Most investors use some combination of the three.

Probably the simplest and most intuitive of the approaches is avoiding "unethical" companies, and the easiest companies to avoid are ones whose basic businesses you disapprove of or oppose. Philip Morris, although praised by *Black Enterprise* magazine for its minority hiring and purchasing programs, won't find favor with antismoking lobbyists, and a person who wouldn't work for a nuclear weapons manufacturer wouldn't want to own stock in a company that makes missiles.

Of the roughly $500 billion invested according to some ethical screen, the lion's share falls into the category of avoidance, the most familiar example of which is the movement to shun companies with South African operations. In the second half of the 1980s, political activists and college students called on corporate America to shed its economic ties to the apartheid regime of South Africa. Two of the nation's largest retirement funds—the Teachers' Insurance Annuity Association/College Retirement Equities Fund (TIAA–CREF) and the California Public Employees' Retirement System—as well as a host of other pension funds and university endowments traded in their investments in companies with South African operations for "South Africa-free" alternatives. The movement to avoid companies that had not taken what was believed to be the socially responsible step of withdrawing from South Africa brought to light the potential power of investors' holding companies accountable for behaving as good corporate citizens.

If you plan to invest at all, buying the good must go hand-in-hand with avoiding the bad. Defining the good then becomes the first hurdle. One investor may consider any company that's not directly harming people, animals, or the environment a possible investment. Another may decide that for an investment to be ethical the company's main business must right a current social wrong. The first investor might avoid American Electric Power because its coal-fired energy emits acid-rain-causing pollutants and instead buy Xerox Corp. The second might buy CRSS Inc. for its system that reduces acid-rain-causing emissions. Investing only in companies you agree with in principle can be a difficult task. First, you must research a company thoroughly enough to be convinced that it *is* responsible and that there are no skeletons in the closet. Next, you must consider whether this highly ethical investment is just as attractive from a financial standpoint. (Most of this book is devoted to this type of analysis.)

The third approach to socially responsible investing, changing the bad into the good, is most often employed by church groups, socially conscious institutions, and activist organizations, although this need not be the case. Concerned individuals who own shares in a company can use their clout to attract attention to a position or issue through much the same routes open to institutional investors. The crux of this approach is that corporations operate on a one-share-one-vote principle, allowing even a shareholder with a small stake in the company to bring up questions about social issues at annual meetings and to file shareholder resolutions. If a shareholder's resolution gains enough support, it can be brought to a proxy vote; if it wins, the company can be forced to reverse its objectionable policy.

A Brief History of Ethical Investing

Ethical investing had its roots in religious groups which found it inconsistent to preach abstinence from certain activities and then invest in "sin stocks"—companies whose primary businesses are gambling, tobacco sales, or alcohol manufacturing. Many church groups continue to be involved in the socially responsible investment movement and have played leading roles in both the South African divestment issue and product boycotts. In 1928 the Pioneer Fund launched the first mutual fund designed specifically to accommodate the social objectives of religious groups. However, the civil rights movement; the women's movement; antiwar issues generated by the Vietnam War; growing concern over the environment, worker safety, and product liability issues created a climate in which a broader range of social criteria could be applied to investments. With the Pax World Fund, the first ethical mutual fund addressing this wide a range of issues was born. Pax was organized in 1970 to accommodate those who had asked founder Luther Tyson where they could invest without indirectly funding the Vietnam War effort. From the start, Pax looked into equal employment opportunities and the environmental programs of the companies it screened. Two years later a major investment firm, the Dreyfus Corporation, introduced its Third Century Fund, which also emphasized social and ethical issues.

The range and possibilities for socially responsible investing were not tested until the issue of exiting South Africa aroused popular sentiment in the mid-1980s. Calling for divestment became a way that antiapartheid activists could make their views known; students staged sit-ins on college campuses and erected shanties similar to those black South Africans inhabited outside Johannesburg. These actions raised legitimate questions of who should control large pools of assets being held in trust for a group. Pension funds, which represented a roughly $2.3-trillion chunk of assets in the late 1980s, turned activist too, and workers began to demand a say in where money wound up that was being put aside for their retirement, since these assets are actually a form of deferred wages.

In response to these concerns, some officers of endowments rid their portfolios of shares of companies with South African ties. The retirement funds for the states of New York, California, Wisconsin, Minnesota, and the cities of Washington and Philadelphia took leadership positions in becoming South Africa-free. And even mainstream money managers began offering services to screen their clients' investments for ties to South Africa. One prominent example is The Boston Company, which introduced its SAFE (South Africa-Free Equity) index.

Despite articles explaining South African divestment and socially responsible investing, many investors remained skeptical of the movement and its methods. Some pension officers argued that to apply social criteria to investment decisions was a breach of fiduciary responsibility, since this was not acting as a prudent man would act. At the time, statistics on ethical investment were scarce, but subsequent studies have shown that socially screened investments generally yield results similar to those of the broad market. An index of 400 major companies screened for social criteria performed in line with the S&P 500 over a five-year period through the end of 1988, according to a study released by Cambridge, Massachusetts-based social investment experts Peter D. Kinder and Amy L. Domini.

Skeptics also argued that restricting the field of investment was bound to take a toll on the bottom line. Many argued that ethical investors would be best off concentrating on financial returns and handing over a portion of profits to charitable causes. After October 19, 1987, the day the stock market plunged more than 500 points within hours, critics of socially responsible investment sounded less convincing. October 19 "leveled the playing field," said Michael Moffitt, who heads Shearson Lehman Hutton's socially responsible investing unit for individual accounts. Those uttering the conventional wisdom against ethical investing no longer appeared quite so wise when their own investments lost 25–50% in one day.

More recently, environmental accidents throughout the country have underscored what socially responsible investors have long been saying: Ethical investing *is* sound investing. Critics of the movement have missed the new reality, according to a June 1989 *Money* magazine article entitled "Tanker from Hell," which pointed out that "In today's world, polluters are far less likely to earn the best results."

Why Ethical Investing Is Sound Investing

The skeptics' arguments overlook the pluses of ethical investing. The first argument in favor of socially responsible investing is the flip side of the skeptic's objection. Everyone agrees that restricting investments to those that jibe with an investor's conscience means passing up some stellar financial opportunities, yet all investors—no matter how high-tech their computer systems or encyclopedic their memories—must somehow restrict themselves. And the investor who takes on the Herculean task of keeping track of every stock traded on every exchange cannot possibly do such a thorough job that no opportunities squeak by unnoticed. If some restrictions are necessary, why not let them be social ones?

In practice, most investors limit themselves to a specific type or group of stocks that they research and then consider for investment. Professional money management firms, which cater to institutional investors such as pension funds, endowments, and foundations, often distinguish themselves from competitors as much by their choice of universe (the group of stocks from which they make investment selections) as by their stock-picking ability. Some firms feature a universe of small capitalization stocks and others offer a universe of large cap stocks like those in the Standard and Poor's (S&P) 100. Still other firms make most of their investment purchases from just one industry; for example, technology and drug/biotech funds all but rule out other industries. Sophisticated institutional investors generally employ several managers with different styles, but even they tend to tilt toward one or two approaches. (Otherwise one manager's style would tend to cancel out the next one's, and over time the returns would approximate those of the broad market.) The confusion of just settling on a universe of stocks justifies the old joke that if you laid all the economists in the world end to end, they wouldn't point in the same direction.

That choosing a universe is something of a coin toss is good news for the socially responsible investor; he or she can define an investment universe according to conscience and be no more handicapped than other investors also ruling out vast numbers of stocks. Restricting the field is therefore not a problem. But why are social screens good ones to use?

Although corporations are not like cowboy movies where good always triumphs over evil, many believe that over the long run companies with sound ethical and business practices will outperform their less responsible (and often less responsive) peers. For example, companies that opted for short-term profits rather than investing in the equipment necessary to clean up or reduce air emissions could soon be hit with big bills to straighten up their acts. In 1989 President George Bush announced a three-part proposal on clean air, addressing acid rain, urban smog, and toxic air emissions. (Acid rain is caused by sulfur dioxide and nitrogen oxide emissions, which come from coal-fired electric utilities and gas-powered vehicles. These emissions enter the atmosphere and return as acid rain, fog, or snow.) The Bush plan mandated a 12-million-ton reduction in acid-rain-causing pollutants by the year 2000. Although the plan will certainly be modified before it is passed, several utility companies will be hurt by this law. Because most ethical investors would have avoided these environmentally irresponsible companies, they are not confronted with the economic impact of this type of legislation.

Examples abound: Most socially responsible investors would have shunned Union Carbide, and so would have remained economically unhurt by the Bhopal tragedy. Ditto for the Exxon *Valdez* catastrophe. In many ways socially responsible investing is a very conservative approach to stock-picking, since investors following their consciences generally steer clear of potential problems before they strike. One ethical investor says that he sleeps better knowing it won't be his companies making the morning headlines for an environmental spill or equal employment lawsuit.

Although this next argument cannot be quantified, it seems clear that companies willing to wrestle with current social issues will be better equipped to grapple with the business issues they're also encountering. Conversely, companies that refuse to tackle these issues might also back away from important business questions and be slower to pick up on industry trends. Often companies that allow their employees the time and resources to be creative come up with innovative new products or strategies. One favorite of ethical investors, Maytag Corp., has had an employee participation program in place since the 1940s. In addition to making for lonely repairmen, Maytag-brand machines have won praise from the environmentally concerned because they now require much less energy to operate than they did years ago.

Given the impending shortage of qualified professionals predicted for the next few decades, companies that haven't taken ample steps to secure special benefits for their employees may find that they've lost many qualified women to companies that made these forward-thinking changes long ago. To its credit, Corning Inc. frankly admitted its shortcomings in this area and has made significant changes to stem its loss of women and black employees. A corporate study revealed that while Corning was doing a good job recruiting and hiring women and minority members, it was not retaining them—between 1980 and 1987 one in six black professionals and one in seven female professionals resigned, while only one in 14 white males with comparable jobs left the company. Responding to this problem, CEO James Houghton introduced a wide variety of work options and told male executives that their own promotions would in part hinge on their ability to help qualified female and minority employees reach their potential. Corning estimated that replacing the minority members and women who left cost them $2 million a year![1] In addition to these bottom-line savings, it seems that a company willing to take the lead on these types of issues will hold onto a more talented workforce and ultimately be stronger financially.

A third argument for the success of an ethical portfolio is based on liquidity—the flow of funds—and is quite speculative. While one socially responsible investor is not about to cripple Royal Dutch/ Shell, the boycotts against it for its South African operations do have a financial impact on the company and on its stock price. Beyond all of the technical and fundamental reasons for a rise in stock price, a company's shares go up because people are spending more money to buy those shares than to sell them. If applying ethical criteria to investments becomes a widely accepted practice, there will be a flow of funds toward stocks considered socially responsible and away from those perceived as objectionable. This translates into the prices of ethical issues rising and of others falling. Therefore, people who've made ethical investments early are likely to make a profit from their principled behavior.

When funds from the over $2-trillion chunk of pension assets—obviously a formidable force in the market—were directed toward companies with South African restrictions, this put pressure on corporations to change their policies on doing business with South Africa. It also meant that funds poured into companies without South African ties and helped push up their stock prices. Because the market is so complicated there are no statistics on the effect of this flow of funds, however, it was an obvious boon. Although the South African divestment movement has slowed, a similar flow of funds could benefit a different group of stocks if social pressure were applied. With activism growing about environmental issues, buying companies with strong records on this issue might be a smart move. Meanwhile, companies whose main business is environmentally attractive, like Imco Recycling or Allwaste, could profit from new legislation, setting tough recycling or cleanup agendas for corporations. As in all investing, being first to spot a trend could mean big profits. That this might coincide with what the investor views as the ethical thing to do makes it even more attractive.

■ 2 ■
THE
ENVIRONMENT

There was a strange stillness. The birds, for example—where had they gone? Many people spoke of them, puzzled and disturbed. The feeding stations in the backyards were deserted....
No witchcraft, no enemy action had silenced the rebirth of new life in this stricken world. The people had done it themselves.
—Rachel Carson, *Silent Spring (1962)*

I
f a single issue will propel socially responsible investing into the headlines in the 1990s, it is the environment. The reasons for this sound like a grim science-fiction tale: the hole in the ozone layer that appears over Antarctica each spring, medical waste washing up on East Coast beaches, shades of Love Canal as children play in toxic waste near Niagara Falls, pools of oil on Prince William Sound, the Greenhouse Effect. And the most frightening part is that this is the nightly news, not a novel.

Yet signs of concern abound. *Time* magazine pictured "Endangered Earth" on the cover of its January 2, 1989, issue instead of its traditional person of the year. The environment was billed as the star of the fall 1989 television season in a *Wall Street Journal* article,[1] and Ben & Jerry's Homemade Inc., a favorite of ethical investors, dubbed one of its new flavors Rainforest Crunch to inform ice-cream eaters about the plight of Brazil's trees. In 1989 both Fidelity Select Portfolios and Tucker Anthony and R. L. Day's Freedom Funds each launched a fund devoted exclusively to environmental investments. Prior to these funds, the New Alternatives Fund, which features alternative energy investments, was the only one tackling issues akin to the environment. And in September 1989 the ethical investment community itself seized the momentum of media attention and popular outrage to post the *Valdez* Principles, a set of standards that corporations are being asked to endorse and adopt voluntarily.

The *Valdez* Principles

Drafted by the Coalition for Environmentally Responsible Economies (CERES), a project of The Social Investment Forum, the *Valdez* Principles "are designed to be a stick and a financial carrot for a new corporate consciousness," according to Joan Bavaria, who co-chairs CERES and is president of Franklin Research & Development.[2] Each of the ten principles asks corporations to recognize their responsibilities beyond the bottom line. The first sentence states: "By adopting these principles, we publicly affirm our belief that corporations and their shareholders have a direct responsibility for the environment." Not only will corporations be told of what steps they should take to become more environmentally responsible, but investors will be able to gauge a company's commitment to environmental issues by whether or not it signs the *Valdez* Principles and what compliance rating it earns.

Although the principles had not yet collected corporate signatures by late 1989, they still are good guidelines for ethical investors to use when evaluating investments on environmental grounds. The following list sums up what is called for by the principles:

Minimizing or eliminating the release of pollutants that harm air, water, the earth, or its inhabitants

Minimizing practices that contribute to the Greenhouse Effect, ozone depletion, acid rain, or smog

Conserving nonrenewable natural resources and protecting wildlife and wilderness

Minimizing the creation of waste, especially hazardous waste

Recycling when possible, and when not, disposing of waste responsibly

Using safe and sustainable energy supplies

Employing safe technologies and taking precautions to minimize health, environmental, and safety risks

Marketing environmentally safe products

Informing consumers of the environmental impact of the products they buy

Compensating victims of damage

Disclosing environmentally harmful operations

Appointing a board member qualified to represent environmental interests

Evaluating progress and working toward environmental audit procedures that will be available to the public

The principles are a reach that exceeds the grasp of most corporations today, yet most agree this area warrants swift and serious action.

Handling Waste

The Environmental Protection Agency (EPA) projects that by 1995 half of the nation's roughly 5400 landfills will be closed.[3] Philadelphia has already run out of room for its refuse and must negotiate to rid itself of the 800,000 tons of waste generated each year.[4] This space shortage is driving disposal costs up and creating an economic incentive, as well as an environmental one, to recycle. A July 17, 1989 *Business Week* article noted that New Jersey cities, which paid only $30 a ton to dump refuse in 1987, were forking over around $100 per ton by the summer of 1989.

Given that several publicly listed companies' main business is environmental cleanup, investors can buy directly into companies that solve the problem rather than just avoiding those that create it. Recycling is one of the best-established alternatives to dumping waste and has been particularly successful for aluminum cans and paper. The United States produces nearly 80 billion aluminum cans each year, and nearly 55% of these are recycled. During the first half of the 1990s, an estimated 75% of all cans will be recycled. Imco Recycling's primary business is aluminum recycling, and other major recyclers include Alcoa, which recycled 16.1 billion cans in 1988, Reynolds Metals, and Anheuser-Busch. Not only does recycling reduce the volume of waste reaching already-crowded landfills, but manufacturing an aluminum can from recycled metal requires only 5% of the energy used to make it from raw materials.

While paper and aluminum have long been successfully recycled, one of the biggest challenges is recycling plastics. Wellman Inc., the nation's largest plastics recycler, buys up most of the roughly 1.5 billion two-liter soda bottles returned each year, recycles the plastic, and manufactures a wide range of products from it, including the fuzz on tennis balls and resins for plastic moldings on cars.[5] Meanwhile, Archer Daniels Midland, a major grain-processing company, has patented a cornstarch-based additive that when blended with normally nonbiodegradable plastic makes the final product degradable.

Growing awareness of the landfill problem is spurring consumer companies to find innovative ways of using recycled packaging. Procter & Gamble, which accounts for an estimated 1% of the nation's solid waste, is selling Spic & Span in a recycled plastic bottle[6] and is considering selling liquid detergent refills in thin envelopes that would allow consumers to reuse rather than throw away the original containers. Meanwhile, P & G is experimenting with recycling disposable diapers; these bulky, nonbiodegradable products have caused great concern because of the space they take up in landfills. In a Seattle landfill, P & G is separating the plastic part of the diaper from the paper and recycling each into new products. One company that is not publicly traded but has attracted attention in the last year is RMed International, which markets what it claims is a biodegradable diaper. RMed came up with the catchy slogan "Change the world one diaper at a time."

Many companies that are not responsive to the country's growing garbage problem are being protested or boycotted by environmental groups. McDonald's has been attacked for its use of plastic Styrofoam boxes, which are not biodegradable and can only be recycled into other materials. Some cities, including Minneapolis and Berkeley, have banned these plastics, declaring themselves polystyrene-free zones. The Golden Arches does, however, use recycled paper for its Happy Meal packages and recycled plastic in some of its trays,[7] and is starting a polystyrene recycling program at some locations.

Other corporations not so visibly involved in the landfill crisis demonstrate their concern for the environment by recycling at the office. Hewlett-Packard's headquarters launched its "Recycling Makes Cents (and Dollars)" program, which saves the company money in two ways: It is paid for paper that would have otherwise been thrown away and it saves on trash removal costs. The computer concern works with an outside recycling coordinator, which sorts the paper and then provides the staff and equipment to remove it.[8] Hewlett-Packard cut its landfilling by 46% just two years after initiating the project. Browning-Ferris Industries began a paper-recycling drive at its Houston headquarters in early 1989, the proceeds of which fund the company's Cares About People charitable program. Other companies provide sorting bins for employees so that recyclable paper and cans can be easily separated from other trash.

Another way of tackling the landfill shortage is waste-to-energy, a process by which trash is burned and the energy generated harnessed and sold to the local utility. The two premier companies in this area are Wheelabrator Technologies, which inaugurated the first waste-to-energy plant in 1975, and Ogden Projects.

Toxic Waste

In addition to the landfill shortage, the disposal of toxic waste poses increasingly serious problems. Methods for handling toxic chemicals once believed to be adequate are now creating unforeseen problems. Love Canal, the community in upstate New York built atop a municipal and chemical waste dump, is one of the most famous examples. Hooker Chemical bought this strip of land in the 1940s and dumped toxic chemicals there until 1953, when it filled in the land. Houses were built both on the land and near the site. Over time the chemicals buried in the canal began to surface—homeowners reported strange smells and high levels of carcinogenic polychlorinated biphenyls (PCBs) were discovered in storm-sewer systems. Women began experiencing unusually high rates of reproductive problems, and eventually all but 86 of the 900 families that lived along Love Canal were evacuated.[9] Occidental Petroleum, which purchased Hooker in 1968, is being investigated for its waste-hauling record, as are three other companies for a toxic waste site just 2.5 miles from Love Canal. In an eerie episode of history repeating itself, carcinogenic compounds associated with rubber production have been found near Niagara Falls, and once more families are faced with the possibility of abandoning the site and their homes.[10]

Although this is not a first for Occidental, waste problems plague even companies with the finest community records. Eastman Kodak, known as the Great Yellow Father for its protective attitude toward its employees, recently found that methylene chloride, a chemical used in manufacturing film, had contaminated groundwater near its headquarters at Kodak Park in Rochester, N.Y.[11] The company agreed in writing to reduce the emission of methylene chloride from its facilities 30% by 1991. It will also spend $100 million on a five-year project to replace or upgrade its chemical-storage tanks.

The responsibility for cleaning up these sites is often a tricky legal issue, although recent suits have determined that companies rather than their insurers are generally liable. Up until the 1980s, companies were rarely called upon to clean up their messes. In 1980 Congress realized that Love Canal was probably the tip of the iceberg and that thousands of other contaminated sites would require remedial action. The Superfund program was designed to set aside money to clean up these sites. The EPA is in charge of deciding which companies are responsible for waste sites that are in urgent need of attention. Typically, a corporation is named a "potentially responsible party" for the cleanup of a site along with other companies that have dumped there, too; the company's share in cleanup costs may not have been determined at the time it is named a potentially responsible party.

One burgeoning area in waste management is companies cleaning up hard-to-handle situations, especially toxic ones. Chemical Waste Management, 79% owned by Waste Management, is one such company, and others include Kimmins Environmental and ENSR Corp. In the field of asbestos abatement several companies have recently emerged—Allwaste and the Brand Companies, to name two profiled here.

Some of the major waste handlers have been environmental offenders themselves. Browning-Ferris Industries, whose reputation has suffered due to environmental violations, cleaned up its image by placing William Ruckelshaus, twice head of the EPA, at its helm. Waste Management, generally regarded as the largest environmental cleanup company, has also had its share of environmental problems, and both are being investigated for having allegedly teamed up to fix prices on containerized waste. For that reason the Parnassus Fund, which specializes in socially responsible investing, has Waste Management on its worst-company list.

Other companies have stepped in with innovative ideas for coping with the hazards of wastes in our increasingly industrialized society. Whether companies respond to these problems out of a sense of obligation or from the realization that tougher regulations will prove costly in terms of violations and remedial action, necessary changes are beginning to take place. The Toxics Use Reduction and Hazardous Waste Reduction Act signed into Oregon state law in July 1989, requires that large companies file a detailed plan for chemical usage reduction by September 1, 1991. Similar legislation is pending in Massachusetts, perhaps the start of a trend toward greater environmental disclosure for corporations. One company, Tektronix, rates its managers on environmental performance and has taken other admirable steps to correct potentially harmful situations. And Baxter International teamed up with Waste Management in 1989 to provide consulting services to health-care organizations and hospitals on the disposal of medical waste, a problem that recently became widely recognized when medical waste washed up on the shores of several beaches.

Air Pollution

The hole in the ozone layer that has appeared over Antarctica each spring since 1979 indicates that ozone depletion is a more serious problem than previously thought. Ozone, the three-atom form of oxygen, is the one atmospheric gas that prevents solar ultraviolet radiation from reaching Earth. This radiation causes skin cancers, cataracts, and global warming. Between 1969 and 1986 the average global concentration of ozone in the stratosphere had decreased by approximately 2% and over more populated areas by an average of 3%.[12] Prime culprits in this warming, scientists agree, are compounds containing chlorine and bromine, which are released by industry. Much of the chlorine comes from chlorofluorocarbons (CFCs) and the bromine from halons. An international agreement signed by 35 countries, the Montreal Protocol, mandates that CFC emissions be halved by 1998 and the emissions of halons frozen by 1992. Many fear this is too little, too late.

CFCs are widely used as a coolant in refrigeration and air conditioning; when vaporized, they form a gas used in puffing up Styrofoam. Many companies have curtailed the use of CFCs and have pledged to phase them out completely as soon as suitable alternatives are found. Aerosol cans are still the largest emitters of CFCs, but many other industrial processes are guilty as well. Du Pont, which marketed CFCs under the trademark Freon, is phasing these chemicals out of several market segments in the early to mid-1990s and completely by the turn of the century. Northern Telecom has said it will eliminate all CFCs by the end of 1990, well ahead of AT&T, which also made an outstanding effort by publicly announcing it will eliminate CFCs from manufacturing procedures by 1994 and halve its usage by 1991. AT&T ranks fifth in CFC emissions, behind General Motors, United Technologies, IBM, and General Electric.[13] Many of these companies have not clearly mapped out how to accomplish these goals, so their willingness to make a commitment is particularly impressive.

Clean Air

The Clean Air Act, which was being amended as of this writing, addresses air emissions, urban smog, and acid rain. As air pollution regulations become tougher, companies that have not made efforts to exceed existing regulations will have to scramble to improve facilities and may still be hit with stiff penalties, while companies with strong environmental controls in place will do well.

Auto manufacturers are faced with two problems: They must reduce pollutants responsible for urban smog and improve fuel economy in order to cut carbon dioxide emissions, a major contributor to global warming. (One way to cut fuel consumption is by reducing the weight of cars.) Automakers are also considering an improved catalytic converter developed by the EPA, which cuts tail-pipe hydrocarbon emissions by 30% and nitrogen emissions by 10%. At the same time, politicians such as Tennessee Senator Albert Gore Jr. are pressing Congress for a higher fuel-economy standard.[14]

Several companies have found ways to reduce air emissions. Atlantic Richfield introduced a reformulated gasoline, EC-1, in Southern California in September 1989. The product is lead-free and has lower levels of benzene, olefins, sulfur, and aromatics than ordinary gas. Arco's EC-1 is designed for older cars; although they are only about 15% of the cars on the road, they generate 30% of exhaust pollution. Arco says tests show that if all leaded-gasoline users in Southern California switched to EC-1, about 350 fewer tons of pollutants would be dumped into the air each day.[15]

Archer Daniels Midland manufactures ethanol from its corn. Ethanol reduces the carbon monoxide emissions of most cars and can be used without adjustment in vehicles. Meanwhile, a third alternative—more cleanly burning natural gas—may power the cars of the future. Pittsburgh-based Consolidated Natural Gas has a fleet of natural-gas powered cars and Brooklyn Union Gas has demonstration buses.

Acid Rain

Manufacturers may also be confronted with regulations to reduce the sulfur dioxide and nitrogen oxide emissions that cause acid rain. The cost of retooling existing manufacturing facilities (equipping these factories with the wet and dry scrubbers or injection systems that clean up emissions) is a costly prospect, but many companies are coming up with creative solutions. American Electric Power, which stands to be hard hit given that most of its energy comes from high-sulfur coal, has found a way to burn coal more cleanly. Its Pressurized Fluidized Bed Combustion process injects powdered limestone into the pulverized coal dust; this cleans up the emissions before they reach the smokestack, so 90% less sulfur dioxide enters the air.

CRSS Inc., through its NaTec subsidiary, is offering a low-cost alternative to expensive scrubber systems. Its solution is a mixture of baking soda and proprietary materials that significantly reduces emissions. NaTec anticipates this system will cut sulfur oxide emissions by 20–80% as well as reduce nitrogen oxide by as much as 40%. Innovative solutions such as this could make it possible to burn coal within allowable emission levels.

Water Pollution

Many of the toxic contaminants discussed in this chapter enter the groundwater and could pollute drinking water. But there is a unique set of water pollution problems dramatically brought to public attention on March 24, 1989, by the grounding of the Exxon *Valdez,* which dumped 10.8 million gallons of oil into Prince William Sound, Alaska. One of the most disturbing facts that emerged from the investigation was that Exxon, and Alyeska, which was responsible for cleaning up the spill, had not prepared to put their cleanup plans into action because computers had predicted that an accident of this magnitude would only occur once every 241 years.[16]

The *Valdez* spill had cost Exxon $2 billion for cleanup alone as of February, 1990—excluding the legal damages it may pay. The company faces 153 lawsuits, including 58 class-action suits. But there is no way to calculate the loss of prestige Exxon has suffered, which goes far beyond the nearly 20,000 customers who mailed their credit cards back to the company cut in half. Awareness of what damage a spill brings not only to wildlife and beaches, but to the company's finances, might spur a change. Meanwhile, new legislation could require all oil companies to be better prepared for spills.[17]

Alternative Energy

Coal has been criticized as a fuel source because its emissions pollute and contribute to acid rain. The sulfur content of coal varies by location: Eastern or Midwestern coal has a higher sulfur content than Western coal. And nuclear energy holds dangers as well: Accidents are devastating and the hazardous waste generated by the process poses a difficult disposal problem. Experts agree that the ideal form of energy would be nonpolluting—solar energy fits the bill.

Photovoltaic (solar-cell) technology has developed to the stage where it might soon be a feasible energy alternative, and prices have fallen as the technology has grown more efficient. While solar energy is the most exciting development in alternative energy according to New Alternatives, the fund cautions that it is a risky investment because it is a rapidly changing area and one company is constantly topping the next. Yet harnessing the sun to heat our homes and power our industries is an alluring solution because no pollution is emitted and the risks seem minimal. Defense giant Boeing is one company that offers a superior solar cell, while Chronar, a smaller company that is not a military contractor is also a leader in this industry.

Many concerned investors agree that protecting the environment must top our agenda for the 1990s. For environmentally aware stock-pickers, there are a wealth of companies tackling the tough cleanup ahead from which to choose. Unlike other areas of socially responsible investing, environmental cleanup companies offer investors an opportunity to participate in the solution rather than avoiding the problem.

■ 3 ■
EQUAL EMPLOYMENT OPPORTUNITY:
COLOR, SEX, AND SEXUAL ORIENTATION

No longer can we afford to spend our hard-earned dollars with those that do not employ us, promote us, use our businesses, support our organizations, and include us on their Boards and policymaking bodies. We must teach our dollars more sense.
—Fred H. Rasheed, National Director, NAACP Economic Development Program[1]

I f you decided to put together a portfolio of stocks in companies either owned or headed by women, right off the bat you'd have to cross off almost all of the companies listed on the New York Stock Exchange: High-profile U.S. companies aren't yet being run by women. This is still the case despite laws opening up the path to the CEO's office for all employees. In fact, in 1989 there were only three women CEOs of *Fortune* 500 companies: Katharine Graham of *The Washington Post* Co., Marion Sandler of Golden West Financial Corp., and Linda Wachner of Warnaco, Inc.[2] That most women-owned businesses are smaller (and therefore riskier investments) is another hurdle in putting together a portfolio of companies exclusively owned or run by women. Although the difficulty of this project underscores how far corporations must still go before equal employment is achieved, investing in companies owned or headed by members of groups that have historically been shortchanged is not necessarily the goal. Instead, the investor concerned with EEO issues generally looks for a sincere commitment on the part of management to protect and promote employees regardless of race, ethnic background, sex, sexual preference, age, and religious belief as well as Vietnam veterans, the physically disabled, and people with AIDS.

Since the Civil Rights Act of 1964 and the emergence of the women's movement, affirmative action has made tremendous strides in reversing hiring and promoting trends that have kept groups that have been historically discriminated against from rising through the corporate ranks. Not only is equal employment opportunity the law, it is increasingly attractive from a business standpoint. As corporations face greater competition, management has its back to the wall: It must either recruit and promote women and minority members or else be outdone by companies that can hold onto these valuable employees. And predictions for the 1990s point to an even more competitive workplace with a shortage of well-skilled employees to fill the growing number of specialized jobs. That's why some corporations are tailoring the workplace to suit the special needs of women and minority members. (As mentioned earlier, what's ethical is often what's wise.)

One area where fewer inroads have been made is discrimination on the basis of sexual orientation. Many companies do not have a policy explicitly prohibiting this, and the law does not always protect homosexual employees from unreasonable job dismissal. However, this could change. Meanwhile, some companies like Time Warner and AT&T have recently taken steps to protect the privacy of employees with AIDS and to make sure they are not discriminated against because of this disease.

Although minorities have made dramatic strides in claiming corner offices of large corporations and gaining entrance into positions of power, there's still progress to be made. An August 1989 issue of *Ebony* identified "The New Civil Rights Movement" as a drive for economic equality. The article argued that to achieve "black/white job parity would mean an additional two million executive, professional, sales and other high-pay, high-status jobs for blacks." *Ebony* quoted U.S. Representative William Gray III (D., Pa.) as saying the racial question has now boiled down to one of economic progress for blacks: "It's not whether Blacks can *get into* Harvard, for example, but whether they can *pay the tuition*.... Not whether Blacks can *drive the bus*, but whether they can *own the bus company*.[3] (Although whenever possible statements include all minority groups such as Hispanics, blacks, Asian/Americans, American Indians, and Pacific Islanders, more data has been collected for blacks than for these other groups and so some quotations and statistics speak of blacks alone.)

For many socially responsible investors, these issues are important both as principle and as a personal matter. Although most investors are men, at least half of ethical investment clients are women. Rian Fried of *Clean Yield*, a socially responsible investing newsletter, says having a woman on the board of directors is "a first cut" in assessing a company. He considers this an appropriate yardstick given that more than half of *Clean Yield*'s subscribers are women. An article on socially responsible investing in *Lear's* magazine estimated that women account for 60 to 70% of all individual social investment clients.[4]

Even though it is not yet common for members of historically discriminated against groups to be running major corporations, there are still meaningful choices to be made. Those corporations addressing equal employment issues by promoting minorities, by making explicit antidiscrimination statements, and by expanding benefits to meet the needs of working mothers can be applauded and nourished by investors choosing them over companies not confronting these issues. Ethical investors can send corporations that ignore these situations a message that their conduct is unacceptable either explicitly, by questioning this situation at annual meetings and through proxy votes, or by selling shares in these corporations and refusing to profit from these practices.

Tallying Up

Counting the number of female or minority individuals in upper management is one of the most straightforward ways of gauging a corporation's commitment to affirmative action. And yet corporate-wide comparisons of men to women or whites to nonwhites are generally not the best indicator of a strong affirmative action program, especially if the percentages of women or minorities at higher levels drop off sharply. A pattern like this might mean yes, women and minorities are being hired, but in more traditional jobs and for one reason or another are not penetrating what has been termed "the glass ceiling." Numbers can be deceiving; a company with one or more women on its board of directors might be taking its affirmative action responsibilities seriously; alternately, it may be trying to avoid equal employment lawsuits. It is easy to place one or two people of color or women in prominent posts, but much more difficult to demonstrate a pattern of minorities and women steadily climbing to upper management. Therefore, trends reveal more than any single set of statistics can. One last problem with statistics is that they differ greatly by industry and by geographic location—it might not be fair to compare a company based in New York City, which has an ethnically and racially diverse population, with one in Kansas.

Gannett, which runs the nation's largest chain of newspapers including *USA Today*, has made impressive strides in promoting women and minorities at all corporate levels. Of the company's 5448 employees considered upper management, 1731 are women and 588 minorities, and on Gannett's 18-member board of directors sit four women and two minority members. Not only does Gannett earn high marks for its EEO commitment, it has also been outspoken about these issues. Instead of placing the traditional photo or other graphic on the cover of its 1988 annual report, these words are the only decoration: "Diversity is strength. By encouraging and expecting a mix of opinions, backgrounds, sexes, races and ideas, Gannett improves results." According to *The Best Companies for Women*, Gannett "candidly agrees women have been historically shortchanged in pay when compared to men" and uses grade adjustments and paybacks to correct past offenses. The company's commitment goes well beyond the cosmetic. Gannett gave up its membership in the Genesee Valley Club in Rochester, N.Y., because of its policy against admitting women and returned only after this policy had been reversed.[5]

As a media company, Gannett operates in an arena in which women have historically succeeded. However, the admirable affirmative action efforts of Hechinger, an operator of building supply stores based in Landover, Maryland, refutes many companies' protests that they cannot lure women into less traditional ventures. Three out of Hechinger's 13 board members are women, as are eight of its 29 corporate officials.

That many companies recognize it as in their best interest to encourage and promote talented female and minority individuals is an encouraging sign, but such companies are not necessarily responsible on other fronts. For example, Philip Morris, which *Black Enterprise* highlighted for its affirmative action initiatives and minority business purchasing program, is under fire for aggressively promoting smoking and alcohol consumption (it manufactures Marlboro cigarettes and owns the Miller Brewing Company). This is frustrating for the ethical investor looking for tobacco-free investments, but the emphasis on affirmative action is a promising trend. Despite the fact that industry analysts predict that minorities and women will be a crucial part of the workforce of the future, 48% of blacks surveyed in *Black Enterprise*'s February 1989 career survey said they believed the chances for black managers to advance were slim, and most felt they were victims of on-the-job discrimination. Companies may be acting in their own self-interest by promoting minorities and women, but this is still a rare enough achievement that it deserves recognition.

Minority- and Women-Owned Business Development

One way that major U.S. corporations can demonstrate their support for minorities and women is through programs to purchase from women- and minority-owned businesses. The National Minority Supplier Development Council works on supporting the growth and expansion of minority-owned businesses as well as helping corporations grow and enhance their programs.

Both the National Association for the Advancement of Colored Persons (NAACP) and Operation PUSH have taken corporations to task for their records on Afro-American issues. Both groups have asked companies to sign agreements saying they will hire and promote blacks, purchase goods and services from minority-owned businesses, and set aside part of their charitable contributions for programs to aid blacks. These voluntary agreements are drafted specifically for each individual corporation. The NAACP's Operation Fair Share program, begun in 1981, has three aims: researching and selecting potential target companies; negotiating and signing formal agreements; and monitoring the company's progress in meeting these goals. The NAACP says it initiated this program after Ronald Reagan was elected president, correctly anticipating a waning in the federal government's role in social and economic programs for the disadvantaged. The rationale is simple—while blacks spend $185 billion each year, only 7.5% of that money is spent with Afro-American businesses. Therefore, white-owned businesses should take the concerns of their black customers seriously in order to hold onto these dollars.

By late 1989 the Fair Share program had signed agreements with 45 corporations. As a result, Fair Share anticipates that $350 million will be directed to Afro-American businesses in procurement contracts over the next five years, as well as $150 million to minority-owned banks, $75 million to black-owned media, and $250 million in insurance coverage through Afro-American professionals. The NAACP also projects an average 7.5% increase in the numbers of Afro-Americans working at the companies that have signed these agreements.

General Motors recently signed a commitment with the NAACP; other corporations that have done so include United Airlines, Toys

"R" Us, Chrysler, Walt Disney, K mart, Commonwealth Edison, and the Adolph Coors Co. These agreements help socially responsible investors gauge a company's commitment to minority issues. When *Black Enterprise* magazine compiled its February 1989 list of The 50 Best Places for Blacks to Work, it compared companies against 1987 Bureau of Labor statistics that said black Americans comprised 10.1% of the nation's more than 112 million employed civilians, 6.2% of its nearly 28 million managers and professionals, and 8.5% of its 3.3 million technical and related support staff.[6] These statistics can be taken as norms against which the progress of profiled companies can be measured.

Other Ways of Demonstrating Commitment

Tallying up the numbers of women and minorities in x job at y time is one indicator of affirmative action progress, but it can be misleading. Although it seems appropriate to applaud companies like Gannett, Hechinger, and Philip Morris for statistically backing up their commitment to equal employment opportunity, companies with less impressive records are not necessarily apathetic. Companies can demonstrate their commitment to affirmative action in a variety of ways. In fact, many of the problems women and minorities say hold them back are social: a lack of female or nonwhite mentors, exclusion from the old-boy network, innuendos from co-workers, inadequate provisions for working mothers, and traveling in different social circles. When companies take steps to counteract these subtle influences by encouraging professional networks for women and minority members or training managers to address these concerns, it can be a sign of commitment just as firm as board representation.

For women, benefits provide a potent sign of whether or not management is willing to accommodate the responsibilities working women must often balance. Working parents face unique responsibilities that some companies are easing by making provisions for child or elder care (either through an on-site or near-site child care center), through financial subsidies for these programs, through flexible benefit programs that allow pretax salary dollars to be directed toward family care, or through referral and information programs. Other companies offer flextime, part-time, and job-sharing options. Companies that have initiated these programs report better performance from their employees. In a 1982 survey Hoffman-La Roche found that

78% of its employees who took advantage of the company's child care center felt their work had improved.[7]

Although some companies have instituted liberalized leave policies on their own, a bill pending in the House and Senate could require them to do so. The Family and Medical Leave Act of 1989 says that employees who have completed one year of service and have worked at least 1000 hours per year will be able to take family leave (10 weeks of unpaid leave over a 24-month period for childbirth, adoption, or serious illness of a child or parent). Employees are entitled to the same position on return and continuation of pre-existing health benefits during the leave. (Small businesses are exempted.)[8]

Although only one woman at Minnesota Mining & Manufacturing holds the title of vice president or above, the company was considered one of "The 60 Best Companies for Working Mothers" in *Working Mother* magazine's October 1989 survey. That's because 3M instituted a flextime policy in 1989, initiated part-time work schedules and has hired a full-time child care administrator. With so few companies taking steps in the right direction, such changes are worth noting.

Again, these corporate practices are sound ones and companies facing challenges like these will likely have a stronger workforce in the 1990s. And the situation is growing more difficult to ignore: From 1989 through the year 2000, it is estimated that two out of three new entrants to the workforce will be women.[9] Corning's candid response to this problem was discussed in Chapter 1; other companies, like Mobil, are responding to similar business imperatives. Mobil is striving to accommodate women employees in order to stem costly attrition—the company's talented women have left at a rate two and a half times that of comparable men. Mobil has initiated a nationwide day care referral service, a spousal relocation service, and a reduced workweek program in an effort to turn the situation around.

Besides benefits, the way new employees are recruited can reveal a company's attitudes toward affirmative action goals. Corporations concerned with recruiting minorities and women often advertise jobs in magazines targeting these groups, participate in minority and women's professional organizations, and offer internships and scholarships. Companies frequently publish EEO booklets that describe their efforts in these areas. And, as noted, some corporations (like Corning) have tied managers' performance bonuses to their ability to recruit and promote women and minorities. This creates a strong incentive for employees to make sure the interests of groups that have been historically shortchanged are adequately met.

Sexual Harassment

Sexual harassment is another area of concern to working women. Because sexual harassment is the action of a single individual, it is not clear whether it is the fault of that individual alone or of the corporate culture. Many companies explicitly forbid sexual harassment and spell out the steps an employee who feels she or he is being harassed should take. However, policies against sexual harassment, no matter how strict, can be cosmetic steps to protect the company from lawsuits rather than a sign of sincere commitment. A *Forbes* article estimated that three out of four companies nationwide have a strict policy against sexual harassment on the books.[10] While having a written policy is certainly better than not, swift action taken against a sexual harassment offender may be more meaningful than even the most forbidding policy. The authors of *The Best Companies for Women* point out that at one company, news that a well-established male employee was fired for sexual harassment sent a loud and clear message that this behavior was not to be tolerated.[11] Although a company's reaction to sexual harassment claims is important, it can't be the only criteria used because it is never published in the annual report or addressed at shareholder meetings.

This tricky situation is simplified by some companies that have gone beyond statements, instituting training programs and holding mandatory management meetings on this issue. CBS conducted a study on sexual harassment, which resulted in the three major networks teaming up and filming a four-hour program against sexual harassment that all employees are required to watch.

Du Pont has also taken creative steps to confront one of the more frightening issues with which women are confronted. In 1985 the company pioneered its personal safety program, which includes an eight-hour, for-women-only rape-prevention workshop. This effort grew out of female employees' concerns about rape given that traveling was increasingly a part of their job duties. Du Pont offers its training workshop to other companies that wish to institute similar programs.

Another issue of discrimination is the appearance requirements some airlines impose on their flight attendants; these rules are often more stringent for women than for men. In August 1989 Pan Am agreed to end periodic appearance checks of flight attendants in order to settle a discrimination lawsuit pending in the San Francisco federal appeals court. The airline will pay as much as $2.8 million to flight attendants who have been fired or suspended because they failed to meet weight requirements. Prior to this decision, Pan Am's flight-attendant check list included such categories as: thighs/hips, figure/physique, and legs/ankles.[12] AMR Corp. is fighting a similar battle with its flight attendants over liberalizing weight requirements.

Sexual Preference

Discrimination against gays and lesbians in the workplace is not an issue that many socially responsible investment funds are currently addressing. That may be because it is such a difficult area to evaluate, or because many companies have done so little in this area that to weigh it too heavily would mean scratching some otherwise good candidates off the list of socially responsible choices.

And yet some of the more notorious corporate actions have become well-known. For example, Adolph Coors has been boycotted for alleged gay-baiting as well as racially discriminatory hiring practices. The AFL–CIO ended its boycott of the company in August 1987, but many groups have continued the protest. Until a few years back, the company screened prospective employees with a lie detector test, which allegedly "assisted the company in anti-gay discrimination."[13] When in 1985 Peter Coors became CEO he sponsored a gay pool tournament and attempted to give San Francisco's Tavern Guild (an association of gay bar owners and employees) $10,000 for an employee benefit, but homosexuals felt the gift was inappropriate.[14]

AIDS

As investment experts point out, AIDS is a tough issue to keep up with given the pace of research and conflicting reports on treatment. AIDS activists are putting pressure on drug companies to speed up the availability and lower the costs of drugs that can battle the disease or its symptoms. Burroughs Wellcome lowered the price of its drug, AZT, in September 1989 after activists accused the company of profiteering. Meanwhile, Bristol-Myers quickly agreed to distribute its new AIDS treatment, dideoxyinosine (ddI), outside formal clinical trials in September 1989. This followed pressure from activists and an announcement from Anthony Fauci, director of the National

Institute of Allergy and Infectious Diseases, recommending selective distribution of AIDS treatments as soon as they've been proved safe.[15]

In general, companies are careful to avoid actions that may be construed as discriminatory, and yet only a handful have taken strong and innovative steps to make sure that historically discriminated-against groups make adequate progress in the workplace. Growing demand for skilled employees could change this. Likewise, the Fair Share program, employees, and activists can all send messages to management that this issue needs to be emphasized if companies want to attract socially conscientious investors.

■ 4 ■
THE
SOUTH
AFRICA
QUESTION

Injustice anywhere is a threat to justice everywhere.
—Dr. Martin Luther King, Jr.

I n the 1980s whether to withdraw from South Africa was probably the hottest ethical issue facing most U.S. multinational corporations. More than 180 companies left South Africa during the decade, according to the Interfaith Center on Corporate Responsibility (ICCR). But as of June 1989, 58 U.S. companies were maintaining operations there and had signed the Statement of Principles, a code of conduct for corporations operating in South Africa. This chapter discusses South Africa exclusively because U.S. involvement and investments there propelled socially responsible investing into public attention. Of course, similar questions could be raised about operations in a variety of countries, and are commonly asked about international corporations operating in Northern Ireland. Although the political situations vary, the fundamental methods of evaluating whether a corporation should withdraw from a country whose practices are considered unethical are essentially the same, no matter what the geographical location.

The South African government's policy of apartheid, which literally means "apartness," is a codified system of racial segregation and discrimination, voted into law in 1948 when the Afrikaaner-dominated National party came to power. The immorality of apartheid is generally acknowledged in the United States; under this policy, the white minority (just over 15% of the population) has claimed for itself 87% of the land and almost all of the wealth. Although some of the most hated laws against blacks (including the ban on interracial marriages and laws requiring non-whites to carry passes) were eliminated in the late 1980s, the state of emergency in effect since July 1985 continues. The freeing of Nelson Mandela, F. W. de Klerk's presidency and the country's deteriorating economic situation are changes that many hope will herald the dismantling of apartheid in South Africa.

Almost everyone agrees that apartheid is morally wrong. The debate arises over what steps the United States should take to end this injustice. Despite pleas for economic sanctions against South Africa by political activists and black leaders, including the 1984 Nobel Peace Prize winner Desmond Tutu, Anglican bishop of Johannesburg, until 1986 the Reagan administration opposed this strategy, opting instead for a policy of "constructive engagement." This policy is based on the assumption that the United States' economic presence in South Africa could be a greater vehicle for change than the message sent by severing ties to that country. Constructive engagement gave way in 1986 to the imposition of partial economic sanctions against South Africa, which Congress pushed for against Reagan's wishes.

In hindsight, economic sanctions are generally agreed to have been successful since they've taken a serious toll on the finances of South Africa, and this has put pressure on the Pretoria government to consider concrete change. The magnitude of economic sanctions is difficult to gauge. However, the American Committee on Africa estimates that there was a $12-billion "capital flight" from South Africa between 1984 and mid-1989, created by economic sanctions such as unrenewed bank loans and the sale of operations in South Africa. The imposition of economic sanctions by the U.S. government had an immediate impact. From the first three-quarters of 1986 to the same period in 1987, South Africa suffered a net loss of $468.6 million in export revenues for products prohibited by sanctions. Ninety percent of these losses were from exports to the United States, according to the *Multinational Monitor*.[1]

Meanwhile, the main question for corporations—whether or not to sell South African subsidiaries and, in some cases, sever licensing ties to and franchising agreements with the apartheid regime—mirrored the political questions of the time. Just as the government had a stake in maintaining good relations with South Africa because of strategic imports, corporations with South African subsidiaries were reluctant to abandon what had been a profitable market. However, antiapartheid activists were convinced that U.S. corporations operating in South Africa perpetuated the system of racial segregation by paying taxes to the Pretoria government, by obeying South African laws, and by providing strategic goods and services to that country. In this instance, student activism pressuring university administrations to divest coupled with a similar movement on the part of many city, state, and union pension funds created an opposing economic argument favoring an exit from South Africa. As of September 1989, the ICCR estimated that roughly $275 billion worth of investment assets were being screened to eliminate companies with ties to South Africa.

The question of whether or not to withdraw from South Africa illustrates how socially responsible companies may easily come out economically ahead of their less responsible peers. Not only were companies with South African operations hurt as institutional investors dumped their stock in favor of South Africa-free alternatives, but apartheid has not proved a very profitable economic environment over the long run. Roger Smith, General Motors' CEO, explained the reasons for the sale of the company's South African operations in an October 3, 1986 *New York Times* opinion piece: "The basic problem— one which all corporations must pay attention to—is the fact that our South African operations have been losing money for several years. Clearly, a major portion of our financial troubles were generated by the very existence of apartheid." Likewise, Goodyear Tire & Rubber, which remained in South Africa until June 1989, attributed its decision to sell off operations to the faltering South African economy, which suffered from a high inflation rate and a devalued rand. And this condition was exacerbated, if not created, by Congress' 1986 partial economic sanctions against the Pretoria government.[2]

The Statement of Principles for South Africa

Despite pressures to sever ties to South Africa, many companies chose to maintain operations there. Many of these corporations repeatedly stated that they were a positive influence against the apartheid system; several spokespeople from corporations that had exited South Africa said the decision had been painful. These corporations believed that their employees, black and white alike, had been hurt by the company's decision to leave, which sometimes resulted in unemployment or harsher treatment under new management.

In 1977 the Reverend Leon Sullivan, a prominent Philadelphia activist in the antiapartheid movement and a member of General Motors' board of directors, proposed a code of conduct for U.S. companies choosing to remain in South Africa. Companies signing this code, known as the Sullivan Principles, agreed to maintain nondiscriminatory work practices such as integrated work spaces and cafeterias, equal pay for equal work, equal opportunities for all employees, and a minimum wage. Signing is voluntary; corporations that do sign are then rated annually by an outside evaluation party on how successfully they have put these principles into practice. Most corporations did participate, although some, like multinational Schlumberger, did not. Schlumberger argued that the task of evaluating the political systems of all the countries in which it operates is too great and balked at the paperwork involved in annual audits.

The well-intentioned compromise offered by these principles sparked even more heated debate. For corporations that wanted to hold onto their South African operations, a good Sullivan rating gave the decision a moral authority it might otherwise have lacked. Therefore, signing often became a way to sidestep, or at least divert, public attention from the issue of an outright exit. On this subject, Bishop Tutu said, "These principles are totally unacceptable. We don't want apartheid made comfortable and acceptable. We don't want apartheid reformed. We want to be rid of apartheid."[3]

It is estimated that fewer than 1% of South African blacks are employed by U.S. companies. Therefore, activists argue, even if the worklives of these blacks are improved by the presence of U.S. employers in South Africa, the vast majority of lives remain untouched. And even that fortunate few must return to apartheid at night. In the mid-1980s, Leon Sullivan announced that if the South African government hadn't taken significant steps to dismantle its racially discriminatory laws in two years' time, he would call for a full exit of U.S. corporations. In 1987 he did just that, renouncing his own principles as not sufficiently effective. Corporations with South African operations still receive ratings for how well they've adhered to what was renamed the Statement of Principles, although most antiapartheid activists and socially responsible investors no longer consider a good rating that meaningful.

Two Approaches: Mobil and Royal Dutch/Shell

Mobil, one of the corporations most outspoken against divestment, announced in April 1989 that it, too, would be leaving South Africa.

Its departure was spurred by a 1988 change in U.S. tax law that no longer permitted companies to deduct the taxes they pay to South Africa from their U.S. returns. In effect, this change taxes corporations twice for their presence in South Africa. Mobil's sale of its South African assets to General Mining Union Corp. (Gencor), a South African company, for $150 million was especially surprising, given the company's public declarations that it would remain in South Africa. As part of the sale, Mobil stipulated that Gencor allot $3 million annually through 1994 to continue the work done by Mobil to create opportunities for nonwhites.

In contrast to this, another major oil company, Royal Dutch/Shell Group, is the target of a highly visible international boycott and a divestment campaign that has not budged the company's policy. Although South Africa is rich in most natural resources, it has an Achilles' heel—it is extremely dependent upon external supplies of oil.[4] Foreign-owned oil companies that continue to operate within South Africa are therefore keeping one of the most painful messages of the sanctions movement from being delivered. Royal Dutch/Shell is considered an especially potent symbol of discontent because it is an international conglomerate with headquarters in both the Netherlands and the U.K., the two countries from which most white South Africans originate. The Boycott Shell Campaign, sponsored by the United Mineworkers of America and supported by the World Council of Churches, charges Royal Dutch/Shell with having shipped large quantities of crude oil to that country in violation of the United Nations-sponsored international oil embargo against South Africa.[5] The company, however, denied these reports in the Spring/Summer 1989 issue of *National Boycott News*.

The Sham Divestment Issue

The sanction argument is tricky enough, but it is only the first hurdle in this complicated situation. Determining which companies are truly out of South Africa is the next challenge. When a company sells off its South African operations, these operations are purchased by another company. The purchaser as well as the terms of the sale then become equally important factors in how responsible the company's exit was. Many companies, like Mobil, make provisions for the acquiring company to maintain the employment practices it has initiated. But others contend that the true yardstick of how socially responsible a company's withdrawal is this: Whether or not the company will continue to sell its products through a licensing or franchising agreement with either the buyer or another willing vendor. Selling off operations and yet maintaining licensing, vending, or franchising ties has been denounced by many ethical investors as sham divestment, an attempt to cloud the issue rather than take a stand. Yet companies frequently protest that without these agreements they have nothing to sell except perhaps a building and some equipment. How investors should treat these partial exits is an individual decision. Many socially responsible investing funds avoid companies that haven't completely severed ties to South Africa, but there's often no absolute way of knowing whether or not a company's products are getting through. Even if the company prohibits sale to South Africa, it's still possible that a European vendor is hawking the company's products in Johannesburg. At some point the ethical investor must accept the company's actions; the tricky question is When?

Another issue that confuses what would already be a far-from-cut-and-dried issue is parent/subsidiary relationships. For example, to boycott U.S. Shell is to boycott a subsidiary for what another subsidiary is doing. In other words, Royal Dutch/Shell owns the South African operations and Shell Oil, its U.S. arm, is just another division. Many times these issues pivot on a technicality; you may be surprised to read that Shell has no South African subsidiaries when you've also read about the boycott. Unless you sort through the parent/subsidiary intricacies, a company can publish factually correct statements that are misleading.

Several U.S. computer companies have sold off their South African assets and yet their computers are still sold there; these include IBM, Unisys, Control Data, and Hewlett-Packard. Computers are considered strategically important for keeping the apartheid government in power, so many antiapartheid activists are concerned about these partial or incomplete divestments. For example, IBM sold its South African subsidiary in March 1987 to an employee trust, Information Management Systems, but maintains marketing, sales, service, training, and distribution agreements with the trust. Other major U.S. corporations tell similar stories. Goodyear's sale of its subsidiary to Consol, Ltd., part of the South African conglomerate Anglovaal Ltd. can only be viewed as a partial victory because Goodyear has signed technical and service agreements with Consol. And the sale of Ford cars to the South African military and police has not stopped even though the company sold off most of its equity in its U.S. Samcor subsidiary to an employee-controlled trust in November 1987 because Ford maintains sales, license, distribution, and technical assistance ties through Samcor. Although it is easy to condemn these companies for obeying the letter and ignoring the spirit of withdrawal, many are caught in a Catch-22 situation. The company has a fiduciary responsibility to protect the interests of its shareholders, and yet some of its shareholders may be telling it to sever all ties to South Africa. And so these demands often create a real dilemma for companies.

What it means to be South Africa-free is blurred by such distinctions. And yet this type of inquiry can go on indefinitely, and at some point becomes quibbling. Coca-Cola has been the target of a high-profile boycott since 1987 because of its presence in South Africa. In 1976 the company began reducing its South African investment and eventually sold off its remaining shares to groups of black South African investors. So why the boycott? The Coke Campaign, organizer of this boycott, argues that until "total economic disengagement" from South Africa is reached by the company's making the product unavailable there, Coca-Cola has not fulfilled its obligations. Is Coca-Cola, which certainly isn't a cornerstone in empowering apartheid as are computers or trucks, obligated to pull its products completely out of South Africa? The decision must be yours. Certainly, it is possible to avoid all companies that have any known ties to South Africa, and this is the route many ethical investors take. But there are in-betweens, reasonable gray areas, and room for legitimate disagreement. Even companies that do not maintain overt ties to a company selling its wares in South Africa cannot police the world carefully enough to make sure that its products aren't winding up there anyway. Apple Computer, which has never had any South African ties, cannot guarantee that an independent European vendor isn't selling its computers to the apartheid regime. And if there are Macs on desks in Johannesburg, can the company really be blamed? Probably not. Potential shareholders can choose to make investments only in companies which are trying to maintain a consistent policy toward South Africa, a policy that matches their own. So one ethical investor might decide to invest in companies with no South African ties whatsoever, while another might decide to invest in companies whose products are nonstrategic. Both decisions are reasonable, and demonstrate that the investor has considered this issue.

■ 5 ■
LABOR
AND
COMMUNITY
ISSUES

Intelligent discontent is the mainspring of civilization.
—Eugene V. Debs

Many socially responsible investors are interested in how a corporation treats its employees, its unions, and its community. A company's policies toward female and minority employees are frequently fair indicators of a company's overall commitment to its workers. But other employment issues, such as how a company reacts to a downturn in business, are not necessarily reflected in its equal employment record. Digital Equipment, a favorite of many ethical investors, has never had a layoff. Although the company says this policy is not chiseled in stone, this tradition makes good business sense to DEC in light of how much is invested in hiring and training its employees. Beyond benefits and salary, companies demonstrate concern for employees through promote-from-within policies; good communication between employees and upper management; fund-matching and profit-sharing programs; minimizing the distinctions between management and entry-level positions; on-the-job-training programs; workshops on social problems like alcohol abuse and rape prevention; and on-site physical fitness centers.

When a company's programs are innovative, management has taken time to consider the welfare of its employees. For example, Federal Express is known for listening to employees' grievances no matter what title the staffer holds. And, in a more offbeat way, it demonstrates its attitude toward employees by holding a lottery after purchasing a new plane and christening the plane with the name of the winning employee's child.[1]

Apple Computer also has innovative programs: All employees from factory workers on up are loaned a computer to take home two months after joining the company; ten months later they are given the computer outright as part of Apple's "Loan to Own" program. Another stand-out in employee relations is Delta Air Lines, a particularly impressive story given the strife-ridden histories of many of its competitors. *The 100 Best Companies to Work for in America* tells how three Delta stewardesses donated $1000 each to help the company buy a new Boeing plane in gratitude for "the way Delta has treated us."[2] Why are employees so loyal to Delta? For one, Delta offers a cradle-to-grave approach to benefits and, although the company has had to relocate and reassign employees, it has a firm policy of no layoffs, something its employees appreciate.

Worker Safety

One vital sign of corporate commitment is a comprehensive safety program and a relatively clean safety record. The Occupational Safety and Health Administration (OSHA) tracks corporate stand-outs in this area through its Voluntary Protection Program. As the name implies, this program monitors companies that have agreed to be tracked and have sustained below-industry-level numbers of accidents over a three-year period. The standards are high, therefore a subsidiary or a plant is generally commended rather than an entire corporation. Likewise, OSHA generally singles out a plant or facility for a citation when it has been found by federal inspection to be violating the Occupational Safety and Health Act. In the case of violations, the company is cited along with the fine incurred.

Not paying sufficient attention to safety can cost a company in hefty penalties, workers' compensation insurance premiums, and even lawsuits, as well as jeopardizing the company's standing with its employees and community. After an employee died from a volatile chemical leak in 1977, H. B. Fuller commissioned a study of its safety standards and found that its practices were well below industry norms, and its accident rate was consequently higher than other chemical concerns'. Fuller, generally recognized as a good corporate citizen, hired a full-time safety director and allocated an annual budget of nearly $280,000 to remedy the situation. Ten years later Fuller boasted only 1.4 lost-time accidents per 100 employees, half the industry average and a quarter of its average a decade earlier. The social message is clear, but the financial upshot is also compelling. Fuller now regards its safety program as a small profit center. If accidents had continued to occur at the 1977 rate, the company calculates it would have been spending nearly $1.4 million annually in workers' compensation premiums by 1987; with the new safety measures, the bill came to only $375,000. This spells a net benefit of about $457,000 even after the expenditures for its new safety programs, on top of the incalculable benefit of good will.[3]

The Role of Corporations in the Future

Experts anticipate that in the 1990s American corporations will be called on to play even bigger roles in their employees' lives than they currently do. The needs of working parents have already spurred some corporations to extend their responsibilities to providing for child care, not so much from kindness as from a desire to retain talented employees. A September 27, 1989 *Business Week* piece entitled "The Password Is 'Flexible'" said: "The complicated lives of workers, for better or worse, will become very much a corporate affair, with employers helping see them through personal crisis or family turmoil. Such assistance will have little to do with benevolence and everything to do with the bottom line." This vindicates the socially responsible investor yet again; even companies that have shut themselves off from social problems will need to grapple with these issues to stay competitive. But the role of the corporation could expand beyond that of taking on duties that two-career families are finding difficult to meet alone. A *New York Times* article pointed out that as the workplace becomes more oriented toward technical knowledge, companies may find themselves driven to educate their employees. There are two reasons for this: a decline in the American school system, which will lead to fewer people with the basic skills employers require, and a slowly shrinking population from which potential employees will be in short supply. Therefore, whether or not corporations feel ministering to social ills is their responsibility, they will have to tackle these problems just to compete.

Motorola, Ford, Xerox, Polaroid, and Eastman Kodak all began teaching employees basic reading and arithmetic skills in the 1980s to meet their internal needs.[4] Aetna Life & Casualty has taken this one step further and is actively recruiting employees who must first be schooled in office skills before they can perform their jobs. Early in 1989 Aetna embarked on its ambitious program to fill 130 positions a year with inner-city residents of Hartford, Connecticut, where the company has its headquarters, in response to slowing growth in the workforce. Candidates for new positions are first enrolled in two months of basic skills training, followed by two months of specific job training. Supervisors say the program graduates are better prepared than recent hires, and the company seems to have hit upon a creative response to a pressing problem.[5] Which corporations will be most successful at preparing and retaining a qualified workforce remains to be seen, although the sensitive corporations of today are likely to have an edge. The following profiles list outstanding or innovative programs for those corporations that have them. Taking a company's treatment of its employees seriously now might determine who will be the most competitive and boast the best bottom line tomorrow!

Unions

Some companies take the welfare of their employees to heart without prompting and others don't. At the latter, employees have often banded together, typically through unions, to bring about changes through collective bargaining. Not all companies are unionized, although many of the larger companies in this book have some partially unionized subsidiaries. The union question is one about which people who share the same beliefs may easily come to opposite conclusions. Many believe that a unionized company will tend to take more progressive positions because the unions will spur them to do so. However, it can also be argued that the company became unionized because of a conflict between management and the workers in the first place and that that struggle will not always translate into a win for labor. Many nonunionized companies have never needed a union because management has been fair and programs are in place to resolve disputes. Perhaps more than any other issue, whether or not a company has a union cannot be broken down to numbers or signs. Each company's story must be interpreted on its own.

For many of the companies discussed in this book, the question of union affiliation is further complicated by the fact that large conglomerates frequently operate in several countries. Working Assets, a socially responsible money market fund, will not invest in multinationals with more than half their employees outside the United States because it believes this is a sign that the company may be taking unfair advantage of cheaper labor markets overseas. Even without considering this, multinationals are tougher to evaluate because labor practices differ by country and company-to-company comparisons do not hold true. The picture is further muddied by takeovers. Some acquiring companies step in and change the policies of the companies they purchase; others operate as holding companies, allowing their subsidiaries to dictate their own policies.

Often unions champion issues of broader social concern than the practices within the companies they represent. For example, the United Mine Workers of America (UMWA) initiated the U.S. Boycott Shell Campaign because of the presence of Shell's parent, the Royal Dutch/Shell Group, in South Africa. While the UMWA's complaint is partially one of self-interest, it is also a broader, ethical appeal to protest the apartheid regime. Specifically, the Mine Workers contend that reduced labor costs in South Africa through the "slave labor" of blacks has created unfair competition with American companies, ultimately leading to mineworker layoffs in the United States. The UMWA targeted Shell to boycott because the campaign contends, despite company denials, that Royal Dutch/Shell ships oil to South Africa in violation of the international oil embargo called by the United Nations.

The American Federation of Labor–Congress of Industrial Organizations (AFL–CIO) is also a powerful force in corporate reform. Its boycott list publicizes companies in conflict with unions. Generally, the AFL–CIO sides with unions that have not satisfactorily resolved disputes with management and is later joined by other organizations crusading for social reforms. Companies profiled in this book and also on the September/October 1989 AFL–CIO "Don't Buy" list are Royal Dutch/Shell, International Paper, and the Continental and Eastern divisions of Texas Air. On the boycott list since 1987, International Paper is an example of a yet-to-be-resolved labor dispute. The company told its workers it would cut pay, reduce health benefits, and subcontract work at lower wages, and its 2300 unionized employees decided to strike. International Paper locked the workers out and hired nonunion workers to fill their posts. This action was ruled illegal by the National Labor Relations Board; the workers have returned to their jobs but have been boycotting the company's products until an agreement can be reached.[6]

One of the headline union battles of 1989 was that waged between the International Association of Machinists and Aerospace Workers (IAM) and Frank Lorenzo, chairman of Eastern Airlines and its parent, Texas Air. After Texas Air acquired Continental Airlines in the early 1980s, Texas Air quickly pushed for and received wage concessions from Continental's employees; employees resisted these concessions, which ultimately led to Continental's filing for Chapter 11 bankruptcy protection, under which all of its union contracts were in effect canceled. When Texas Air acquired the financially troubled Eastern Airlines in 1986, history repeated itself. In March 1989, pilots and flight attendants decided to honor the machinists' strike for higher wages at Eastern and, five days later, the company filed for bankruptcy protection. Changes in bankruptcy law prevented the canceling of union contracts, but Texas Air could—and did—sell off much of Eastern's assets or transfer them to other subsidiaries.[7] As of late 1989 the pilots and flight attendants had ended their strike, although the machinists continued.

Often the interests of a corporation's management and its union are in opposition, and tension can be expected. But a prolonged strike indicates that problems between labor and management run deep and could not be negotiated away by less drastic steps. Again, the nature of each strike varies—an investor might not take a strike over wages so seriously as a strike for safer working conditions. Another important thing to consider is the extent of the strike. If the truck drivers of one particular plant strike, that is not necessarily a sign of widespread discontent; however, if other unions honor the strike and unions from other areas back the action, something is seriously amiss.

Charitable Contributions

Historically, corporations have made charitable contributions to educational, community, and cultural organizations. Some companies do so because it is a tradition passed down from their founders; others make charitable contributions because they want to assume a leadership role in society; most recognize the tax benefits of these gifts; and many have an eye on the public relations impact these contributions make. Frequently, a company makes a gift to counterbalance a social problem it is accused of creating or aggravating. For example, Anheuser-Busch, which has been criticized for promoting and glamorizing alcohol, asserts that it, too, is concerned about accidents caused by drunk driving and it backs this up by supporting

Students Against Driving Drunk (SADD). And companies like Avon Products made large contributions in the early 1980s to organizations studying alternatives to live animal testing in product development. (As of the summer of 1989, Avon announced it had ended all phases of animal testing.)[8] There's no question that these gifts are positive demonstrations of corporate commitment, yet each has a PR angle as well.

Perhaps gift horses shouldn't be treated so cynically. If a company makes donations to curry favor with the public, that's the essence of socially responsible investing: bringing corporate policies in line with shareholders' beliefs. Many point out that Merck's free distribution of Ivermectin, its river blindness drug, made for good public relations, but this doesn't diminish the gift. After all, other companies have the same opportunities for the positive press a good deed attracts and haven't done what Merck has.

The size of corporate charitable giving programs varies greatly. Some profiled in this book donated a fraction of a percent of a year's pretax income, others as much as 5%, and Ben & Jerry's tips the scales with the hefty 7.5% it scoops out to charitable organizations each year. On average, corporations gave 1.6% of worldwide pretax income in 1987, according to the New York-based Council on Economic Priorities.[9] Investors should also look at how wide a range of activities the company supports, and whether these go beyond traditional outlets such as the United Way and college donations. Innovative community gifts are often of interest to ethical investors because the giving projects the company emphasizes most likely reflect its social philosophy. If published, a company's charitable giving program offers a glimpse into the social activities the company values and those it ignores.

One company that takes an unusual approach to charitable giving is H. B. Fuller. Not only does this chemical concern earmark around 2% of its annual U.S. pretax profits for charitable giving, but it allows employees to allocate these funds. Overseas employees take part in the decision-making process too, so the company's contribution list includes projects as varied as a day care center for children of low-income working mothers in Brazil and a gift to a Chilean foundation for handicapped children. McCormick is another company that draws employees into the corporate giving process. On one Saturday a year designated C (for Charity) Day, employees work for wages that are matched dollar for dollar by McCormick, and this doubled paycheck is then donated to whatever charity the employee chooses.

Although these programs are fairly unusual, many companies have matching-gift programs through which they lend support to activities that employees are already funding.

Charitable contributions provide a wonderful peek into a corporation's priorities, but this information is not always public. The *Taft Corporate Giving Directory* is a good source because it lists the size and projects funded by many major companies. When asked by an investor, most companies are willing to name selected beneficiaries of gifts, but they do not always disclose the size of these gifts. Others are more forthcoming about this information, and several have foundations that publish records. Although these foundations may be dedicated to philanthropic causes, they may not invest these assets in a manner the individual deems socially responsible. Foundation portfolios frequently invest in companies with ties to South Africa, the military, or other areas the investor might find objectionable.[10]

There are several ways a company can demonstrate its interest and commitment to its employees and its community. Benefits are just one component of the equation: labor relations, charitable giving, and employee programs should all be considered as well. As declining literacy rates and a shrinking population compel corporations to assume a more significant role in the lives of their employees, how corporations meet these challenges is one way investors can make a more informed judgment about whether this is the type of company they want to add to a portfolio.

■ 6 ■
CORPORATE
CULPABILITY

The issues discussed in the previous chapters are broad and apply to virtually all companies; even corporations with no South African operations may have at some point severed these ties or taken conscious steps to withhold products from South Africa while apartheid exists. However, there are also several narrow ethical issues upon which only specific companies or industries act. In this chapter, we examine issues of product liability, defense contracting, nuclear energy, political action committees, and animal testing.

Product Liability

Socially responsible investors generally assume that companies they perceive as ethical are much less likely to be involved in litigation over misconduct or product liability than are other companies. Although companies with some ethical black marks already against them seem to be embroiled in controversy more often than the darlings of social investors, occasionally a company with an excellent reputation comes under fire. One of the most bitter and costly medical product-liability class action suits in American history centered around the Dalkon Shield intrauterine device made by A. H.

Robins, a company known as a generous corporate contributor to charity. Nearly 200,000 women stand to be compensated for injuries from the company's IUD, many of whom had to have hysterectomies, became infertile from serious inflammatory infections, or became pregnant and suffered septic abortions, from which some 20 U.S. women died. The Dalkon Shield was dubbed "the Bhopal of the women's health movement" by attorney Sybil Shainwald of the National Women's Health Network.[1]

The Dalkon Shield was recommended in the early 1970s both in the United States and abroad. Although Robins had no experience in the birth control market, it did not hire an on-staff gynecologist to supervise and test the product, and internal memos reveal that it knew its advertised 1.1% contraceptive failure rate was exaggerated. A *Ms.* feature article on the Dalkon Shield case quotes Wayne Crowder, quality control supervisor for the IUD, as telling his boss in March 1971 that "he couldn't 'in good conscience' approve of 'something that I felt could cause infections.' His boss said that 'my conscience didn't pay my salary.' "[2]

Robins has also been criticized for not taking swift and effective enough steps to resolve this problem once it was made known. In 1974 the company withdrew the shield from the market and recommended it be surgically removed from any pregnant women in whom it had been inserted. However, it was not until several years later that Robins contacted doctors to advise removing the shield from all women, and not until 1984 that the company launched a full-fledged campaign to remove the IUD at its own expense. As claims and lawsuits mounted, Robins opted for protection under Chapter 11 of the bankruptcy code in August 1985. After a protracted class action suit, claimants will receive $2.375 billion in compensatory (but not punitive) damages. American Home Products (AHP) acquired Robins in late 1989 and is establishing the claimant trust as partial payment for the company. Robins' stockholders will receive roughly $30 per share for stock worth $8 at the company's bankruptcy, and the Robins family stands to collect $294 million from the sale of the company, according to *Ms.* magazine.

In many ways the Dalkon Shield case doesn't play out as a cautionary tale. Prior to the shield, A. H. Robins boasted an excellent reputation in the pharmaceutical industry and was praised for its generous philanthropic programs. In short, it was the type of company that would grace many ethical investors' portfolios. And yet the lengthy unfolding of the Dalkon Shield drama gave socially responsible investors plenty of time to abandon the stock and send management a message that its conduct was unacceptable. True, investors who hung onto their shares received a bigger return than those who sold at Robins' low, but this is little incentive to stick with companies involved in product liability suits. An investor would have made more money still by investing in another pharmaceutical company like Merck, one whose price appreciated because it introduced several new socially useful drugs.

A case like this frequently implicates other companies along the way. Robins' insurer, Aetna Life & Casualty, was named defendant in several lawsuits, and as of 1989 had paid $75 million to the claimants' trust. At the same time, American Home Products is now linked to the Dalkon Shield tragedy, and along with some strong products has acquired a company infamous in the world of product liability.

Named one of "The Ten Worst Corporations of 1988" by the *Multinational Monitor*, Pfizer is another company entangled in product liability suits. More than 200 victims or their families have initiated suits against Pfizer for strut fracture or failure of its Bjork-Shiley convexo-concave heart valve, which has allegedly resulted in 252 deaths. Corporate memos indicate that Pfizer knew more about the potential dangers of this valve than it publicized, according to the Public Citizen Health Research Group. Meanwhile, an employee report and an inspection of manufacturing facilities revealed that workers were not adequately trained about how defects could arise and how properly to test the valves.[3] In response to these charges Pfizer noted that the valve was withdrawn from the market in 1986 and the number of reported strut failure cases is small in view of the fact that 85,000 valves were implanted worldwide. The financial impact of these suits on Pfizer cannot yet be determined but is something investors should consider.

When a company's irresponsibility lands it in court, its finances are jeopardized along with its reputation. However, other unethical actions will never be litigated and may even boost a company's bottom line. One complaint against multinational drug companies is that they sometimes ship drugs banned by the FDA to developing nations where regulations are less strict. In these instances the company generally offers medical evidence that the drug is safe, but many ethical investors would avoid a company for this practice.

A similar problem that came to the attention of activists and concerned investors in the 1970s and 1980s was the aggressive marketing of infant formula in developing nations. For many years, manufacturers of breast-milk substitutes distributed free samples of their products to overseas hospitals, thereby committing new mothers to buying the formula once their own milk dried up. Because the formula is costly, poor women sometimes dilute it, causing malnutrition, or mix it with impure water, which can result in illness or death. An activist group, INFACT (Infant Formula Action Coalition), called for a boycott of Nestlé, blasting its infant-formula marketing practices, and won. In 1984 the company agreed to observe the infant-formula marketing code spelled out by the World Health Assembly. However, Action for Corporate Accountability, a board created by INFACT to monitor compliance with infant-formula codes, reinstated the boycott in 1988, charging that Nestlé continues to dump more formula in hospitals than is necessary for the 1% of infants who legitimately need it. The group is also boycotting American Home Products, another infant-formula manufacturer, for allegedly violating the World Health Organization code. AHP denies this. Action for Corporate Accountability estimates that the lives of one million babies each year could be saved by breast- rather than bottle feeding. Although these marketing practices do not land manufacturers in the courtroom and may even fatten bottom lines, many ethical investors avoid these companies on principle.

One of the most infamous industrial accidents ever occurred at the Union Carbide plant in Bhopal, India in 1984. Methyl-isocyanate was released into the air, killing between 2000 and 5000 people, and injuring as many as 200,000 more. Although many of the facts are under dispute, Union Carbide is charged with having an inadequately designed plant and having improperly trained workers to handle an emergency of this magnitude. Union Carbide has certainly been financially punished for Bhopal although the final settlement of $470 million fell far short of the Indian government's initial request for $3.3 billion, and came about five years after the tragedy.

In all of these instances a social problem has been created or aggravated by the actions of big business. Some of these problems have taken a calculable toll on the bottom line through legal settlements or boycotts; in others, the damage was to reputation rather than the balance sheet.

Defense Contracting

Supplying weapons or systems to the Department of Defense is not solely the domain of defense companies; multinational giants like

General Electric, AT&T, and IBM all do business with the military. The simplest route for investors concerned about the arms build-up is to cross all companies that have any exposure to defense off the potential investment list. However, many investors favor arms reduction—a slowing of defense spending rather than elimination of it altogether. In this case is it consistent to avoid investing in any company that does defense contracting?

Naturally, even an investor who believes that some military work is necessary might decide that this is not an area in which he or she wants to invest. While defense contractors argue that government alone should decide what systems are necessary to keep the country secure, others contend that these contractors actively market to the government, convincing officials that larger and more costly weapons are vital. As John Kenneth Galbraith has said, corporations provide the demand for their products along with the products themselves. That a shrinking defense budget hurts contractors is undeniably true. INFACT takes the aggressive marketing of the B-1 bomber, which was exorbitantly expensive and on the brink of obsolescence, to exemplify this point. Rockwell International called its campaign for the bomber Operation Common Sense, a name that smacks of public relations hype, and spread the contracts and subcontracts out over 48 states so that any cuts in the B-1's budget might cost constituents' jobs throughout the country.[4]

In the mid-1980s INFACT launched a visible boycott of General Electric because of the appliance company's military contracting work. It selected GE because this well-known consumer company has several lucrative business lines, and its existence does not depend upon the defense industry. At the same time the difficulty of finding a light bulb whose manufacturer has no ties to military contracting highlights how pervasive the defense industry is. Westinghouse, GTE/ Sylvania, and North American Philips all have ties to defense, although none is so heavily involved as GE. Brands made by weapons-free companies include Duro-Light (made by Duro Test), ABCO (made by Angelo Bros.), and ACE Hardware, according to the Spring/ Summer 1989 issue of the *National Boycott News*.

Another reason why socially responsible investors might shy away from defense contractors is recent governmental charges that several have procured contracts in unethical and even illegal ways. A government investigation called Operation Ill Wind is examining the marketing practices of several industry giants.

Political Action Committees (PACs)

Political Action Committees (PACs) provide corporations an opportunity to advertise their interests to political candidates, and therefore have been accused of allowing big business to buy political influence. While it is illegal for a company to contribute directly to a political candidate or campaign, the Federal Election Campaign Act of 1974 states that PACs can raise money from individuals to disburse to candidates. Either employees or shareholders can contribute to these PACs, but no more than $5000 can be given to any one individual in a federal election. In 1984 PAC dollars constituted 59% of representatives' campaign spending.[5]

Corporations present PACs to their employees as a way like-minded individuals can send a forceful message to candidates. For example, General Motors says that by combining funds, candidates receiving Civic Involvement Program/General Motors' "contributions view them as representing the collective interests of GM employees who care about the political process." However, companies have other avenues of influence—for instance, lobbying—and not all companies believe in or have PACs. Whether or not a company has a PAC, how large it is, and the types of candidates it supports are all ways investors can get a more complete picture of a corporation's philosophy and workings.

Nuclear Energy

Nuclear power has the considerable advantage of being a relatively clean energy source; the risks associated with it, however, are so great that many investors choose to avoid utilities that generate power this way. The dangers of nuclear technology were vividly brought to public attention by the explosion at the Chernobyl reactor in the Soviet Union in April 1986, in which seven tons of radioactive material were spewed into the atmosphere with far-reaching consequences. Vegetables in Northern Italy were declared unfit for consumption following the accident, and 100,000 Soviets were forced to abandon their homes, according to the *State of the World 1989.*

Currently, nuclear power provides around 15% of the world's electricity,[6] and even though it is a more common energy source in Europe, several U.S. utilities also derive energy from nuclear plants. In this country, Commonwealth Edison operates the largest network of nuclear facilities.

Many of the challenges associated with nuclear power have yet to be satisfactorily resolved. No nuclear power plant has ever been decommissioned, and the question of where to dispose of nuclear waste generated in the reaction process (much of it is radioactive or contains highly poisonous elements like plutonium) has not been decided. Currently, most of the U.S.'s nuclear waste is sitting in pools of filtered water next to the reactors that created it because no permanent disposal method has been found.[7] Not only must nuclear waste be kept out of contact with people, it must also be isolated from anything that will later become part of the food chain or water supply.

The electricity that reaches your house could be generated by nuclear energy without your even knowing it. And yet it is possible to research whether a utility generates its energy from nuclear power plants with one caveat: avoiding this area means eliminating most electric utilities from your investment choices. One non-nuclear utility profiled in this book is Citizens Utilities, which passes most other social screens as well.

Animal Testing

Live animal testing is one of the more emotional issues with which some corporations are confronted. Partially resulting from activist pressure, some companies have phased out the practice completely; the toy and cosmetic industries have scrambled to find alternatives and many have ceased animal testing altogether. In the summer of 1989 Avon Products halted all tests on live animals, either off-site or on, as has Hasbro. And yet the ingredients that Avon purchases have already been tested—generally on animals.[8] The FDA requires pharmaceutical companies to perform very thorough product experiments, which usually means animal testing. Those calling for drug companies to eliminate tests that are not medically essential and to reduce the number of animals used in necessary tests have scored some points. Procter & Gamble has been honored by the Council on Economic Priorities for reducing the number of live animals in testing 30% over five years. Many of these changes are made possible by new technology—for example, computer modeling and tests performed on tissue can in some cases offer valid results without involving live animals.

One of the most visible antianimal-testing campaigns waged against a corporation is aimed at Gillette. One of its caretakers, Leslie Fain, taped and filmed information about the alleged suffering of animals at Gillette's lab. The company vigorously denied that the footage was of its facilities. Since then, Gillette has closed down its on-site lab, but the boycott continues because the company still uses live animals in testing even though the tests are performed by outside labs.

Investors concerned about animal testing can ask companies directly if their labs have been accredited by the American Association for Accreditation of Laboratory Animal Care. And most companies that do perform live animal testing have an informational brochure on the conditions under which the tests are performed.

Although each of these issues applies to only a small band of companies within the spectrum of investment choices, they are issues that most concerned investors say bear consideration. Just the same, the decision to avoid a company or industry should be made intelligently. If you benefit from these practices, perhaps it is inconsistent to take a stance on them only when investing. Most ethical investors are attempting to bring their investment actions in line with their principles; how to accomplish this is an individual decision.

■ 7 ■
THE
ECONOMICS
OF ETHICAL
INVESTING

The economics of ethical investing need be no different than that of any other type of investing. However, the economic approach should fit the social one—that is, if an investor has decided to invest in smaller companies with shorter track records, taking a straightforward and less risky approach to stock selection may be wise. Still, socially responsible investing is often regarded as a conservative approach to stock-picking because negative surprises such as environmental violations and liability suits should be weeded out by the ethical screening process itself. Socially responsible investors may also feel that they are applying unusual criteria to determining a universe of stocks and so should be traditional about the financial aspects of their investment decision.

For ethical investors favoring smaller companies that perform a socially useful service, it is important to assess the greater risks these investments bear. It is possible to temper this risk in a number of ways: by including some more stable investments in the portfolio, by earmarking some money for a secure investment like a money market account, or by researching the companies thoroughly enough for the risk to be acknowledged and deemed acceptable. How much risk you want to assume depends upon your overall financial situation and temperament and will certainly influence what investments you make. This chapter explains some of the key concepts in financially evaluating a stock as well as the other types of investments you might choose to make. Two excellent sources examining this subject in much greater depth are Amy L. Domini and Peter D. Kinder's *Ethical Investing*, a nuts-and-bolts approach to socially responsible investing, and *How to Buy Stocks*, Louis Engel and Brendan Boyd's classic explanation of the intricacies of investing.

Economics of Stock Investing

Doing your homework on the social dimensions of a company can also keep you apprised of its financial status. The daily newspapers, especially business-oriented ones like *The Wall Street Journal*, and financial magazines are invaluable sources for monitoring the social developments shaping the companies you follow. And these sources will also keep you informed about major financial changes or news that could affect an investment's bottom line.

Ethical investors must put more energy into defining a universe than most other investors because researching the social dimensions of companies is so time-consuming. A working universe should contain several times as many companies as you plan to invest in so that you can make final decisions based purely on financial criteria. To research too few companies is a mistake. That makes it more difficult to sell a stock if the company's finances or social policies change because there are no alternatives at hand. Not all of the companies in your universe need be painstakingly researched, but you must have several with which you feel comfortable.

The first rule of investing is that the price of a given stock rises because the demand for shares exceeds their availability, driving up the price of these shares. It sounds simple, but the trick is to recognize when a stock will soon be in greater demand.

The price of a stock is often driven by earnings growth. However, a history of steadily mounting earnings may not always be a good indicator of future growth. In some instances, a five-year record of earnings growth indicates that the company is well managed and could continue to post superior gains for quite a while. Buying at that point will position you to gain as the company continues to grow. However, a solid earnings growth history does not guarantee that the future will bear the same results as the past. For example, a pharmaceutical company might launch a drug that cures the common cold, hiking annual earnings dramatically for several years. However, earnings could drop off sharply if another company introduces a one-time inoculation against colds and the first company has no blockbuster drug with which to replace its now-obsolete one. Of course, it would have been wonderful to have owned shares of the first drug company as it was launching its common cold cure. Five years later, the competitor with the sure-fire one-time shot is the smart investment.

To make these judgments, the investor needs a thorough knowledge of the workings of the company (or its fundamentals). This knowledge can be obtained from several sources. If you plan to conduct transactions through a full-service brokerage house, the reports of the firm's analysts will be available to you. This professional information gives you many of the facts with conclusions already drawn. However, one word of caution: Brokerage houses make money when investors buy and sell stocks; their reports therefore often recommend frequent trading. Remember, each time you swap one stock for another you must pay a fee to sell the first and buy the second. If you plan to put this information together yourself, periodicals, newspapers, and magazines will help you form a picture of the company. What's more, most public libraries have a set of S&P guides, which profile the key financial aspects of publicly traded companies. Some investors choose to subscribe to specialized stock market newsletters, a few of which are designed especially for ethical investors. The latter are listed in the Directory.

Although the internal workings of a company will certainly influence its stock price, stocks are also driven by macroeconomic factors. For example, a company that exports products will financially benefit from a falling dollar making its prices internationally competitive. And markets themselves tend to move in cycles. A typical bull market lasts three to five years and is generally followed by a downturn, or bear market. While it is not impossible to make money in a down market, it is certainly more difficult.

Some investors focus on technical rather than fundamental factors. A common Wall Street saying is that the market is governed by emotion. Technicians have found that stocks track patterns and that by charting a stock over a stretch of time, they can predict whether its price should rise or fall regardless of new products or business conditions. Just as fundamental analysts rely on certain criteria for understanding the business conditions of companies, each technical analyst relies on his or her own indicators. Some track the new highs stocks hit, others look for specific trading patterns or political trends, and some even link price movement to astrological phenomena.

Although both fundamental and technical approaches deserve consideration, neither type of analysis has consistently posted the kind of results that would convert one camp to the other. As an investor you will have to decide what your particular investment philosophy is and then apply it. If you do not want to plot stock paths or study balance sheets, you still have several investment options. There are both socially responsible investment brokers who handle individual accounts and socially responsible mutual funds. A list of both is in Chapter 10.

Mutual Funds

Socially responsible mutual funds are generally tailored to avoid most of the major don'ts in ethical investing—typically, these funds avoid companies with ties to South Africa, Department of Defense contracts, major product liability suits, even live-animal testing. Depending on the fund, it may or may not take EEO and labor issues into consideration. The advantage of a socially responsible mutual fund is that it does all of the homework for you, and the fund managers can keep up to date on corporate policy changes in a way that might seem mind-boggling to the individual. It also removes the onus of evaluating the company from a financial standpoint, and the investor automatically has a diversified portfolio without having to invest the large sums of cash it would normally take to achieve this. Another selling point is that the fund is managed by a professional who often has extensive research capabilities and can devote full attention to this task.

Mutual funds, however, are no recipe for success. If they were, money managers could contentedly invest their own funds and live off the profits. Another drawback is that your specific ethical concerns might not be addressed by a given fund. A mutual fund is a type of potluck—you buy "stock" in the investment company, which in turn buys shares of other companies. Depending on the type of fund, these investments may be mixed with bonds or cash to temper the result. For the ethical investor, it is particularly important to know what the mutual fund is setting out to do, something that should be clearly spelled out in the company's prospectus.

There are two types of mutual funds: loads and no-loads. A load fund typically charges a commission (in the 8.5% range) and is sold through a full-commission brokerage house. A no-load fund charges an annual management fee rather than a commission. Fees on no-loads are reasonable, frequently ranging from 1.0–3.0%. Some no-loads do charge a withdrawal fee, although this "back-door" fee decreases over time.

Individual Accounts

For the socially responsible investor with sizable assets to invest, an individual account managed by an ethical investment specialist is another option. Several large investment houses (Shearson Lehman Hutton and Smith Barney, to name two) have individual account managers who screen for social criteria, as do the Atlanta, Georgia-based Social Responsibility Investment Group and United Trust Company in Boston. An individual account manager can tailor your investments to your own particular beliefs, something a mutual fund obviously cannot do. And these managers are willing to match the risk of investments with the special needs of the client.

Fixed-Income Investments

Just as most people are unwilling to lend money to an acquaintance who intends to use it for an unethical end, some investors refuse to loan money to companies whose purposes they don't agree with by buying that corporation's bonds. Corporate bonds are considered the most risky area in fixed income, although the fixed-income market is generally regarded as safer than the equity (stock) market. In addition, an investor can gauge how risky a fixed-income investment is by the issue's debt rating. Bond prices rise when interest rates fall and seesaw down when interest rates rise; since bond prices hinge on interest rates the fixed-income market is heavily tied to economic factors.

Of all fixed-income investments, U.S. Treasury bills are regarded as the safest because it is the U.S. government that pays off the debt. T-bills fund U.S. governmental projects, ranging from social programs to defense or foreign relations. The investor has very little ethical control over this form of debt and for that reason many socially responsible investors shy away from treasuries.

Municipal bonds are debt issued by state or local governments. These can be attractive as a way of helping fund a project you support such as the construction of a school or specialized housing. While municipals carry risk, most have special tax advantages.

Money Market Funds

Money market funds are similar to mutual funds except that they grant investors ready access to their money. The main advantage of a money market account over a bank account is that money markets pay higher interest, although the rate fluctuates. These funds generally invest heavily in bonds, but unless you select an ethical money market fund like Working Assets, you have no control over how your money is put to use.

Bank Accounts

Opening up a savings account is actually loaning money to the bank at a specified interest rate. Once the money is in the account, you have no say in who borrows it or for what reason. That's why some ethical investors put their money in socially responsible bank accounts like the ones listed in the Directory.

The social implications of what investors do with their money are farther reaching than they first appear. And yet the principle behind all of these investments is fundamentally the same: Investors want some say in what happens to their money once it leaves their wallets. For example, Working Assets, which makes all its investments according to socially responsible criteria, offers a VISA card it calls "the only credit card that works for peace, human rights and the environment." The company donates five cents to nonprofit organizations every time the cardholder makes a purchase with it. As the idea spreads that social-responsibility concerns are legitimate, there will most likely be a wider range of investment vehicles from which ethical investors can choose.

■ 8 ■
PROFILES
OF THE
S&P 100

The Standard & Poor's (S&P) 100 index comprises the hundred largest capitalized, publicly traded companies in the United States. The capitalization of a stock is the number of shares outstanding multiplied by the price of these shares. Naturally, the market capitalization of a stock fluctuates daily, depending on how the stock trades; the S&P 100, therefore changes, too. In fact, Standard & Poor's issues a new index list monthly. The companies in this chapter were the hundred largest capitalized ones for September 1989. Unless otherwise specified, all information given was accurate as of late 1989.

The S&P 100 is considered a good representation of the broad market, most of these companies have readily recognizable names and operate in a variety of industries. Although these companies are all large, they represent a random sampling and, unlike the companies profiled in Chapter 9, have not been hand-picked. Many of these companies would automatically be screened out of professional socially responsible investors' buy lists because of military contracting or ties to South Africa. At the same time, these companies have often taken other admirable initiatives, ones that must be understood in order to weigh the issues fairly.

The information provided by the companies themselves has not been attributed, although sources of all other information are noted. Often profiles refer to a major corporate survey such as *Black Enterprise's* list of the 50 best workplaces for blacks or *Fortune's* survey of the reputations of 305 major American corporations. The write-ups also indicate whether a company has been mentioned by socially responsible investment specialists like Calvert or Franklin's *insight*.

AMP INC.

AMP, the world's leading maker of electrical and electronic connectors with around 20% of global market share, is considered a "responsible corporate citizen" by the Calvert social investment fund. Because of its quality-oriented culture, AMP has been described as a Japanese company in the middle of Pennsylvania.[1]

One social area AMP has emphasized is the environment. In 1985 AMP established a professionally staffed environmental department and performs an annual environmental audit of all facilities. Annual testing disclosed that small amounts of solvents had entered drains ten to twenty years ago, and AMP set to work cleaning up and rehabilitating groundwater. It has also replaced underground waste-oil tanks with new above-ground systems at all plants, as well as cutting waste oil and chlorinated solvents by up to 97%.

Although AMP says its charitable giving is in line with other comparable corporations, it would not reveal annual contributions. AMP matches employee gifts to education on a generous two-for-one basis.

AMP has no women or minorities on its board of directors or at the management level. AMP does, however, have a program to ensure women- and minority-owned businesses an opportunity to compete fairly for business, although this is not a formal minority purchasing program. Because the materials AMP purchases must meet technical specifications, decisions must be made on the basis of which companies can supply these materials.

FAST FACTS:
- No South African operations.
- No direct sales to the Department of Defense, although it does supply prime contractors with components.
- No unionized members of 15,700 domestic employees.
- 24,000 employees worldwide.
- Responded with information.
- Harrisburg, PA.

AT&T

Even after the break-up of this telecommunications giant, AT&T remains "the right choice" for women and minorities, who are well-represented throughout the company. It may, however, be the wrong choice for investors concerned about nuclear weapons: AT&T ranked eleventh largest nuclear weapons contractor for 1988, according to Nuclear Free America's listing. The company disputes this.

New union contracts negotiated during the summer of 1989 offered only "a modest wage hike but granted an unusually extensive 'family benefits' package."[2] Employees are allowed up to a year of unpaid leave to care for infants or ill dependents and are reimbursed for up to $2000 in adoption costs. Additionally, AT&T is setting up a $5 million fund to finance child care centers. Of 298,000 employees, 46% are women, although this percentage drops to only 6% of the 800 individuals considered upper management. *Working Mother* included AT&T as one of "The 60 Best Companies for Working Mothers," and it was one of 52 companies profiled in *The Best Companies for Women*, which praised its forceful policy against sexual harassment, implemented in 1987. There are two women and three minority members on its 19-person board of directors.

AT&T was named one of the 50 best places for blacks to work by *Black Enterprise* magazine. "Recently installed CEO, Robert E. Allen, has steadfastly reaffirmed the communication company's commitment to affirmative action," the February 1989 article noted. Around 21% of all employees and 5% of upper management are minority members. Meanwhile, AT&T purchases around $1 million a day in goods and services from minority-owned businesses.

AT&T's Bell Labs division was profiled in *The 100 Best Companies to Work for in America*. Throughout AT&T, managers are schooled in sensitivity toward groups that have been discriminated against historically. The company has also issued a formal statement protecting the privacy and other rights of employees with AIDS.

Nuclear Free America says that AT&T's prime Department of Defense and Department of Energy nuclear weapons contracts totaled $1,189,747,000 in 1988. The company vigorously disputed this in the *National Boycott News*. James Olson, former chairman of the board, said that less than 6.5% of AT&T's total 1986 revenues came from the federal government. He also pointed out that the DoE owns Sandia National Laboratories, and AT&T only provides management services for the facility on a no-fee basis. However, these management services include "full spectrum nuclear weapons research," according to recently retired Sandia president George Dacey.[3] The Interfaith Center on Corporate Responsibility issued a shareholder proposal asking for a written report on AT&T's Strategic Defense Initiative Organization efforts at the 1989 annual meeting. The directors recommended voting against the proposal, saying: "The selection of systems to defend the nation is the responsibility of officials of our government who are accountable to the electorate."

AT&T publicly announced its plans to eliminate all chlorofluorocarbons from manufacturing processes by 1994 and to halve their use by 1991.[4] This is well ahead of what was called for by the Montreal Protocol, and is an especially admirable step given that few companies have staked their reputations on a tough-to-meet agenda like this. The company has a high-ranking post—environment and safety engineering VP—designed to oversee these decisions.[5]

AT&T's unions have praised the company for hiring on-staff health and safety specialists and for sharing information with employees. But future union demands may be harder for the company to accommodate. For example, the Communications Workers of America wants AT&T to reexamine jobs that involve repetitive motion, affecting as many as one-quarter of all employees. And the International Brotherhood of Electrical Workers, representing 25,000 AT&T manufacturing workers, is concerned about shaping future policy on Video Display Terminal (VDT) use.

AT&T generally donates around 1.2% of pretax earnings to charitable causes. In 1988, the AT&T Foundation made grants in support of educational, health care, social action, and cultural organizations worth around $30 million.

AT&T has had no ties to South Africa since 1986, although government regulations require it to supply long-distance service there. AT&T has asked one of its European partners, Olivetti, to reconsider doing business with South Africa.

FAST FACTS:

- Around 54% of employees are unionized—160,000 out of roughly 284,000 total.[6]
- AT&T said 1989 job cuts would total about 25,000, according to December 11, 1989 *Wall Street Journal* article.
- Responded with information.
- New York, NY.

ALCOA

Alcoa, an aluminum products manufacturer, has also made its mark in recycling, having recycled around 16.1 billion aluminum beverage cans in 1988. The company is the largest manufacturer of the sheet aluminum from which these cans are made and recycles 40% of all cans annually recycled. Meanwhile, in its 1988 annual report Alcoa boasted of leading the aluminum industry in safety performance, with a 20% decline in serious injuries that year.

Alcoa was named one of the 11 largest emitters of carcinogenic chemicals unregulated by the Clean Air Act by the Natural Resources Defense Council. The trouble stemmed from its Riverdale, Iowa, plant, which uses perchloroethylene.[7] An Alcoa spokesperson explained that the high level of emissions occurred during the 1987 installation of new control equipment, and that these emissions now are under control.

The Alcoa Foundation donated $10.76 million to charitable organizations in 1988. The funds were directed to education (44.6%), cultural (12.1%), health and welfare (23.1%), civic and community (10.8%), youth organizations (6.0%), and the remainder to miscellaneous.

Alcoa sold off its Alcoa Defense Systems to McDonnell Douglas in the late 1980s but continues to perform research and development for the Department of Defense.

Alcoa has a "cafeteria" approach to benefits; one choice is setting aside funds for child care. At each of Alcoa's major locations there is an Employee Assistance Program counselor to handle both family and job-related problems.

In 1988 Alcoa settled new labor agreements with its major unions covering 15,000 employees at 14 plants. In all the company employs 59,000, a little over half of whom work in the U.S.

Alcoa has a good reputation—it ranked most admired of ten in the Metals category of *Fortune's* January 29, 1990, survey of corporate reputations.

FAST FACTS:
- No South African operations.
- Profit-sharing plan.
- Responded with information.
- Pittsburgh, PA.

AMERICAN ELECTRIC POWER

American Electric Power was selected as one of five "likely losers" from the growing emphasis on environmental issues by *Money* magazine. That's because the company generates electricity by burning American coal, which contains high levels of sulfur and gives off acid-rain-causing emissions. The Clean Air Act, which is expected to tighten the regulations on these emissions, could cost the company as much as $8 billion, estimated the June 1989 *Money* article entitled "Tanker from Hell." AEP will likely be hit hard by these regulations because almost 90% of its capacity is coal-fired (the remainder is nuclear).

AEP is currently working on technology to burn American coal more cleanly. Its process, Pressurized Fluidized Bed Combustion (PFBC), injects limestone powder into the pulverized coal dust during combustion, and the limestone neutralizes the pollutants in the coal. This differs from other technologies by eliminating sulfur during combustion rather than in the smokestack. The company says the PFBC process cuts sulfur dioxide emissions 90%. American Electric expects its demonstration plant for PFBC technology to be completed by 1992, and when older plants are due to be updated it will retrofit them with the equipment for the PFBC process. AEP is also working on an in-duct scrubbing pilot unit that reduces 40–50% of the sulfur dioxide emissions and is suitable for retrofitting older plants.

AEP's Ohio Power Company turned 30,000 acres once mined for coal into ReCreation Land, a free camp and park.

The company has 15,000–16,000 employees, the vast majority of whom work in the U.S. Some employees are unionized and belong either to the United Mineworkers or the International Brotherhood of Electrical Workers.

FAST FACTS:
- No South African operations.
- No arms-related contracts.
- Would not release charitable contributions; emphasis is on higher education.
- Two women on 12-person board of directors.
- Responded with information.
- Columbus, OH.

AMERICAN EXPRESS COMPANY

The Work Force Challenge is what American Express calls its project to address employment issues pinpointed in employee polls and a 1988 year-long study. American Express (which includes IDS Financial Services and Shearson Lehman Hutton) already treats its female employees well. It has expanded its child care referral service, initiated a pilot elder care referral service, and offers a lunchtime series on work and family issues. One innovative project is its support of Gentle Care, a project through which Fort Lauderdale employees of the Travel Related Services' (TRS) division can drop off mildly ill children to receive special attention. Women interviewed in *The Best Companies for Women* date changes at the company to CEO James D. Robinson III, who among other things issued a strong statement against sexual harassment. American Express was one of the 60 best companies in the October 1989 *Working Mother* survey and the most admired of ten in the Diversified Financial category of *Fortune*'s January 29, 1990, survey of corporate reputations. The company devoted seven pages of its 1988 annual report to Public Responsibility.

American Express also has its critics. Working Assets halted all business with the company because its credit-card services continue to be offered in South Africa through a franchise arrangement. American Express is an endorser of the Statement of Principles, which entails making an annual contribution in support of the program.

The United Brotherhood of Carpenters & Joiners of America (UBC) Local 2230 called for a boycott of AmEx in the spring of 1986 because the company used nonunion contractors to construct its $60 million credit-card processing facility in Greensboro, North Carolina. In the Spring/Summer 1989 issue of *National Boycott News*, the company pointed out that over the past several years 86% of the dollars spent on U.S. facilities went to union contractors. It further noted that union bids were accepted in Greensboro and numerous other contracts were awarded to union bidders.

FAST FACTS:
- Philanthropic contributions totaled $21 million in 1988, roughly 1.58% of pretax earnings for that year. Although there was heavy emphasis on traditional giving through the United Way, AmEx also supported more innovative projects such as the Living with AIDS Fund and Bangladesh flood victims.

■ Of 77,000 employees, 43,000 are women, and women account for
42% of managers and officials.[8]
■ Responded with limited information.
■ New York, NY.

AMERICAN INTERNATIONAL GROUP

American International Group, a U.S. international insurance and
financial services company, derives half of its operating income from
other countries, and 37% of its assets are located outside of North
America. Even though the company has operations around the world,
it sold its sole South African subsidiary, American International
Insurance Co. Ltd., to Johannesburg Insurance Holdings Ltd. in 1987,
and no longer has operations there.

There is one woman, but no minority members, on AIG's 17-person
board of directors.

AIG ranked second most admired of ten in the Diversified Financial
category of *Fortune*'s January 29, 1990, survey of the reputations of
major U.S. corporations.

FAST FACTS:
■ More than 30,000 employees, over half of whom work overseas.
■ Responded with printed materials.
■ New York, NY.

AMERITECH

Ameritech, one of the nation's leading communications companies, is
a "responsible corporate citizen," according to the Calvert social
investment fund. This Baby Bell, which serves the Great Lakes
region, is attractive from several social perspectives.

Ameritech makes charitable contributions through its Ameritech
Foundation and subsidiary programs, which contributed more than
$18 million in 1989. However, each of its operating companies is in
the process of hiking corporate giving from current levels of between
1.0–1.5% to 2.0% by 1995. Each company decides how to allocate these
funds, but the general emphasis is on health and social services,
education, and economic development. Employee gifts to higher education, culture, public TV, and (in some states) private grade-school
education are matched two for one for the first $500, then one-and-a-
half to one for sums up to $4500. In 1989 Ameritech was awarded the
Business Community on the Arts' Outstanding Citizen award.

Some 45,000–50,000 of Ameritech's 77,000 employees belong to one of two unions: the Communications Workers of America or the International Brotherhood of Electrical Workers. In the summer of 1989 these workers went on strike for two-and-a-half weeks over wage and benefit packages before a new contract could be signed. On Ameritech's 15-member board of directors sits one woman— Hanna Gray. Women are well represented at Ameritech: 53% of all employees and 46% of managers are women. And a woman, Betty Elliott, is president of Ameritech Credit Corp. Certain areas of Ameritech have cafeteria-style benefits and employees can put aside pretax dollars for child care. Although policies vary by company, some form of flextime is available throughout the corporation. Ameritech also has an employee referral program to counsel employees on child and elder care decisions and for relocation assistance.

Recycling is a firmly entrenched practice at Ameritech. The company uses recycled paper in its offices and recycles directories and office paper at most locations.

FAST FACTS:

■ No South African operations; all operations are in the U.S.
■ No weapons-related businesses.
■ Responded with information.
■ Chicago, IL.

AMOCO

Amoco has been vocal about the need to strengthen student achievement. Improving standards is vital for "our nation's ability to compete successfully in an increasingly competitive global environment," wrote Richard M. Morrow, chairman of the board. To combat the problem of minorities not receiving sufficiently high-quality educations to compete in the workforce, the Amoco Foundation supports the National Action Council for Minorities in Engineering as well as other projects aimed at keeping minority youth in school. In 1988 the foundation made a total of $21.901 million in grants (0.66% of its $3.307 billion in pretax earnings), almost half of which went to education. It also sponsors the University of Chicago School Mathematics Project, an effort to develop a new curriculum to spur student interest in this field.

Numbers of minorities and women employed have steadily increased: Minorities totaled 19.5% of the workforce in 1988, up from 17.7% in 1984, and 8.6% of the officials and managers, up from 7.0%.

In 1988 26.7% of Amoco employees were women, against 24.2% four years earlier, and women made up 8.1% of the company's officials and managers in 1988, compared to only 5.2% in 1984.

The Republic of France and related parties have sued Amoco and certain subsidiaries, seeking damages for pollution from the stranding of the Amoco *Cadiz* on March 16, 1978, off Portsall, France. Amoco will pay damages, but the amount has yet to be fully settled.

FAST FACTS:

■ No South African operations.

■ An *insight* social recommendation as of October 1989.

■ Announced it would pump more cleanly burning, compressed natural gas at four Denver service stations in 1990.

■ No weapons manufacturing, although Amoco does bid for Department of Defense fuel contracts—a very small percentage of business.

■ One of eight companies forming the $16-million National Polystyrene Recycling Co. to provide companies with recycled plastic.

■ Ranked second most admired of ten in Petroleum Refining in *Fortune*'s January 29, 1990, corporate reputation survey.

■ Responded with information.

■ Chicago, IL.

ATLANTIC RICHFIELD

Rather than trying to beat the clean air agenda, Atlantic Richfield joined the environmentalists by introducing a reformulated gasoline called EC-1 Regular in California on September 1, 1989. This product is lead-free and benzene, aromatics, olefins, and sulfur have all been dramatically reduced. In a full-page ad in the October 11 *Wall Street Journal* the company said that if all leaded gasoline users in Southern California switched to EC-1, around 350 fewer tons of pollutants would enter the air each day. The reformulated gas is for older cars, of which there are about 1.2 million in the South Coast Air Basin of Southern California; although these account for only 15% of the cars on the road, they contribute 30% of the area's vehicular pollution.[9] It costs the company two cents more per gallon to manufacture EC-1 than regular leaded gas, but Arco is not charging its dealers more for the product in order to promote it. *Fortune* magazine cited EC-1 as one of its "Products of the Year" in its December 4 issue. Arco has been on recent buy lists of Calvert, *GOOD MONEY*, and *insight*.

Arco is included in *The 100 Best Companies to Work for in America*, where it is praised for having one of the best corporate newspapers, *The Spark*, and for its emphasis on excellence. Arco is considered a good place for both minorities and women to work, earning places on both *Black Enterprise* and *Working Mother*'s honor rolls. *Black Enterprise* cites its system of internal audits for reviewing the progress of individual affirmative action programs throughout its operating companies. Despite a 55% overall reduction in the workforce since 1981, the number of black and female employees has increased. Around 8.3% of Arco's U.S. employees are black, and blacks hold 3.5% of Arco's 4500 managerial positions. In 1988 Arco purchased $98.3 million worth of goods and services from minority vendors.

Women make up 11.2% of Arco officials and managers, and *Working Mother* said women are more prominent at Arco than at the other major oil companies. Unpaid leave of up to six months is available for dependent care.

FAST FACTS:
- No South African operations.
- No arms-related businesses, but Arco does sell jet fuel to the Department of Defense.
- 27,000 employees worldwide, the majority of whom work in the U.S.
- Gives between 1.0–2.0% of pretax income in charitable contributions; the Arco Foundation made nearly $10 million in direct grants in 1988.
- Arco Chemical was one of eight companies to form the National Polystyrene Recycling Company to provide industry with recycled plastic through five regional processing centers.[10]
- Most of Arco's oil comes from Alaska; *Money* cited it as one of five "likely losers" from the renewed emphasis on the environment since a ban on drilling in the Arctic National Wildlife Refuge is probable.[11] Arco, meanwhile, is exploring other potential drilling sites on Alaska's North Slope.
- Responded with information.
- Los Angeles, CA.

AVON PRODUCTS

The make-up of Avon's workforce is unique—women are in the majority of the 7300 person employee roster, and nearly 32% of the roughly 181 officers and directors are women. Minorities are also well represented. Blacks made up around 12.5% of total employees and 9.4% of officers and directors at Avon in 1989. *Black Enterprise*, which numbered the company among the 35 "best of the best" workplaces for blacks, ascribes the success of minorities and women at Avon in part to open access to corporate training programs that allow employees to advance.[12] On the company's 11-person board of directors sit three women and one black.

The Best Companies for Women praises Avon for taking a strong stance against sexual harassment.[13]

In June 1989 Avon announced it had ended all phases of animal testing of its products, and no testing is done in outside laboratories.

Avon, which ran into financial troubles once it diversified into the health-care area, sold off most of these businesses at a loss of $404.5 million in 1988 and is now focusing on its core beauty-care businesses again noted a company spokesperson.

FAST FACTS:

- No South African operations.
- No defense-related work.
- A social recommendation of Franklin's *insight* as of October 1989.
- Workforce is not unionized.
- Made $1.7 million in charitable contributions in 1988—a smaller figure than usual because of a difficult business year, according to an Avon spokesperson.
- Responded with information.
- New York, NY.

BAKER HUGHES

Baker Hughes provides equipment and services to the petroleum and construction industries and is the world's largest producer of drilling bits.

Baker Hughes has three South African subsidiaries employing around 500 workers, roughly half of whom are black. The company sold off one of its four divisions there in July 1989. It has signed the Statement of Principles and received the second-highest rating, Making Progress, for compliance for the three years through June 1989.

The company employs 21,000 worldwide, only 5–10% of whom are unionized. One Texas plant has 1200 employees who belong to the United Steelworkers union. There are no women or minority members on the board of directors, and out of 14 corporate officers, there is one woman, but no people of color. Of total employees, only 13% are women, something the company attributes to the industry. Numbers for minorities were unavailable. Pretax dollars may be put aside to pay for child care, and although policies vary by division, the company has a flextime option.

Baker Hughes makes charitable contributions through its charitable foundation, although it declined to specify the extent of its giving.

FAST FACTS:

■ No arms-related businesses or prime contracts with the Department of Defense.

■ Complies with OSHA and other regulations.

■ Responded with information.

■ Houston, TX.

BANKAMERICA CORP.

While BankAmerica's aggressive marketing of its retail products was termed "combat banking" by *The Wall Street Journal* in an October 2, 1989, article, the company's social initiatives have been more moderate, although on a wide range of fronts. If one area were to stand out, it would probably be equal employment efforts. Bank-America's numbers of minorities and women in upper management are good, even relative to banking, which is a field that has historically attracted both groups. Out of approximately 55,000 employees, roughly 40,000 are women and 20,000 minority members; of the 3253 employees considered upper management, 995 are women and 391 minorities. Likewise, two minority individuals and one woman sit on BankAmerica's 18-person board of directors.

In its "Equal Opportunity at Bank of America" publication, Chairman A. W. Clausen points out that 65% of the company's officials and managers are women and 30% minorities, relative to the average 45% and 16%, respectively, for the top 50 banks across the country. BankAmerica recruits at schools and organizations for minorities and women and has a written policy of holding no membership in clubs that discriminate on the basis of religion, race, or handicap status. In 1988, the company did $32.4 million worth of business with minority-owned businesses, and in 1989 was awarded the Minority Enterprise Development award.

FAST FACTS:

■ Never had South African operations; it ceased all lending to that country's public sector in 1983 and has made no new private-sector loans there since July 1985.

■ Bank of America is not unionized, although some subsidiaries are.

- Generally 1% of annual pretax earnings goes to charitable contributions.
- Won the United Way National Award in 1987 and 1988.
- Responded to questionnaire.
- San Francisco, CA.

BAXTER INTERNATIONAL

A manufacturer and marketer of health-care products, systems, and services, Baxter International performs a beneficial role by pioneering products such as treatments to extend the lives of kidney patients and hemophiliacs. It has also taken opportunities to do what good it can; in the fall of 1989 Baxter made a $100,000 donation to the American Red Cross to help victims of the San Francisco earthquake and made more than $750,000 worth of cash and supply donations to Hurricane Hugo victims. In other years it gave products and supplies to victims of the Armenian earthquake and Chernobyl. In 1989 Baxter earmarked $3 million for charitable contributions, primarily in the health-care and education areas—a below-average 0.6% of 1988 pretax income. Baxter is one of 60 corporate contributors to the Corporate Community School, a no-fee, full-curriculum school for underprivileged children in Chicago.[14] Baxter was a selection of both Pax and *Clean Yield* as of the summer of 1989, and was a social pick of Franklin's *insight*.

There are two women but no minority members on Baxter's 18-person board of directors. Of its 28 corporate officers, three are women, one of whom is black. Michele Hooper, a black woman, is president of Baxter's Canadian subsidiary. In 1988 the company instituted a management-incentive program for the recruiting and promoting of minorities and women. Baxter began publishing its EEO numbers as of its 1988 annual report. In 1988 minorities equaled 24.1% of the workforce and women 55%. As for officials and managers, 9.1% were minorities and 32.4% women.

Baxter was listed in *The 100 Best Companies to Work for in America*, published in 1985. One employee perk is its fitness centers at headquarters and at its primary R&D facility. Currently, employees can allocate money toward day care through Baxter's flexible benefits program. Chairman Vernon Loucks Jr., assigned a task force to study work/family options, and so the system may be revamped in 1990.

In 1989 the board of directors mandated that Baxter reduce all toxic emissions 80% by 1996. The Lakeland Audubon Society gave

Baxter a citation in 1988 for its environmental protection of the Lake Lulu Wetlands, Wisconsin. Baxter has joined forces with Waste Management to provide consulting services to health facilities on the disposal of medical waste.

FAST FACTS:
- No South African operations.
- No weapons manufacturing.
- Minimizing the number of animals used in testing through computer modeling; Baxter was accredited by a voluntary peer evaluation group, AAALAC.
- Responded with information.
- Deerfield, IL.

BELL ATLANTIC

One of the seven regional operating companies created out of the AT&T break-up, Bell Atlantic was a pick of Calvert as of early 1989 because of the company's strong employee/union relationship. More than two-thirds of Bell Atlantic's employees are represented by unions, primarily by the Communication Workers of America (representing 41,000 Bell Atlantic workers) and the International Brotherhood of Electrical Workers (representing 9100 workers in New Jersey and approximately 1900 workers in Pennsylvania).[15] In the summer of 1989, the unions went on a 23-day strike until a new contract could be reached. The primary issue at stake was health-care benefits, the cost of which the company wanted its employees to share.

Bell Atlantic's telephone directories are recyclable, something that had earlier been impossible because the inks used in printing the directories destroyed recycled paper.

FAST FACTS:
- No South African operations.
- No arms-related work.
- Contributions, the size of which it declined to specify, made through its foundation.
- Ranked second most admired of ten in Utilities category in *Fortune* survey.[16]
- Responded with information.
- Philadelphia, PA.

BETHLEHEM STEEL CORPORATION

Bethlehem Steel has taken several moderate social initiatives and recently strengthened its emphasis on the environment. The company has an environmental affairs department that reviews the policies of operating units, and its environmental policy goes hand in hand with the company's guiding principles: "We will require strict adherence to the letter and the spirit of all laws applicable to the conduct of our business." Bethlehem has recently increased its efforts to facilitate the recycling of used steel cans in addition to recycling steel plant wastes, and was granted a U.S. patent for the chemical stabilization/detoxification of certain waste materials generated within a steel plant. The company estimates its environmental equipment costs will run $60 million in 1990, up from roughly $10 million in 1988.

As for equal employment, there are 1800 women and 4400 minority members among the company's 30,000 employees. The numbers drop off sharply in upper management—there is only one woman and no minorities among the 200 employees considered upper management. In part, this is due to the industry, not historically one that's attracted women. Bethlehem does have a formal Minority Business Enterprise program, which has been in effect for 17 years. In 1988 the company purchased $10 million worth of goods and services from minority-owned businesses as well as $30 million from women-owned businesses. Corporate policy puts purchasing managers in charge of preparing and maintaining lists of possible minority-owned businesses and making sure they have the same opportunities as other contractors.

FAST FACTS:

- No South African ties.
- 78% of workforce is unionized.
- Since the beginning of the 1980s, Bethlehem laid off more than 39,000 workers.
- In fiscal 1987 Bethlehem had $23.3 million in arms-related defense contracts.[17]
- Did not release charitable contributions, but in 1989 60% went to United Way and other health and human service groups, two-thirds of the remaining 40% went to higher education, and the rest to cultural, public policy, and civic organizations "with close relationships to the company."
- Responded to questionnaire.
- Bethlehem, PA.

BLACK & DECKER

In a major turnaround Black & Decker successfully pulled itself out of a several-year slump, but economic stress took a toll on the company's social initiatives. In recent years charitable contributions have been reduced, according to a company spokesperson who declined to cite figures. This is an about-face for the company: In 1985 B&D was a member of the Baltimore Five-Percent Club, meaning that it contributed at least 1% of pretax income to charitable organizations and had pledged to increase this to 5% within three years.[18] Currently, employee gifts are matched dollar for dollar.

To turn the company around, CEO Nolan Archibald closed five plants, putting more than 2000 employees out of work.[19] The merger with Emhart in 1989, however, considerably swelled the total number of B&D employees to 36,000 worldwide. Of these, roughly half work in the U.S. Although domestic employees are not unionized, some of the Emhart plants have union affiliations.

The company sold off its South African subsidiary in the late 1980s but maintains what it termed "arms-length" distribution agreements that allow its products to be sold in South Africa.

B&D has been praised for emphasizing employee innovations and listening to its customers. This feedback system is formalized through dealer advisory councils, which help the company develop new products.

FAST FACTS:
- An Emhart subsidiary that does business with the Department of Defense is expected to be sold in 1990.
- One woman on 11-person board of directors.
- B&D did not release EEO numbers.
- No child care provisions at headquarters.
- Responded with limited information.
- Towson, MD.

BOEING

Boeing has several ethical strikes against it, but it also deserves gold stars for its generous charitable-giving budget and its ethics program.

Boeing ranked twelfth in Nuclear Free America's list of the top 50 nuclear weapons contractors for 1988, with prime Department of Defense and Department of Energy contracts worth $1,122,355,000. This diversified aerospace company's arms-related products include the Short Range Attack Missile (SRAM II), the Advanced Tactical Fighter, and automated information systems for the military.

Boeing's reputation suffered in the fall of 1989 when the company pleaded guilty to criminal charges related to unauthorized use of internal Pentagon planning documents in the early 1980s. The documents were obtained by Richard Fowler, a Boeing marketing manager, who was convicted in 1989 on fraud, conspiracy, and other charges for illegally funneling more than 100 classified documents into the company from 1978 to 1986, when he was fired. Prosecutor and court records contend that these documents gave Boeing and other large defense contractors unauthorized access to some of the military's most sensitive budget and acquisition information. Boeing is one of several defense contractors thought to be involved.[20]

By the late 1980s, Boeing was reemphasizing corporate ethics. Its efforts included CEO involvement, a toll-free number for reporting ethics violations, and an ethics committee that reports to the board.[21]

In late 1989 Boeing also had internal problems—57,000 unionized workers struck in early October 1989 and did not return to work until late November. The conflict revolved around employees wanting higher paychecks rather than management's offer of fatter lump-sum payments. The final contract did, in fact, increase payments more than the 4% wage increase but may have cost the company as much as salary concessions would have.[22]

Boeing is a generous corporate contributor and gave $16.75 million in cash and $3.5 million in in-kind donations to charitable organizations. Boeing's annual contributions are generally 1.5–2.0% of pretax earnings. Higher education and health are priorities for funding.

The Natural Resources Defense Council named Boeing one of the 11 largest emitters of carcinogenic chemicals unregulated by the Clean Air Act for its trichloroethylene emissions at its Wichita, Kansas, plant.[23] Yet Boeing makes a positive environmental contribution as a leader in photovoltaic and solar-energy technology. It had a solar cell with 37% efficiency in lab tests as of September 1989, which puts it in the ballpark of more conventional power sources.[24]

In 1989 Boeing agreed to pay $200,000 to the Federal Aviation Administration in connection with the miswiring of fire-protection systems on some 757 jetliners. In this civil suit the FAA alleged that Boeing didn't notify the agency until months after it discovered these problems, even though regulations require defects be reported within 24 hours of discovery.[25]

FAST FACTS:
- No South African operations.
- Most admired of ten in Aerospace category of *Fortune*'s January 29, 1990, survey of corporate reputations.
- 150,000 employees.
- No women on the 13-person board of directors.
- In 1988 Boeing purchased more than $166 million from minority-owned businesses and around $2.191 billion from small businesses.
- Responded with information.
- Seattle, WA.

BOISE CASCADE

"Sensitivity to the environment is a daily concern" at Boise Cascade because of its business: paper and forest-product manufacturing. The environmental steps the company has taken are moderate, as are its other social initiatives. About 10% of its pulp use is from recycled or secondary fiber, in line with the industry; its paper mills are 60% energy self-sufficient and are driven by the steam generated from the paper-milling process. In 1988 the company continued to support Project Learning Tree, a national environmental education program, with a $20,000 grant to the American Forest Foundation. Boise Cascade contributed over $3 million to educational and charitable organizations in the U.S. and Canada in 1988, a 36% increase over the previous year and a giving record for the company. Education and literacy was the company's top funding priority, receiving 36% of its allocations, including $200,000 for a new Ready to Read Program, which will purchase books for elementary schools in the communities where employees live.

The Occupational Safety and Health Administration (OSHA) is proposing $1.6 million in fines for the company's Rumford, Maine, pulp and paper mill, where it cited 535 violations. A spokesman for OSHA said the company showed "a substantial disregard...for the safety and health of its employees at the mill."[26] Boise Cascade will contest all the allegations and believes it will win on around half, although there will be things that "need to be fixed," according to a company spokesperson.

FAST FACTS:
- Of 2063 employees considered upper management, roughly 324 are women and 125 minorities.
- 51% of workforce is unionized—71 labor agreements with 17 different unions.

- Corporate headquarters provides referral service for child care.
- Up to two months unpaid parental leave for birth/adoption/to care for seriously ill child.
- Responded to questionnaire.
- Boise, ID.

BRISTOL-MYERS SQUIBB COMPANY

The 1989 merging of Bristol-Myers and Squibb joined together two major pharmaceutical companies, both of which have taken several positive social steps, although each has also known controversy. The agreement between the companies was friendly, although the new company will adopt what are essentially Bristol-Myers policies.

In 1989 Bristol-Myers agreed to provide its new AIDS drug dideoxyinosine (ddI) free of charge to all AIDS patients ineligible to participate in formal clinical testing. It made this decision on the heels of a suggestion by Anthony Fauci, director of the National Institute of Allergy and Infectious Disease, that AIDS treatments be selectively distributed as soon as shown to be safe, and he named ddI as a good candidate. The decision also followed a demonstration by AIDS activists from ACT UP in front of Bristol-Myers' Toronto office, which the company says did not affect its decision.[27] The drug, whose brand name is VIDEX, is being tested on AIDS patients who cannot tolerate AZT.

Meanwhile, Bristol-Myers is being boycotted by some medical professionals over its new infant formula, which it is marketing directly to the public. Although the quality of the product, a joint effort between Bristol-Myers Squibb and Gerber Products, isn't in dispute, infant formula has not traditionally been pitched directly to women. Some doctors fear the ads will encourage women to give up breast-feeding, and a few have even threatened to stop recommending any Bristol-Myers products over this.[28] Bristol-Myers explained that Gerber's advertising directs parents to a physician before making a decision on infant feeding and positions breast-feeding as the ideal method. Although Bristol-Myers markets infant formula to developing nations, it is not being boycotted for that, and in fact, was the first U.S. infant formula manufacturer to adopt the World Health Organization (WHO) International Code of Marketing of Breast-Milk Substitutes.

Bristol-Myers was named one of 15 companies to watch in *Black Enterprise*'s corporate survey. The company has an active minority recruitment program and in the first quarter of 1988 filled new openings with one minority member for every two nonminorities. Of Bristol-Myers' 34,100 employees, 18.6% are minority members, and minorities account for 10% of officials and managers. B-M has deposited more than $69 million with minority- and women-owned banks.[29]

Bristol-Myers has one South African subsidiary and has signed the Statement of Principles. It received the highest (Making Good Progress) compliance rating for four consecutive years through June 1989. Squibb has two subsidiaries, both of which also received the highest rating for compliance with the Statement of Principles for the past four years. Bristol-Myers Squibb's South African operations account for less than 1% of total company sales and employ roughly 580 people, 60% of whom are nonwhite. Bristol-Myers has asserted that the progress generated by signatory companies is part of the solution, not the problem.

Bristol-Myers Squibb does perform laboratory tests on live animals. In 1982 the company established a permanent subcommittee on animal welfare, which calls for minimizing the number of animals used whenever possible, reducing the severity of the tests, and using nonanimal or in vitro testing methods. Less than 1% of its lab-animal use is for consumer-product testing, and its labs are all accredited by the American Association for Accreditation of Laboratory Animal Care.

An annual environmental coordinators' conference allows the company to share information and reaffirm its commitment to this area. Some steps taken are the removal of underground storage tanks at one division and a paper-recycling program at a facility.

FAST FACTS:
- No weapons-related businesses.
- Bristol-Myers Squibb projects contributions of $16.5 million for 1990, almost half of which will go to medical and health organizations. It also has earmarked nearly $3 million for business contributions to professional organizations.
- Responded with information.
- New York, NY.

BRUNSWICK CORP.

Brunswick Corp., the world's largest manufacturer of recreational boats and a maker of machine engines, is unstinting when it comes to quality: The company declares it "will either be the highest quality producer in every market we serve or we won't be in that business."

Essentially a recreation/leisure company, Brunswick also has a defense division that was awarded over $12 million worth of prime contracts in 1988. One division ranked 203rd in terms of DoD contracts that year. It produced the Forward Looking Infrared (FLIR) system for the U.S. Navy and was developing the Rifleman's Assault Weapon (RAW) in 1989.

Brunswick made $1,215,969 million in charitable donations through its foundation in 1988, a below-average 0.4% of pretax income, with education receiving the bulk of the funding. By making grants to organizations at which employees volunteer and by matching gifts to education, cultural organizations, and the FishAmerica Foundation on a generous two-for-one basis, Brunswick involves its employees in the funding process. Brunswick was one of only 70 companies to receive the 1989 Presidential Citation for Private Sector Initiatives in recognition of the Brunswick minority scholarship program.

Since 1983 Brunswick has boasted an active employee stock ownership plan, which recognizes employee contributions to the company's well-being.

FAST FACTS:
- No South African operations.
- No women on ten-member board of directors, although there are two female corporate officers.
- Around 23,000 employees.
- Responded with information.
- Skokie, IL.

BURLINGTON NORTHERN INC.

In a return to its roots, Burlington Northern Inc. spun off its energy and natural resource businesses to shareholders as a separate corporation on New Year's Day, 1989, and is again solely a railroad system. BNI has taken several moderate social steps and has demonstrated in a variety of ways that it is a good corporate neighbor.

BNI generally hands out 1.5% of pretax net income to charitable organizations each year. Funds are distributed through its foundation; areas of emphasis include education, youth services, culture, civic programs, and hospitals. Through its foundation grants program employee gifts to education are matched two for one and faculty achievement awards are granted to professors for excellence. In 1988 the Second Harvest network of food banks honored the railroad for providing free transportation for its food drives.

There are no women on BNI's 11-person board of directors. Of 33,416 employees, 2260 are women and 2608 are minorities. And there are 304 women and 142 minorities among BNI's 3227 professionals, officials, and managers. Pretax dollars may be put aside for child care.

The company has been confronting soil and water pollution problems stemming from spills or buried storage tanks that leaked diesel fuel and lubricating oil over the years. It is cooperating in joint cleanup projects with state and local governments.

FAST FACTS:

- No South African operations.
- Around 90% of BNI's workforce is unionized.
- Responded with information.
- Fort Worth, TX.

CAPITAL CITIES/ABC

Capital Cities/ABC has used its position as a news-media company to help some worthy causes. Its media capabilities have supported Partnership for Drug Free America, with broadcast and print advertising for this program in 1988 worth more than $27 million. It is also very active in Project Literacy U.S. (PLUS). In another socially positive step, ABC teamed up with the other networks to put together a taped discussion on sexual harassment, which it shows to all employees.

Capital Cities/ABC has no South African operations or assets, although it does have a news bureau there to report South African stories.

FAST FACTS:

- No Department of Defense contracts.
- One woman on the 17-person board of directors; no women or minorities among eight executive officers.
- 19,000 employees.
- Gave approximately $1.5 million to charitable organizations in 1987,[30] around 0.27% of that year's pretax income.
- Matches gifts to higher education dollar for dollar up to $2000 annually.
- Currently reviewing day care, although no provisions at this time.
- Responded with information.
- New York, NY.

CHAMPION INTERNATIONAL

Champion International, a forest-products company, has been praised for opening an on-site day care center at its Stamford, Connecticut, headquarters in 1988. The center is cost-subsidized, and pretax dollars can be set aside to help employees pay the bill. Current enrollment: 40 children with 46 more on the waiting list, according to *Working Mother*, which pronounced the company one of the 60 best for working mothers in its October 1989 survey. Benefits for working parents are generous, allowing up to six months of unpaid parental leave and offering flextime and job-sharing options.

Champion is carefully regulated by federal and state environmental standards, which it meets with "a little bit extra" in some areas, according to a company spokesperson. The company is taking interesting strides in wildlife preservation. In the fall of 1989 it added a full-time wildlife biologist to its staff. Owning 6.5 million acres of land, Champion believes it can make a difference in this area. Its program began with a forester in Maine making mating boxes for wood ducks and includes allowing beekeepers to keep hives on Champion land.

In 1989 the company expected charitable contributions to total around $6.4 million (pretax income for 1988 was $730 million). In September 1989 the company extended its dollar-for-dollar matching gifts program to include all nonprofit organizations rather than just education, and it opened up the program to retirees. Its Champion Fund for Community Service hands out grants to employee volunteers to fund pet projects; a panel of employee peers decides which projects to support. Another interesting twist to Champion's charitable giving is the Community Needs Assessment Program. Employees interview community members and put together projects based on their findings. The grants range from $30,000–$200,000, and fund projects such as a Michigan project to combat high rates of alcoholism in the Upper Peninsula by offering a rehabilitation counseling service and by supporting traveling arts projects there.

Chairman Andrew Sigler headed the Business Roundtable's ethics program to examine different ethics programs at ten major corporations.[31]

FAST FACTS:
- No South African operations.
- No weapons businesses.
- Franklin social pick as of October 1989.

- Roughly 4000 women out of 21,609 employees; women make up 7.8% of 200–300 managers.
- Responded with information.
- Stamford, CT.

CIGNA CORPORATION

CIGNA, a multinational insurance and financial services company, has taken several admirable community and employee initiatives. In September 1989, New Pendel, the regional arm of the National Minority Supplier Development Council, named CIGNA Corporation of the Year. All purchasing department employees are expected to increase the number of minority businesses from which the company purchases goods and services. Out of CIGNA's $144 million purchasing budget for 1988, 10.1% went to minority-owned businesses.

Meanwhile, the insurer is tackling social problems well beyond the traditional. In 1988, Philadelphia Mayor Wilson Goode presented the company with a citation for its involvement in literacy teaching. CIGNA established the first corporate on-site learning center to train CIGNA employees as literacy tutors. And a regional study it funded on AIDS in the workplace resulted in a manual for employers. CIGNA also provided grants for outreach to black children and youths in Philadelphia. Through its matching gifts program, CIGNA matches employees' contributions of up to $5000 a year dollar for dollar. In 1988 the company provided more than $8 million in grants, including matching gifts.

CIGNA also has several attractive employee programs. For example, its Wellness Program, dating back to 1979, offers exercise classes, medical examinations, counseling on marital and alcohol abuse problems, and even a seven-week stop-smoking course taught on company time. CIGNA's confidential Speak Easy program allows employees to talk with upper management about work-related problems, including sexual harassment.

FAST FACTS:

- CIGNA divested its South African insurance subsidiary in 1987 and former employees now own the operation.
- Ranked second least admired of ten for Diversified Financial in *Fortune*'s January 29, 1990, survey.
- At year-end 1988, 48,615 employees total; for a group of 30,000 with statistics available, women are 70% of total and 16% of upper management, and minorities are 21% overall and 8.5% upper management.

■ Less than 1% unionized.
■ CIGNA PAC contributed $200,000 in 1988.
■ No-cost child care referrals and an on-site day care facility in Bloomfield, Connecticut, one of its two major locations.
■ Responded to questionnaire.
■ Philadelphia, PA

CITICORP

Citicorp, a bank holding company the largest unit of which is Citibank, is known as a trend-setter in its industry. But although first to launch a large network of automated teller machines in the late 1970s, Citicorp has not always fared so well in the public eye. Citicorp has come under fire for continuing to provide loans to South Africa long after most other banks had cut off that country. Antiapartheid activists boycotted the company; in the later 1980s it was estimated that U.S. churches closed down over $125 million worth of Citibank accounts because of the company's lending policy toward South Africa.[32] The company said that while some religious community depositors withdrew funds from Citibank, it "would put the figure much lower" than at $125 million. In 1989 the company stopped extending new credit to South African borrowers for all purposes. In mid-1989 Citicorp was an endorser of the Statement of Principles, which means it makes an annual contribution to the program; it was a charter signatory of the original Sullivan Principles.

Others have challenged the tough repayment schedule Citicorp set for Brazil, which called for the repayment of $436 million in debt in the last quarter of 1988. Some link this to Brazil's cutting its social programs and further exploiting its rain forests.[33] Citicorp noted that the schedule was negotiated between the 15 largest commercial bank creditors, of which Citicorp is one, and the Brazilian government.

Just the same, Citicorp has its champions. It was the second most admired of ten in the Commercial Banking category of *Fortune*'s survey.[34] And Citicorp was profiled in *The 100 Best Companies to Work for in America*. The authors praised the company for its fast-paced, go-getter ambience and its lack of an old boy network.

Citicorp made $22 million in charitable contributions in 1989, or 1.43% of its pretax earnings. This represents a noteworthy increase from the $15.89 million donated in 1988, which equalled 0.59% of pretax earnings. In 1989, 57% of this funding went to education.

FAST FACTS:
- Of 26 people considered senior management, two were women and one a minority member.
- Almost half of 89,000 employees work outside the U.S.
- Responded with limited information.
- New York, NY.

THE COCA-COLA CO.

Minority development "is it," at Coca-Cola. In the early 1980s Operation PUSH and Reverend Jesse Jackson reached an agreement with the company that ended a brief boycott. As part of its long-time commitment to minority development, Coke agreed to increase the number of black-owned distributorships, to put a black on its board of directors, and to establish a venture capital fund for black-owned businesses. The program worked. Coca-Cola was recently listed as one of the top corporations in *Black Enterprise*'s survey and was praised for its management-development and promote-from-within policies. The February 1989 article notes that 20% of the beveragemaker's nearly 10,000 domestic employees are black, as are 8% of its 1522 managers. Coca-Cola also spends more than $70 million each year with minority vendors. Coke received the 1988 National Urban League's Equal Opportunity Day Award for its commitment to opportunities for minorities and women. Of 41 corporate officers, nine are women. The company has the Child Care Information and Referral Service to help working parents.

Coca-Cola runs an active recycling program at corporate headquarters and in 1988 sold back more than 500,000 pounds of cans, glass containers, plastic soft drink bottles, white office paper, cardboard, and newspaper for $26,000, which it donated to local charities. For these efforts Coke received Keep America Beautiful's National Award for Local Business and Industry and the American Paper Institute's Best Paper Recycling Story of the Year, Corporate Category, award.

The Coca-Cola Foundation announced it would focus its charitable giving for the 1990s exclusively on education, donating between $4 and $6 million each year and a total of $50 million for the decade, with minority education receiving a significant portion. This is in addition to Coke's traditional $6 million in annual corporate giving.[35] The combined $11 million Coke annually earmarks for philanthropic causes was around 0.7% of its 1988 pretax income.

Coca-Cola's South African disinvestment was particularly well thought through and innovative. However, the Coke Campaign has launched a visible boycott of the company for selling its products in South Africa. Coca-Cola has disinvested, or sold off, its South African assets. Those boycotting the company are not satisfied with this because the company supplies Coke syrup to South Africa and has trademark agreements there. "The Campaign contends that the company simply sold away its South Africa investment while maintaining operations there."[36] Coke points out that it helped a group of black South Africans buy the majority share of its Coca-Cola bottling factory. As part of its disinvestment plan, Coca-Cola made a $10-million donation to establish the Equal Opportunity Foundations, South Africa-based funds dedicated to laying the groundwork for postapartheid South Africa. Trustees on the board include prominent black leaders Archbishop Desmond Tutu and Reverend Allan Boesak. In disinvesting, Coke moved its bottling plant from South Africa to Swaziland, one of the black-ruled homelands, so it wouldn't contribute taxes to the apartheid regime. Critics contend that this is another attempt to skirt the issue of full divestment from South Africa. Although the Coke Campaign has grabbed national attention, prominent Atlanta civil rights figures like Coretta Scott King and Mayor Andrew Young have accepted the company's efforts as sufficient.[37]

FAST FACTS:
- No weapons-related operations.
- Ranked eighth most admired of 305 companies in *Fortune*'s January 29, 1990, survey of corporate reputations.
- Implemented HealthWorks as well as a headquarter-based fitness center.
- Employee gifts of up to $4000 each year are matched on a two-for-one basis.
- Boycotted by the International Society for Animal Rights since 1985 for sponsoring and promoting rodeos.[38] Coke contends that the members of the Professional Rodeo Cowboy Association follow rigid rules for prevention of injury.
- Responded with information.
- Atlanta, GA.

COLGATE-PALMOLIVE

Worldwide consumer giant Colgate-Palmolive is a challenge to evaluate because 60% of its employees work outside the U.S. It's therefore not surprising to find the company in South Africa. Colgate-Palmolive has signed the Statement of Principles and received the highest compliance rating, Making Good Progress, for every year from inception.

Colgate-Palmolive gives over 2% of annual pretax income to charitable organizations, according to *Shopping for a Better World*. Colgate's worldwide dental health programs cover 25 million children each year. It also sponsors youth athletic programs around the world, including the Colgate Women's Games, a track and field event for girls and young women from the inner-city neighborhoods of New York. Meanwhile, it is helping support affordable housing in Jersey City, N.J., at the site of a former factory.

FAST FACTS:

■ Two women on 12-person board of directors.
■ Responded with printed information.
■ New York, NY.

COMMONWEALTH EDISON

Commonwealth Edison operates the nation's largest network of nuclear facilities with six plants and 12 nuclear units. For the first nine months of 1989 around 82.6% of the utility's energy was nuclear, up from 77% the previous year. Commonwealth Edison pointed out that for all but one of its fossil stations its emissions of acid rain-causing sulfur dioxide were well below federal and state standards. That's because the company imports cleaner-burning Western coal rather than the high-sulfur Eastern or Midwestern coal on which other companies depend. As regulations of these emissions tighten, the company will be well ahead of competitors because nuclear energy does not give off emissions. Of course, nuclear energy has the problem of hazardous waste, which C.E. stores in spent-fuel stations on company property. Ultimately, the Department of Energy is responsible for the storage and disposal of spent nuclear fuel from reactors.

Commonwealth Edison signed a Fair Share Agreement with the NAACP, which sets goals for strengthening corporate practices on minority issues.

The utility is working toward greater public safety through Edison's E-Team. Posters saying "Look out for the Supertruck" instruct people that Edison employees will assist people in need. The program received a recent presidential citation as one of the top 100 community service programs in the country.

FAST FACTS:
- No South African operations.
- No business with the Department of Defense.
- 18,000 employees.
- Most hourly employees belong either to the International Brotherhood of Electrical Workers or the United Mineworkers.
- No day care provisions.
- No numbers available on women and minorities in the company.
- Responded with information.
- Chicago, IL.

COMPUTER SCIENCES CORP.

Computer Sciences provides consulting and communications services on information systems technology, primarily for federal, local, and foreign governments; however, it derives around two-thirds of its revenues from the U.S. government. In 1988 it ranked 44th in terms of Department of Defense prime contracts for research, development, testing, and evaluation, with contracts worth a total of $79,573,000, according to the DOD.

In 1988, all of Computer Sciences' divisions together gave around $500,000 in charitable contributions, 0.57% of the pretax income for FY89 (March), which was $84,464,000. Each division makes donations on a request basis, and local operations determine where to distribute funds.

Women and minorities are represented at around industry average, said a corporate spokesperson, who would not provide numbers. There are neither women nor minorities on the eight-person board of directors.

The company does not work with South Africa.

FAST FACTS:
- Around 20,000 employees.
- Responded with information.
- El Segundo, CA.

CONTROL DATA

Although Control Data—a provider of computer products and services—was known for its social welfare programs in the 1960s and 1970s, tougher times in the 1980s spurred it to cut back many of these programs, according to *The Best Companies for Women*. For this reason, in conjunction with conversations with employees and the sketchy data given for women in upper management, the authors excluded Control Data from its 52-company roster. Control Data told the authors that 11% of 4466 employees in upper management were women but declined to give statistics for the highest levels of the company.[39] Still, there are two women on the company's 14-person board of directors.

This computer concern has some attractive policies on the books. It sent letters and brochures to employees about spouse and child abuse, announcing that corporate counselors were available to help with family violence problems.[40] In 1974 it introduced EAR, a 24-hour counseling service available to employees and their families. *The 100 Best Companies to Work for in America* pointed out that in the late 1960s the company chose to build a plant in a depressed North Minneapolis neighborhood and to recruit employees from there.

Control Data supplies its products to the government and was the 41st largest nuclear weapons contractor in 1988 in terms of prime contracts from the Department of Defense and Department of Energy, according to Nuclear Free America. These contracts were worth $87,777,000.

Working Assets has accused Control Data of sham divestment because it maintained the full range of computer sales to South Africa after selling off those assets.[41]

Financial problems in many of its markets have hurt the company in the eyes of the financial community. In the *Fortune* survey of corporate reputations, Control Data ranked third from the bottom in a field of the country's 305 most admired companies.[42]

FAST FACTS:
- Responded with limited information.
- Minneapolis, MN.

DATAPOINT

Datapoint, the computer concern that pioneered local area networking in the 1970s, was undergoing financial difficulties at this writing, and evaluating ways of maximizing shareholder value including putting the company up for sale.[43] One interesting aspect of Datapoint is that the chairman of its board is Asher Edelman, more famous as a corporate raider than as a corporate leader. That didn't stop another raider—Martin Ackerman—from waging a proxy battle for the company.[44] The outcome of this will surely shape Datapoint's social policies. However, few positives could currently be located for this company, which did not respond to calls for information on programs.

Datapoint has two South African sales offices, PunchLine (Pty) Ltd. and PowerNet Services (Pty) Ltd., both in Johannesburg. Datapoint was not a signatory of the Statement of Principles as of June 1989.

Datapoint's CEO and president is Michael Michigami, an Asian-American, and one woman, Doris Bencsik, sits on Datapoint's seven-person board of directors.

FAST FACTS:
■ Responded with limited information.
■ San Antonio, TX.

DELTA AIR LINES

A no-layoff policy and a cradle-to-grave approach to benefits have earned Delta a loyal following among its employees. Around 10% of the workforce is unionized—Delta's 6000 pilots—and, as *The 100 Best Companies to Work for in America* points out, most Delta employees haven't felt the need to organize because they are already well treated. The airline's exemplary record with employees stands in contrast to the bitter strife of other industry members.

In July 1989 Delta introduced an employee stock ownership program (ESOP).

Delta was a Parnassus pick and a social recommendation of Franklin's *insight* in 1989.

FAST FACTS:
■ No operations in, or flight routes to, South Africa.
■ One woman and one minority member of 14-person board of directors.
■ No defense-related contracts.
■ Delta gave approximately $450,000 in charitable contributions for 1987, around 0.1% of its pretax earnings.
■ Responded with information.
■ Atlanta, GA.

DIGITAL EQUIPMENT CORP.

Digital Equipment Corp. is one major company with an immediately recognizable name that's still found its way into many socially responsible investors' portfolios—*GOOD MONEY*, Parnassus, Calvert, Franklin, and Shearson Lehman Hutton's ethical investment specialists all count, or have counted, it as one of their picks. Digital won one of five Corporate Conscience awards from the Council on Economic Priorities in 1988 and has been cited for excellence in *The Best Companies for Women*, *The 100 Best Companies to Work for in America*, and the corporate surveys of *Working Mother* and *Black Enterprise* magazines.

One key to Digital's ethical success is its treatment of its employees. This extends to women and minorities, who are not only hired on an equal basis but are actively sought out through advertising in minority and women's publications and by maintaining ties to these groups' professional organizations. A signed policy statement from president Kenneth Olsen in July 1989 read: "We will provide a work environment free from discrimination and harassment of any kind." Period. The statement explicitly includes veterans, homosexuals, and the disabled, something many other corporations do not. Digital has one black on its board of directors and one female officer of the company.

Digital has been generous in terms of corporate giving, contributing $35 million in FY89 (June), or nearly 2.5% of that year's pretax earnings. Additionally, it gave out $5.5 million in matching employee gifts to nonprofit organizations.

One last, particularly impressive fact about Digital is that it's never had a layoff. Even though sales growth has recently slowed as competition has toughened,[45] this tradition has not been broken.

FAST FACTS:

■ Never had South African operations.
■ Digital's sexual harassment program is "highly regarded," according to *The Best Companies for Women*.
■ No direct business with the Department of Defense, although it does sell to prime contractors.
■ Responded with information.
■ Maynard, MA.

THE WALT DISNEY COMPANY

The Walt Disney Company, which has turned magic and illusion into big business, is not perceived the same way by all corporate watchdogs. Both Pax and *GOOD MONEY* counted it among their socially responsible picks in 1989. Disney has no South African ties and is not a weapons manufacturer or a heavy polluter. But *The 100 Best Companies to Work for in America* decided to exclude the company from the top U.S. corporations profiled, saying that a strike in the mid-1980s typified worker bitterness. "Nearly all said they felt Disney has lost 'the family touch' and is becoming overly concerned with making money, with the result that it has begun to seem little different from other big companies."[46]

Disney *does* have several social positives. It signed a Fair Share agreement with the NAACP, indicating its willingness to strengthen its policies on black people's concerns. Child care is available to employees through KinderCare. And two women sat on Disney's 14-person board of directors as of year-end 1988.

In its 1988 annual report Disney described its co-sponsoring trips for 10,000 disadvantaged children from nine countries, including the Soviet Union, to its theme parks for Mickey Mouse's 60th birthday celebration.

FAST FACTS:
■ 46,000 employees.
■ Responded with limited information.
■ Burbank, CA.

DOW CHEMICAL

Dow Chemical is no stranger to controversy, and yet the company has made admirable efforts in recent years to turn around its image. One sign is the openness Dow projects when asked for information and the wide range of pamphlets it has published on social issues. Although Dow literature does not inform you of the company's historical conflicts, it doesn't entirely skirt the issue. In its 1985 Public Interest Report, a Dow official addresses its environmental record this way: "We've been through some contentious times in the past, but I believe they are largely behind us. Today, we're focused on improved understanding of those who sometimes differ with our view, and on developing positive programs for the future."

Dow manufactured napalm during the Vietnam war and later made the defoliant commonly called Agent Orange, which Vietnam veterans blame for physical and psychological problems as well as birth defects in their children. One of seven manufacturers of this defoliant, Dow agreed to help establish a $180-million Agent Orange claimant trust as part of a May 7, 1984, court-directed settlement; however, the company maintains that the amount of dioxin in the defoliant was insufficient to create health problems and says it is "certain their [Vietnam veterans'] problems were not caused by

Agent Orange." In another controversy, Dow stopped manufacturing Bendectin, an antinausea drug, because of numerous lawsuits alleging links to birth defects. Dow asserts the drug is safe and cites epidemiological studies and FDA reports to support this. As of mid-September 1989 28 judgments stand in favor of Merrell Dow, of which 21 are final, and three verdicts stand in favor of individual plaintiffs, none of which were final at this writing.

Rather than battling regulatory agencies, the Dow of the later 1980s was pitching in on some of the tougher environmental challenges the country faces. Dow is one of eight polystyrene manufacturers teaming up to form the National Polystyrene Recycling Company, which has set a goal of recycling 25% of all disposable polystyrene products by 1995. In 1986 Dow formalized its commitment to reducing waste through its WRAP (Waste Reduction Always Pays) program. From 1974 to 1988, Dow's Michigan Division had reduced air emissions by 92%. *GOOD MONEY*, a newsletter reporting on social responsibility issues, praised Dow for joining with the Sierra Club to endorse a proposed federal law that would sharply reduce hazardous-waste production.[47] And the World Environment Center awarded Dow its 1989 gold medal for international environmental achievement. And yet Dow is far from perfect—*Forbes* reported that in 1989 it was partially responsible for 31 toxic-waste sites identified by the EPA as in urgent need of attention.[48]

Dow has also taken outstanding steps to improve employee benefits, underscored by its being named one of the 60 best companies for working mothers. Women represent 10.1% of the company's 3545 officials and managers. The company has provided two-thirds of the support for Child Care Concepts, an agency that provides help in finding child care. And in 1989 it placed a full-time family issues coordinator on staff. Meanwhile, up to $5000 in pretax income can be set aside annually for dependent care through a government program, and Dow's president championed a diversity effort to address these issues.

FAST FACTS:

- ∎ Dow sold off its South African operations in the later 1980s and has no licensing agreements there.
- ∎ Second most admired of ten in Chemicals category of *Fortune's* January 29, 1990, survey.
- ∎ Has PACs.
- ∎ Purchased around $24.5 million from minority-owned vendors in 1988.

- Sponsors a health program called Up with Life and has an employee development center with training capabilities and health and fitness facilities.
- Performs live-animal testing and is accredited by the American Association for Accreditation of Laboratory Animal Care. It has spent more than $10 million since 1980 in investigating and developing alternatives to animal testing.
- A well-above-average safety record, with only .129 lost time injuries per million work hours in 1988 compared to 3.1 reported by the chemical industry in 1987.
- More than 50% of Dow's sales are from overseas operations.
- In 1988 Dow contributed more than $20 million to U.S. charitable organizations, more than half of which went toward education. That represents around 1.11% of domestic pretax income.
- Responded to questionnaire.
- Midland, MI.

DU PONT

Du Pont's chemistry is complicated. On the one hand, it was the tenth largest nuclear materials contractor in 1988, according to Nuclear Free America; on the other, it's one of only a few companies disseminating information on rape and child abuse to its employees. Du Pont was the third most admired of 305 large U.S. corporations for community and environmental responsibility in *Fortune* magazine's January 29, 1990, survey of corporate reputations. Du Pont pioneered its personal safety program in 1985, which includes an eight-hour rape prevention workshop for women only. There is also a class for managers to discuss how to give sensitive and informed support to abuse victims. A Du Pont employee who's been raped is given up to six months of paid leave to recuperate and access to the company's legal department.

Working mothers are also treated exceptionally well at Du Pont, as is clear by its ranking as one of the top ten companies in *Working Mother*'s October 1989 survey. It has invested more than $1 million in child care facilities over the past three years in New Castle, Delaware, where 25% of its employees work. Of Du Pont's 28,000 managers and professionals, over 12% are women and over 8% minority members—a 24% increase within five years. On its 20-person board of directors sit two women and one minority member.

On the vital environmental issue of chlorofluorocarbons (CFCs),

Du Pont has pledged to phase them out of several major market segments in the early 1990s and completely by the turn of the century. This is in response to the finding that CFCs may have contributed to a 2% decline in global ozone depletion since the 1970s. In 1989 the company announced it would build a plastics recycling plant with Waste Management.

As admirable as these steps are, Du Pont is also estimated to have 64 toxic waste sites designated by the EPA as in need of urgent attention.[49] These are Superfund sites, and involvement is frequently shared with other companies. Du Pont disposes of more than 95% of its waste on company property. When Du Pont announced it no longer wished to operate the Department of Energy's nuclear materials facility in Savannah River, South Carolina, it promised the plant could be operated safely. Structural flaws and accidents were later uncovered, although the Department of Energy took responsibility for keeping the mishaps from the public.[50]

Du Pont has a 30-person sales office in South Africa; it is a signatory of the Statement of Principles and received the highest (Making Good Progress) rating in June 1989.

FAST FACTS:
- Managed $1,206,987,000 in DoE and DoD contracts in 1988, according to Nuclear Free America.
- Gave an estimated $31 million in 1988 charitable contributions, 51% of which went to education, according to the *Taft Corporate Giving Directory.*
- Responded with information.
- Wilmington, DE.

EASTMAN KODAK COMPANY

Kodak's social picture isn't always clear. Its record on affirmative action is excellent; in fact, the company won one of five Corporate Conscience Awards from the Council on Economic Priorities in 1988 for its equal opportunity programs. Both *Working Mother* and *Black Enterprise* cited the company as among the best for working mothers and blacks, respectively. As of March 1989 the company had 78,803 employees, 11.7% of whom were minorities and 25.5% women. Minorities accounted for 5% and women for 9.2% of the company's officials and managers. Meanwhile, two women and one black sit on its 16-person board of directors. Kodak's benefits and programs are also impressive—it offers a comprehensive family-oriented benefits package, including up to 17 weeks of unpaid leave for family obligations, child care, and resource referral services, alternative work schedules, and a dependent care expense plan in pretax dollars. In 1988 Kodak made a $1-million commitment to the United Negro College Fund, and in 1989 50% of company scholarships went to minority students.

On environmental issues, Kodak's record is murkier. The Natural Resources Defense Council found Kodak one of the 11 largest emitters of carcinogenic chemicals unregulated by the Clean Air Act, for its methylene chloride air emissions. Used in making film, methylene chloride was also shown to have contaminated groundwater in the vicinity of Kodak Park.[51] Kodak agreed in writing to reduce the emission of methylene chloride from its Kodak Park facility 30% by 1991 and 70% by 1995. It already recycles 96% of that chemical used. And the company, known as the Great Yellow Father, has announced a program to guarantee the value of homes near Kodak Park that may have been affected by methylene chloride ground seepage. Kodak will also embark on a $100-million, five-year project to replace, upgrade, or eliminate all chemical storage tanks at its primary manufacturing site.

In 1988 Kodak acquired Sterling Drug, which makes Bayer aspirin; the company had come under fire for selling its painkiller dipyrone to developing nations after the USFDA withdrew it in 1974 for possible severe side effects related to blood disorders. A shareholder resolution in 1984 asked that dipyrone products be removed or reformulated worldwide, but the vote was defeated by 92.7%. Sterling maintains that dipyrone's association with agranulocytosis is extremely slight; a five-year study by the International Agranulocytosis and Aplastic Anemia Study in 1986 revealed that the excess risk of this disorder is only an estimated 0.0003% in 14-day users and no risk of aplastic anemia is posed. Furthermore, Sterling offers an international information sheet to users.

FAST FACTS:
- Listed in *The 100 Best Companies to Work for in America*.
- Offers an annual wage dividend to employees.
- Spends millions each year on basic reading and arithmetic skills for employees.[52]
- Devoted 1.1% of 1988 pretax earnings to charitable contributions.
- No union, although, as of late 1989 there was a drive by The International Union of Electrical Workers to organize.
- Sold off South African operations.
- Directed $20–25 million toward minority-owned businesses in 1989.

■ Uses in vitro methods of animal testing to minimize numbers of live animals involved.
■ Ranked 341 in Department of Defense prime contracts for FY88, at $3,458,000.
■ Responded to questionnaire.
■ Rochester, NY.

EXXON

Exxon, the world's largest energy company, is linked in many concerned investors' minds to the running aground of the Exxon *Valdez* tanker off Alaska on March 24, 1989, and the spilling of 10.8 million gallons of oil into Prince William Sound. In early 1990, Exxon was indicted by the U.S. government on criminal counts—two felony charges for violating laws about the mental capacity and competency of ship crew and three misdemeanor charges.[53] Its reputation, which was fairly good before the spill, has suffered. Although *Fortune* magazine ranked Exxon most admired of ten in the Petroleum Refining category of its corporate reputation survey in early 1989, it sank to sixth in the same category for the magazine's January 29, 1990, survey.

Exxon estimated that cleanup costs for the *Valdez* spill had cost over $2 billion by year-end 1989, excluding potential liabilities from litigation, making it one of the most expensive industrial accidents in history. (As of January 1990 there were 170 lawsuits filed against the company over this alone.) Although nearly 20,000 angry Exxon customers returned their credit cards to the company, the cost of boycotts and irate customers is difficult to gauge. In the months following the spill, Exxon's stock hovered while similar companies gained 20–25%, according to Michael Young, an international oil analyst at Smith Barney, Harris Upham.[54] And the approximately 500,000 gallons of heating oil leaking from an Exxon pipeline into New York's Arthur Kill in early January 1990 is bound to reinforce the negatives against the company.

How harshly to judge a company for such errors is an individual decision. Alyeska, the company that operates the pipeline, and Exxon have been charged with being inadequately prepared for implementing cleanup plans.[55] Until the lawsuits are tried, Exxon's responsibility for the *Valdez* accident is difficult to gauge. An Exxon proposal not to release evidence to the public might mean that less is known about this than most investors would wish.[56] Exxon did respond to shareholder protests by naming an environmentalist to its board of directors in August 1989.

Prior to the *Valdez* spill, Exxon was included in *The 100 Best Companies to Work for in America*. The authors praised Exxon, saying that "sensitivity to the needs of minorities, females and other protected groups" is part of employee reviews. Exxon was also named one of "The 50 Best Places for Blacks to Work" in *Black Enterprise* magazine. In 1988 minorities made up 11.4% of officials and managers and 22.9% of the total workforce. Likewise, women accounted for 10.0% of officials and managers and 25.9% of total employees. The *Black Enterprise* article also highlighted Exxon's system for making sure that talented employees advance.

In 1988 Exxon made contributions of $34.8 million in the United States and $14.2 million outside, for a total of around 0.57% of that year's $8.3 billion in worldwide pretax earnings. More than $3 million was donated to environmental, public information, and policy research organizations and projects.

FAST FACTS:

■ Exxon sold off South African assets at year-end 1986 but has subsequently sold some chemicals and solvents to its South African successor on a spot basis.

■ Signing the MacBride Principles was put to a proxy vote at the May 18, 1989, annual meeting. The company recommended a vote against the proposal, saying that its subsidiary already had fair employment practices in Northern Ireland.

■ Another proxy requested that all further investments in Malaysian subsidiaries be suspended until that government reverses its dictatorial acts; Exxon recommended voting against the proposal.

■ One woman on 15-person board of directors.

■ Responded with information.

■ New York, NY.

FEDERAL EXPRESS

FedEx is a high flier on many social investors' buy lists. The company's Guaranteed Fair Treatment (GFT) program, which handles everything from employee/management disputes to sexual harassment cases, has attracted attention. One unique feature of the program is that all disputes are decided by top officers.

The Best Companies for Women says that one-third of FedEx's workforce is women, "many in non-traditional jobs."[57] Also counted among "The 50 Best Places for Blacks to Work" in *Black Enterprise's* February 1989 survey, Federal Express earned praise for the dramatic leap in contracts awarded to minority vendors from $2.7 million in 1987 to $9.3 million in 1988. The article says blacks make up 24% of 56,098 employees and 8% of 3657 managers. *Clean Yield, GOOD MONEY,* and Parnassus recommended the stock in 1989, and it was awarded one of five Corporate Conscience Awards by the Council on Economic Priorities.[58]

In early 1989 Federal Express went global with its $880-million acquisition of Tiger International. This move touched off labor problems; the 960 Tiger pilots, longtime members of the Air Line Pilots Association, called for a vote on union representation at FedEx, which had never been organized. Only 709 pilots voted for unionization, which was considered "a resounding victory to the company's founder and chairman, Frederick W. Smith," who supports high wages and good conditions rather than unionization.[59] The union was considered a threat to FedEx's gung-ho spirit, described as "perhaps the closest thing in corporate America to the Green Berets" by *The Wall Street Journal.*[60]

The company publishes an annual Social Responsibilities Review in which it chronicles its charitable and employee volunteer programs. In 1988 the company made $2,382,535 in charitable contributions, divided among civic, health and human services, education, and arts projects—roughly 0.8% of that year's pretax income. Meanwhile, the FedEx Corporate Neighbor Team Program received a 1988 President's Voluntary Action Citation.

FAST FACTS:
■ No South African operations.
■ 80,000 employees worldwide.
■ Responded to questionnaire.
■ Memphis, TN.

FIRST CHICAGO CORPORATION

First Chicago, owner of the 11th largest bank in the country—First National Bank of Chicago—as well as several other financial service businesses, has taken several positive social steps.

First Chicago is committed to the goal of annually donating 2% of pretax earnings to charitable organizations. However, actual contributions have ranged from 1% to 5%, depending on earnings of the year prior to contribution. In 1989 First Chicago set aside $5 million for direct and in-kind giving, and projected its funds would include social welfare, education, communities and neighborhoods, culture and the arts, and civic activities. Employee gifts to colleges and universities are matched by the company.

There is one woman on the 19-person board of directors. First Chicago helps employees find child care through the First Reimbursement and its referral plan.

FAST FACTS:

- No South African ties; the company has ratified the Statement of Principles.
- No military businesses.
- Employs around 16,000.
- No unionized employees.
- Has a minority-business purchasing program through which it did approximately $8 million in business in 1989.
- Has a PAC.
- Responded to questionnaire.
- Chicago, IL.

FIRST INTERSTATE BANCORP

As part of First Interstate's restructuring, it pared employees by 3000 in 1988—an 8% reduction in its overall workforce. Further changes were brewing in early 1990 as Joseph Pinola announced his retirement as chairman. Meanwhile, two class actions have been launched against the company for allegedly misleading stockholders about the status of the company's loans.[61] A company spokesman noted that it is not uncommon for such actions to be filed against a major corporation.

The country's eighth largest banking company in terms of assets has proclaimed itself the most conservative of the top ten banks in the country and is avoiding leveraged buyout transactions.

There is one black woman, Dr. Jewel Plummer Cobb, on the company's 15-person board of directors.

FAST FACTS:

- No South African business.
- No defense-related businesses.
- Employs roughly 36,000.
- Ranked ninth most admired of ten in Commercial Banking category of *Fortune*'s January 29, 1990, survey.
- Responded with limited information.
- Los Angeles, CA.

FLUOR CORPORATION

Fluor Corp., one of the world's largest international engineering and construction companies, received awards of $154 million from the federal government in 1988, some for defense and aerospace-related contracts. However, the company also broadened its environmental service work to encompass hazardous waste remediation, disposal, and cleanup. It was selected in 1988 as a prime contractor for the EPA and a program manager of the Alternate Remedial Contract Strategy (ARCS) program, which will tackle Superfund projects.

Fluor contributed an estimated $1.7 million in 1988 to charitable organizations, according to the *Taft Corporate Giving Directory*. This represents a generous 4.76% of its 1988 pretax earnings. Education received the lion's share of funding, at 43%, social services 30%, civic and public policy projects 16%, arts and humanities 9%, and the remainder miscellaneous.

FAST FACTS:
- Approximately 43,000 employees.
- One woman on 16-person board of directors.
- Responded with annual report.
- Irvine, CA.

FORD MOTOR COMPANY

Ford has taken admirable strides in the advancement and hiring of minorities and in minority-vending or supplying programs. It was awarded the 1989 NAACP Corporate Fair Share Award as well as the 1989 Minority Business Enterprise Legal Defense and Education Fund Corporation of the Year Award. In addition, it was described in *Black Enterprise* as one of the 35 best workplaces for blacks. Ford's corporate safety programs are also innovative; management teamed up with the United Auto Workers and established a $750,000 fund to promote research on occupational health and safety concerns associated with manufacturing processes.

At the same time, Ford has come under fire for maintaining licensing, supply, technical assistance, and managerial agreements with SAMCOR, the South African company that bought its operations. And since 1986 the Irish National Caucus (INC) has boycotted Ford for discriminating against Catholics in its West Belfast plant, vowing the boycott will continue until Ford signs the MacBride Principles. Ford maintains that it hires the same percentage of

Catholics as exist in the Northern Ireland workforce, but the INC challenges this hiring record: The community it operates in is 85% Catholic and its employees are nearly two-thirds Protestant.[62]

Ford's Aerospace division ranked 27th in Department of Defense prime contracts for research, development, testing, and evaluation in 1988 with contracts totaling $141,968,000.

Ford's social disclosure is outstanding, and for this was awarded a national Corporate Conscience Award by the Council on Economic Priorities in 1987. It is one of only a handful of companies that publish equal employment numbers in their annual reports. In 1988 women made up 16% of the workforce (up from 15.2% in 1987) and 5.8% of upper management, up from 5% in 1987. Minorities totaled 20.0% of the workforce in 1988, up from 19.5% in 1987, and made up 10.7% of upper management, against 10.1% in 1987.

Although Ford has been criticized for resisting tougher air emissions standards, it has taken some environmentally positive steps such as constructing 14 new wastewater treatment plants to reduce sludge volumes and limit the amount and discharge of hazardous materials. It is also working to eliminate the use of chlorofluorocarbons (CFCs) in all areas as soon as acceptable substitutes are available, a positive commitment that nevertheless falls short of many other corporations' efforts. Ford entered into a five-year agreement with Waste Management to use methane gas produced at their Woodland Meadows Landfill as a substitute fuel for coal currently being used.

FAST FACTS:
- In the U.S. nearly all hourly employees and 1.5% of salaried personnel are unionized.
- Most admired of ten in the Motor Vehicles and Parts category of *Fortune*'s January 29, 1990, survey.
- A well-below-average 0.34% of pretax earnings went to charitable contributions in 1988.
- $481 million sourced to minority businesses and vendors in North America in 1988.
- Responded to questionnaire.
- Dearborn, MI.

GENERAL DYNAMICS

The third largest nuclear weapons contractor for 1988, General Dynamics received $2,810,987,000 from Department of Defense prime contracts that year, according to Nuclear Free America's tally. The company's products include the F-16 Fighting Falcon, the A-12 Advanced Tactical Aircraft, and the Tomahawk cruise missile. Stanley Pace, current CEO, is credited with having cleaned up the company's image after the Pentagon procurement scandals in the mid-1980s. However, the company is still one of four under preliminary grand jury investigation for illegally using Pentagon planning documents, according to *The Wall Street Journal*. General Dynamics' new CEO, expected to take over January 1, 1991, is former astronaut William Anders.[63]

General Dynamics Pomona (California) Division boasts an innovative environmental program that has reduced the annual discharge of hazardous wastes by 96% through new control systems. It also has drastically cut air emissions, and after installation of aqueous cleaning systems, expects to reduce waste solvents sent offsite for recycling by 61,000 pounds.[64]

General Dynamics gave around $5.4 million in corporate contributions in 1988, 1.2% of that year's pretax income. Forty percent of this budget was allocated to education and 20% to community projects; other categories included health care, arts and culture, youth, special projects, and public policy. Soup kitchens, literacy programs, and a University of Missouri–St. Louis program for economically disadvantaged students are a few examples of what General Dynamics funds.

In July 1987 OSHA fined the Electric Boat Division, Quonset Point, Rhode Island, $615,000 for record-keeping violations under the Occupational Safety and Health Act. William Bennett, manager of that facility, responded: "In reviews and investigations during the past 13 years, OSHA has given us no reason to believe that we were not satisfying requirements."

FAST FACTS:
- No South African operations or ties.
- Of 101,000 employees, 22.8% are women and 15.6% are minorities.
- No women or minorities on the 16-person board of directors.
- Responded with information.
- St. Louis, MO.

GENERAL ELECTRIC

General Electric's motto, "We bring good things to life," has been turned on its head in *INFACT Brings GE to Light*, a book-length look at GE's role in the defense contracting business. On Nuclear Free America's list of the top 50 nuclear weapons contractors, GE ranked second, with nearly $3.4 billion in prime Department of Defense and Department of Energy contracts. GE operates the government-owned Pinellas plant, where neutron generators, the triggering mechanism for nuclear bombs, are made. INFACT, which launched the Nestlé boycott and has now taken on GE, wants the company to exit the nuclear weapons business altogether. Despite this criticism, GE has been praised in *The 100 Best Companies to Work for in America* and named one of "The 50 Best Places for Blacks to Work" by *Black Enterprise* magazine.

Of course, GE is not the only major weapons contractor that has an interest in landing more defense contracts. INFACT selected GE because it is primarily a consumer company and could exist without its defense business, from which only slightly more than 20% of GE's revenues are generated. INFACT also charges that GE's cozy relationship with Ronald Reagan (he was on the payroll as host of *The GE Theater* starting in 1954) exemplifies the close corporate/political ties that call the size of the defense budget into question. During the years of Reagan's presidency, GE's prime contracts increased dramatically from $2.2 billion in 1980 to $6.8 billion in 1986, according to INFACT. A GE spokesperson asserted that the company believes only the government is in a position to decide how large the defense budget need be.

Separately, General Electric agreed to pay the government around $2.5 million to settle a criminal case charging unauthorized use of classified Pentagon documents through the mid-1980s. At the time of the wrongdoing the unit in question belonged to RCA, which GE acquired in 1986. The RCA employee, Philip Jackson, received unauthorized documents from Richard Fowler of Boeing, who is currently in jail.[65]

GE has a mixed record on environmental issues. On the one hand, GE Environmental Services manufactures pollution-control equipment such as smokestack scrubbers and electrostatic precipitators. And its technological strides enable it to make much more energy-efficient appliances. At the same time, environmentalists are dissatisfied with the company's plan to offset CFCs released by its major refrigerator compressor replacement program by reducing or eliminating CFCs in other unspecified areas. GE argues that the technology to capture CFCs is not yet effective, something environmentalists dispute.[66] GE is also partially responsible for 41 toxic waste sites designated by the EPA as in urgent need of attention.[67]

Because it has so many different lines of business, GE is particularly susceptible to charges of conflicts of interest. For example, in March 1987 GE-owned NBC broadcast a one-hour documentary, *Nuclear Power in France: It Works,* without disclosing GE's relationship to the nuclear power industry. One month later NBC did not report stories of injuries to seven French workers at nuclear facilities.[68]

All the same, GE was named in *The 100 Best Companies to Work for in America* and in "The 50 Best Places for Blacks to Work." Eleven percent of GE's total employees are minorities, as are around 4.7% of its 20,940 managers. In 1988 10% of GE's contracts were awarded to minority firms.[69] Yet in 1989 General Electric Capital Corp. settled FTC charges that it discriminated against certain credit applicants on the basis of age, sex, and marital status by requiring applicants to be employed full-time in order to qualify for GE Credit's instant credit program. The penalty—$275,000—was the largest the commission had levied to date in a credit-discrimination case.[70]

GE has an extensive employee assistance program, which has among other things taken a stance on issues of spouse and child abuse. The company gave nearly $39 million to charitable organizations in 1988, 55–60% of which went to education, according to the *Taft Corporate Giving Directory.* This is around 0.82% of that year's pretax income.

FAST FACTS:
- Sold South African operations in 1984–1985.
- Two women on 18-person board of directors.
- Most admired of ten in Electronics cateogory of *Fortune*'s January 29, 1990, survey of corporate reputations.
- 298,000 employees worldwide, 255,000 of whom worked in the U.S. as of year-end 1988.
- Responded with information.
- Fairfield, CT.

GENERAL MOTORS

General Motors, synonymous with big business for many, has been involved in several major controversies but has also taken a number of socially positive steps.

In the 1960s consumer advocate Ralph Nader wrote a scathing denunciation of the company's Corvair in his book entitled *Unsafe at Any Speed.* GM tried to discredit Nader personally, according to *Everybody's Business*; he sued GM for invasion of privacy and the company eventually had to pay him $425,000.[71] More recently, GM was named one of the 10 worst corporations of 1988 in the December 1988 issue of the Nader-founded publication *Multinational Monitor*, because the gas tanks of one model of car were vulnerable to puncture during some high-speed crashes. In addition, the magazine charges that GM said changing this would be too expensive, although the estimated cost could be less than $11.59 per car. GM contends that cost was not the main consideration in its decision and noted that it won a 1987 lawsuit over this issue, in which its car was declared safe.

The company aroused rancor in Detroit in 1981 when the city leveled some 1500 homes so that GM could build a new plant in a Polish-black neighborhood known as Poletown. The neighborhood fought hard to stop the project, but the city of Detroit and the company prevailed.

GM has won praise for its efforts on minority development. Reverend Leon Sullivan, the antiapartheid activist who drafted the Sullivan Principles, has been a GM board member since 1971. The company is one of the 50 best for blacks, according to *Black Enterprise* magazine. Although there is only one minority among GM's top 54 officers, there are 89,064 minority members among its U.S. workforce of 430,687. GM's minority purchasing program is impressive: more than $1 billion worth of business with 1550 minority-owned firms in 1988. In early 1989 it signed an agreement with the NAACP's Fair Share program to strengthen what is already considered a genuine commitment to minority development. However, GM also settled a lawsuit alleging discrimination against black salaried workers by agreeing to between $20 and $40 million in raises. All but around 15% of black employees were satisfied with the settlement.[72] As of January 1990 the case was on appeal.

Meanwhile, there are two women on GM's 18-person board, and three of its 54 officers are women. Women account for 81,039 of total U.S. employees. Pretax dollars can be set aside for child care expenses, and resource referral is available at many locations.

Since 1970 GM has published an annual Public Interest report on its corporate and social responsibility efforts. In 1987 the company's charitable giving was $65 million, according to the *Taft Corporate Giving Directory*, nearly 1.5% of that year's pretax income. The 1989 report focused on environmental issues, much of which was a plea for moderation in placing restrictions on industry. The company has had an environmental activities staff since 1971. GM announced that all its dealers will install equipment to capture and purify CFC coolants from car air conditioners under repair. GM also points out that emissions have been cut significantly—currently, 85% of auto air pollution comes from the oldest 50% of cars on the road. Nonetheless, the company is partially responsible for 140 toxic waste sites that have been designated by the EPA as in urgent need of attention.[73]

Nearly 100% of GM's hourly employees are unionized. Agreements between the United Auto Workers and the company have led to efficiencies in several plants.[74] Profit sharing is one incentive, but GM and the UAW have teamed up on projects, including a corporationwide educational project on AIDS.

In order to restructure, GM has cut worldwide employment by nearly 100,000 since 1981, the devastation of which was pointed up in a recent documentary film, *Roger and Me*. Since 1984, GM and UAW have committed more than $960 million to education, training, and retraining programs that help both active and laid-off employees.

Although the company sold its South African unit in 1986, one of its European subsidiaries has a licensing agreement with Delta Motor Corp. in Point Elizabeth to build certain model Opel vehicles.

General Motors was the 16th biggest nuclear weapons contractor in 1988, according to Nuclear Free America, with DoD and DoE prime contracts worth $565,071,000.

GM agreed "in a reluctant about-face" to recall 1.7 million cars in the summer of 1989 in order to repair a cruise-control defect that might have hampered the driver's effort to slow down. GM rejected the national Highway Traffic Safety Administration's earlier request to recall these cars.[75]

FAST FACTS:

- GM has a PAC, called the Civic Involvement Program/General Motors.
- The GM Cancer Research Foundation annually sponsors an award to cancer research.
- Responded to questionnaire.
- Detroit, MI.

GREAT WESTERN FINANCIAL

Not only does Great Western Financial treat its employees well, but it also has several programs in place to help the disadvantaged. The company, which owns the nation's second largest thrift unit (Great Western Bank), is involved in consumer finance, mortgage banking, and real estate lending. When employees' houses were damaged in

the San Francisco earthquake, the company extended lower-interest
loans and waived its loan payments for them. In early 1990 Great
Western was relocating its headquarters to Northridge, California,
where it will have an on-site day care center accommodating up to
100 children.

The core of Great Western's charitable giving is the community,
with affordable housing programs for the disadvantaged an area of
emphasis. It declined, however, to specify the extent of its contributions. Great Western's Chairman, James Montgomery, was awarded
the first annual Duke Award from the John Wayne Cancer Clinic in
Orange County, California, in recognition of the time and corporate
donations put toward this project. Montgomery is a director of the
Neighborhood Housing Services of America and the Local Initiative
Support Corporation, a nonprofit organization that helps finance
housing for low-income families.

FAST FACTS:
■ No ties or loans to South Africa.
■ Roughly 12,700 employees.
■ No unionized employees.
■ Ranked most admired of ten in Savings Institutions category of
  January 29, 1990, *Fortune* survey.
■ One woman on its 12-person board of directors.
■ Ten-person executive management committee is all-male and all-white.
■ Responded with information.
■ Beverly Hills, CA.

HALLIBURTON

Few socially positive programs could be found for Halliburton, a
diversified oilfield services, engineering, and construction company with
two-thirds of revenues derived from services to the energy industry.

Halliburton contributed $1.07 million to charitable organizations in
1987, according to the *Taft Corporate Giving Directory*. Its foundation, which made the grants, donates the overwhelming majority of
its funds to education, three-sevenths of which is handed to science
and engineering schools and departments.

A Halliburton subsidiary, NUS Corp., provides a broad range of
engineering and consulting services to the EPA, the Department of
Energy, and other government agencies. Meanwhile, Halliburton performs environmental audits to make sure specific concerns and
regulations are met in different areas.

FAST FACTS:
- No South African operations or employees, although sometimes agrees to work there.
- No arms-related businesses.
- One woman sits on the 12-person board of directors.
- Over 70,000 employees worldwide.
- Responded with limited information.
- Dallas, TX.

HARRIS CORP.

The U.S. government is Harris Corp.'s biggest customer for its four core businesses—advanced electronic systems, semiconductors, communications, and office automation equipment; in 1988 51% of sales were to Uncle Sam. Harris ranked 46th in terms of Department of Defense contracts in research, development, testing, and evaluation in 1988, with contracts worth a total of $69,441,000.

Harris is a generous corporate contributor. In 1988 the company made an estimated $8 million in charitable contributions, 85% of which went to computer grants programs, mainly for technical equipment, according to the *Taft Corporate Giving Directory*. This represented around 5.4% of the company's pretax income. Harris also matched employee gifts dollar for dollar and funds community organizations, drug prevention programs, and blood drives. In 1989 Harris was given the Florida Chamber of Commerce outstanding partner award.

FAST FACTS:
- No South African operations.
- 33,000 employees, 30,000 of whom work in the U.S.
- No women on ten-person board of directors.
- Some acquired businesses had unionized employees.
- Responded with limited information.
- Melbourne, FL.

H. J. HEINZ

The world's number-one ketchup maker is known for treating its employees well. That is what earns it a place in *The 100 Best Companies to Work for in America*, which points out that the company has even included employees' poetry in its annual report.[76] The 1988 report features eight families from different countries describing their lives. Heinz has no South African ties or any links to the military, and is therefore a candidate for many socially responsible investors. Pax included it on its buy list as of the summer of 1989.

In April 1990 Heinz pleased animal rights activists and environmentalists by announcing that it would no longer buy tuna caught in a manner that could injure or kill dolphins. Since the winter of 1988, the company's StarKist Seafood unit had been boycotted by the International Marine Mammal Project for purchasing tuna that had been caught by fishing methods that knowingly drowned more than 100,000 dolphins yearly.[77]

FAST FACTS:
- Charitable giving in 1988 was an estimated $4.9 million, around 0.79% of that year's pretax income.[78]
- Limited use of recycled materials.
- 6.8% of officials and managers are minorities and 13.8% women.
- One woman on 17-person board of directors.
- Responded with information.
- Pittsburgh, PA.

HEWLETT-PACKARD

Hewlett-Packard takes its commitment to affirmative action seriously; it was cited as one of *The Best Companies for Women*, one of the 60 best companies in *Working Mother*'s 1989 survey, and one of 15 companies to watch in *Black Enterprise*'s "The 50 Best Places for Blacks to Work." Of the company's 9668 managers and supervisors in 1989, 26.3% were women and 11.4% minorities, up from 25.2% and 10.7%, respectively, in 1984. The company is also included in *The Best Companies to Work for in America*.

One likely reason HP hasn't been on more socially responsible investors' buy lists is that up until early 1989 the company had a South African sales subsidiary, headquartered in Johannesburg and employing 245 people. It sold these assets and operations to Siltek Ltd., a South African manufacturer and distributor of computer products, which took over the marketing, distribution, and servicing of all HP products there. This move has come under fire by some, including Working Assets, as a sham divestment because HP's full range of strategically important products is still available in South Africa.

"Recycling Makes Cents (and Dollars)" is the slogan for HP's white-paper recycling drive at its Palo Alto headquarters. The computer concern hooked its employees on recycling by pointing out that money is saved by having less trash to haul away and by selling some of the paper for cash—good news for the employees at profit-sharing time. Within two years of starting this program, HP reduced its land-filling by 46% and since 1983 has cut the volume of its hazardous waste by around 30%. Two HP divisions won awards from the California Water Pollution Control Association for the design and construction of industrial wastewater treatment plants.

FAST FACTS:
- In FY89 (Oct.) Hewlett-Packard gave roughly $70 million in cash and equipment grants, a very generous 6% of its estimated $1.151 billion in pretax earnings (85% to education, 12% to health and human services, 2% to arts and culture, 1% to civic).
- HP PAC gave $23,700 to Republicans and $16,500 to Democrats in the House and Senate from 1987–1988.
- Most admired of ten computer companies in *Fortune's* January 29, 1990, survey.
- HP has a formal sexual harassment statement.
- Purchased in excess of $50.3 million in goods and services from minority-owned businesses in FY89.
- Responded to questionnaire.
- Palo Alto, CA.

HOLIDAY CORPORATION/THE PROMUS COMPANIES

This leading hotel and casino company is difficult to evaluate because it is emerging from a major restructuring. A number of the old Holiday Corp.'s businesses—Embassy Suites, Hampton Inns, Homewood Suites, and Harrah's casino/hotels—were spun off into a new business, The Promus Companies, immediately prior to the January 1990 acquisition of its Holiday Inns by Bass PLC of Great Britain.

Promus will employ roughly 25,000 of Holiday Corp.'s former 44,000-member staff. Corporate headquarters operates an on-site day care center that can accommodate up to 120 children and is subsidized by the company. The company has maintained pay and benefits above industry norms to attract a quality staff. At Promus these policies should continue. The new company will maintain the employee stock purchasing plan, its employee stock ownership plan, and its dollar-for-dollar matching for its 401(k) plan.

One of its environmental/charitable programs is collecting aluminum cans from its hotels. The proceeds from recycling these cans are donated to Give Kids the World, a nonprofit organization that works with wish-granting organizations, taking terminally ill children on special trips. Holiday Inns donated $1 million to Give Kids the World toward building Holiday Inn Kids Village, which is fully equipped for handicapped and terminally ill children and is located near Walt Disney World in Florida.

On Promus' 13-person board of directors sit one black man and one Asian-American woman.

FAST FACTS:
- Holiday Inn operates in South Africa through a licensing agreement.
- Small number of employees unionized.
- No arms-related businesses.
- Holiday Inc. made $1.6 million in charitable contributions in 1988.
- The growing labor shortage and a "recognition of increasing cultural diversity" spur Holiday Inns to hire the handicapped. At one recently opened New York City facility, one in ten employees is hearing-impaired or has a learning disability.[79]
- Responded with information.
- Memphis, TN.

HOMESTAKE MINING

Homestake Mining may be good as gold to investors looking for a company with no ties to South Africa or to the Department of Defense, but less attractive to the investor concerned about minority and female representation in upper management; neither group is present on the company's 13-person board of directors. Homestake is an international gold-mining company with interests in Canada, Australia, and Chile.

Although Homestake says it is very environmentally aware, it is subject to cleanup expenses under the Comprehensive Environmental Response, Compensation and Liability Act (CERCLA). In September 1988 the EPA notified Homestake that it was a potentially responsible party for a site in South Dakota. The EPA is also studying indoor radon levels near the company's Grants, New Mexico, uranium mill, for which the company was also named a potentially responsible party in 1986. Homestake has submitted to the Nuclear Regulatory Commission a plan for decommissioning the Grants mill.

The focus of Homestake's charitable giving is community projects. The company matches employee gifts to education dollar for dollar.

FAST FACTS:

- 2179 employees as of September 1989, 1725 of whom work in the U.S.
- Miners at the Lead, South Dakota, plant are unionized—about 1200 employees at that location.
- Responded with information.
- San Francisco, CA.

HONEYWELL

Honeywell is considered a good community member and has been credited with responding to diverse employee issues through counseling and referrals for victims of spousal abuse. It also boasts an active women's council that has direct input to upper management and was established in the late 1970s. Its community activities are well documented—the company was awarded the President's Citation for Private Sector Initiatives in 1985 for community service and again in 1987 for its Neighborhood Improvement Program. In 1983 Ronald Reagan granted Honeywell the President's Citation Award in recognition of employees' outstanding community involvement. The company has a minority internship program and the Honeywell procurement department has a minority representative to help reach its corporate goal of making 7–10% of outside purchases from minority vendors.

Honeywell makes products, systems, and services for a variety of markets, including defense. As of this writing Honeywell was reducing its dependence on the weapons business and might sell part or most of its defense businesses except for the aironics business, which complements its commercial avionics group. Prior to this, the company ranked 20th for DoD prime contracts in 1988, with around $285,930,000 worth of contracts.

Although the company has no workers in South Africa (it sold its subsidiary there to Murray & Roberts in 1986), under the sale agreement the company will distribute Honeywell controls, systems, and services for commercial buildings and industrial plants in South Africa through 1996. Honeywell helped draft the Sullivan Principles.

FAST FACTS:

- In 1988 Honeywell made $8.8 million in charitable contributions, with an emphasis on early childhood education—it posted a loss that year.
- 14% of U.S. workforce is unionized, one-third unionized in Minneapolis headquarters.

- No strikes since mid-1960s.
- The HW Employee Citizenship Fund gave $82,000 to candidates in 1987–1988.
- Of 57,000 U.S. employees, 19,864 are women and 7498 minorities; of 22,320 upper management, 4508 are women and 2068 minorities.
- Included in *The Best Companies for Women*.
- Office recycling program began in June 1989, in Golden Valley, MN.
- One of seven companies to keep an eye on in October 1989 *Working Mother* survey.
- Least admired of ten in Electronics category of *Fortune*'s January 29, 1990, corporate reputation survey.
- Responded to questionnaire.
- Minneapolis, MN.

HUMANA INC.

As one of the largest health-care service firms in the world, Humana Inc.'s main business is socially beneficial. Many of the hospitals it operates are geared toward elderly patients, and the company offers a variety of health benefit plans for employee groups and Medicare beneficiaries. Humana has initiated 29 Centers of Excellence to provide specialized care and accomplish clinical research and education in focused areas such as adolescent psychiatry and women's medicine. Yet many people are disturbed by the trend of for-profit hospital chains becoming big business. Humana points out that being investor-owned allows it to pour resources into special projects such as its Centers of Excellence program.

At the Humana Hospital–University of Louisville, hospital care is provided for all adult indigent patients of the city and surrounding areas. During the first six years of the partnership, the hospital provided more than $66.5 million in unreimbursed indigent care. However, all Humana hospitals treat emergency patients, regardless of their ability to pay. Humana also runs the Seniors Association, a national not-for-profit organization designed for people 55 and over. As of September 1989 there were 192,150 members participating at 76 Humana hospitals—members receive benefits that make health care simpler and less expensive and receive discounts on services.

FAST FACTS:

- No women or minorities on the company's 11-person board of directors.

- 55,100 employees total.
- No South African operations.
- Does not release numbers on charitable giving.
- Responded with information.
- Louisville, KY.

IBM

Top-dollar pay, generous benefits, and an exemplary equal employment record make Big Blue a responsible corporate citizen in several key respects. However, IBM was also the 29th largest nuclear weapons contractor in FY88, with $195,919,000 worth of DoD and DoE prime contracts, according to Nuclear Free America. And it has been criticized for selling off its South African assets and yet signing a distribution agreement there.

Cited as one of the ten top companies in "The 60 Best Companies for Working Mothers," IBM has a nationwide child and elder care referral service and in November 1989 set up a new $25-million IBM Funds for Dependent Care Initiatives to develop new and expand existing child and elder care programs nationwide. The company also introduced what the October 1989 issue of *Working Mother* called "one of the most advanced leave programs in U.S. industry"; employees can take up to three years off with company-paid benefits, but are expected to be available to work part-time during the second and third years. Of 223,000 employees at year-end 1988, 66,000 were women, and women account for 20% of all managers. *The Best Companies for Women* points out that the company has a mandatory program on how to handle sexual harassment.

Black Enterprise named IBM one of the 35 "best of the best" companies for blacks. Seventeen percent of total employees are minorities, as are 3750, or nearly 10%, of 38,000 managers. This strong record should grow even stronger—in 1989 minorities accounted for 29% of new hires. In 1988 the company purchased more than $155 million worth of goods and services from minority-owned businesses, $90 million from firms owned primarily by women, and more than $25 million from companies whose workforce consisted of primarily handicapped employees. The company recruits at historically black universities and minority career expositions.

IBM has a generous corporate giving program and made $135.4 million in cash and equipment donations worldwide to charitable organizations in 1988, nearly 1.5% of pretax income. Education is the major area of emphasis, as is evidenced by a recent five-year, $25-million grant program to help improve elementary and secondary education through more effective use of technology. Since 1971 IBM has had a community-service leave program through which employees can work full-time at community organizations and earn their regular IBM salaries. Around 1000 employees have taken advantage of this. Since 1968 the company has run a U.S. job training program that has graduated nearly 20,000.

In 1987 IBM sold its South African operations to a trust established by a group of former IBM employees. IBM has been criticized because its distribution agreement with its former company allows the full range of IBM products to be sold in South Africa. However, the agreement does guarantee that all U.S. export regulations must be honored, and therefore prohibits sales to any apartheid-enforcing agency such as the military or the police.

IBM is one of the five largest U.S. emitters of CFCs; the company has set an internal goal of eliminating all CFCs by 1993, well ahead of what is called for by the Montreal Protocol.[80]

FAST FACTS:
- One of the top ten companies in *The 100 Best Companies to Work for in America.*
- Responded with information.
- Armonk, NY.

ITT CORPORATION

ITT, once considered the quintessential diversified conglomerate, has shed some of its divisions but still has fingers in several pies. Its main businesses are automotive, electronic components, fluid technology, defense, pulp and timber, and services, which encompasses insurance, finance, hotels, communications, and information services. While defense accounts for 5–7% of ITT's annual income, the company makes no weapons or weapons systems but rather develops and manufactures defensive (primarily electronic) equipment such as radar and night-vision goggles.

ITT has been embroiled in several controversies. A 1973 book entitled *The Sovereign State of ITT*[81] describes the early history of the company and its intervention in foreign governmental affairs, although more recently it has avoided this type of controversy. ITT sold off its South African operations in December 1986, but maintains licensing agreements with the acquiring company. It says it does not receive revenues from South Africa and the agreements are for nonstrategic products.

Like many large companies, ITT is entangled in its share of lawsuits. It is subject to Superfund-site proceedings by state agencies; however, it is considered a "de minimis contributor" in these cases and expects its share of the cleanup to cost less than $100,000.

ITT has two women and one minority member on its 14-person board of directors. To promote affirmative action goals, effectiveness in recruiting and promoting minorities and women is part of executives' performance evaluations.

ITT donated a total of $6 million in 1987 to charitable causes. It has totally underwritten the children's television series *The Big Blue Marble* and sponsored a special, *From the Heart,* which featured the first International Very Special Arts Festival at the Kennedy Center in Washington.

FAST FACTS:
- 117,000 employees in 1988.
- Responded with information.
- New York, NY.

INTERNATIONAL FLAVORS & FRAGRANCES

The company that brings the flavor to McDonald's salad dressing and the scent to Calvin Klein's Eternity perfume[82] is the second most admired of ten in the Soaps, Cosmetics category in *Fortune* magazine's January 29, 1990, survey of American corporations. IFF has sales, manufacturing, and creative laboratory operations in Roodepoort, South Africa, employing some 20 local workers. IFF is a signatory of the Statement of Principles and received the highest rating, Making Good Progress, for the year ending June 1989. In 1988 sales to foreign countries were nearly twice that of domestic sales.

The testing of flavors and fragrances is not done on animals.

FAST FACTS:
- No Department of Defense contracts.
- One woman on 10-person board of directors; would not release equal employment numbers.
- No live-animal testing.
- Would not release size of charitable giving or recipient projects.
- Responded with limited information.
- New York, NY.

INTERNATIONAL MINERALS & CHEMICAL CORPORATION

International Minerals & Chemical, a medical products, specialty chemicals, and animal nutrition company, is a generous corporate contributor, giving 2% of pretax earnings to charitable organizations each year. Areas of emphasis are youth and family programs, arts and culture, and education. In 1988 the company was awarded the President's Citation Program for Private Sector Initiatives C-Flag in recognition of its Community Partnership Program.

IMC has a flex benefits program so that money can be put aside for child care expenses.

FAST FACTS:
- No South African operations.
- No Department of Defense contracts.
- One woman on 15-person board of directors.
- Just under 10,000 employees, around half of whom work in the U.S.
- "Very small" percentage of plants are unionized.
- Responded with limited information.
- Northbrook, IL.

INTERNATIONAL PAPER

International Paper, one of the nation's largest producers of paper products, has been on the AFL–CIO's Don't Buy list since 1987, when 2300 union members went on strike. "Despite record profits of nearly $1 billion . . . International Paper told its workers they must take huge pay cuts . . . absorb high health insurance costs . . . and allow unlimited subcontracting of their jobs at lower wages," reported the *Label Letter*, the AFL–CIO's newsletter.[83] The union refused these conditions and struck; management locked them out and hired non-union workers. The union members returned even though the National Labor Relations Board ruled the company's actions illegal; the union is boycotting IP products until a new agreement is reached, according to the *Label Letter*.

International Paper has also been involved in its share of environmental problems. It is one of four companies under investigation by the EPA for its waste-hauling practices near Niagara Falls, where high concentrations of carcinogenic compounds have been found. Its Androscoggin Mill (Jay, Maine) was charged with violations of the Occupational Safety and Health Act on July 28, 1988, and was cited for $242,000 worth of violations again on October 26, 1988. On the other hand, between 1982 and year-end 1988 International Paper had reduced energy consumption by almost 13% per product ton. And, by emphasizing safety, the company had 13% fewer lost-time accidents in 1988 than for the preceding year.

An area of social strength for IP is its minority and female representation at high levels of the company. There are three minority members and one woman on its 14-person board.

IP has a South African subsidiary through Masonite Corp. that employs almost 2000 workers. It is a signatory of the Statement of Principles and has received the middle compliance rating, Making Progress, for the three years through June 1989.

FAST FACTS:
- No weapons-related businesses.
- IP's charitable foundation donated an estimated $1.95 million in 1988, according to the *Taft Corporate Giving Directory*, a well-below-average 0.17% of that year's pretax income.
- Responded with limited information.
- Purchase, NY.

JOHNSON & JOHNSON

Johnson & Johnson demonstrated a key trait of social responsibility—flexibility—by rolling out a brand-new Work and Family program in 1989. It even expanded its corporate ethics declaration, "Our Credo," for the first time in its history, adding: "We must be mindful of ways to help our employees fulfill their family responsibilities." J&J was praised in the October 1989 issue of *Working Mother* for making the most notable advances of any corporation in a single year. It is building an on-site day care center for its New Brunswick, New Jersey, headquarters; it instituted a nationwide referral service for day and elder care, extended unpaid personal leave from three months to a year, initiated management training to increase sensitivity to these issues, and put alternative work options into place. Prior to this, the company already had several strong employee programs, including its LIVE FOR LIFE health program.

Women account for half of J&J's 33,000 employees, 11% of upper management, and 5% of top executives. There are two women, one of whom is black, on the company's 17-person board of directors. J&J was cited as one of the 35 best workplaces for blacks in the *Black Enterprise* survey, with blacks accounting for over 11% of the total domestic employees and 6.3% of managers.

A crisis need not undermine a company's reputation. When seven people died in 1982 from taking J&J's Extra-Strength Tylenol capsules that had been laced with cyanide, the company immediately issued a nationwide recall, even though the tampering happened after the medication had left its plant. *Rating America's Corporate Conscience* estimated the cost of the recall at over $100 million. A similar incident in 1986, in which one person died from taking a poisoned Tylenol capsule, spurred the company to stop making Tylenol in capsule form. Far from tarnishing J&J's reputation, these crises reinforced its image as a company concerned with the public welfare. Johnson & Johnson was voted the most admired company out of 305 for the Community and Environmental Responsibility category of the January 29, 1990, *Fortune* survey.

J&J's creed, adopted in the 1940s, has been credited with providing a moral rudder to weather these types of crises. And yet in 1975 CEO James Burke called for companywide meetings to challenge the creed. This ongoing approach to ethics is considered important for making employees consider these issues.[84]

J&J is, however, a large U.S. employer in South Africa, with 1400 employees and three operations there. The company is a signatory of the Statement of Principles, and received the highest rating, Making Good Progress, for the three years through June 1989.

This pharmaceutical concern asserts that live-animal testing is necessary, although, from 1983 through 1988 it reduced the number of animals used in toiletries and nondrug testing by more than 80%.

FAST FACTS:
- Cited in *The 100 Best Companies to Work for in America*.
- Gave $6.753 million in 1987, according to the *Taft Corporate Giving Directory*—0.57% of that year's pretax income.
- No weapons manufacturing.
- Four to five unions at the company.
- Responded with information.
- New Brunswick, NJ.

K MART

K mart, the world's second largest retailer, has taken some socially responsible steps. In 1988 K mart increased its purchases from minority- and female-owned businesses a whopping 46% to $374 million. In addition, it did more than $4 million worth of advertising in minority trade media and banked with 40 minority- or women-owned banks. Chairman Joseph Antonini has served as chairman of the National Minority Supplier Development Council. Meanwhile, there are two minority members and two women on the company's 14-person board of directors. And the retailer has signed a Fair Share agreement with the NAACP.

The company made $9 million in charitable contributions in 1988, 0.73% of its $1.24 billion pretax income for that year. It supports the battle against illiteracy through projects like Win America and a two-year pledge to Read America. In addition, the retailer provided merchandise for Armenian relief and cash donations to the American Red Cross for disaster relief following Hurricane Hugo and the San Francisco earthquake in 1989.

In 1987 K mart paid $94,000 in state fines and penalties as a result of a sexual harassment case. The company has a detailed policy against sexual harassment in the workplace, established in June 1980.

FAST FACTS:
- No South African operations.
- No defense-related businesses.
- Responded with information.
- Troy, MI.

THE LIMITED, INC.

Women play key roles in upper management at The Limited, Inc., which encompasses eight retail women's-apparel store chains including Victoria's Secret and Lane Bryant. Three store lines are headed by women, all of whom hold the title president: Verna Gibson of Limited Stores (the largest division), Sally Frame Kasaks of Abercrombie & Fitch, and Cynthia Fedus of Victoria's Secret Catalogue. Two women sit on the Limited's 11-person board of directors. The company both operates apparel stores and distributes clothing through its catalogues.

Few other social initiatives could be identified for the company. However, the company's CEO Leslie Wexner is a generous charitable contributor, having donated $25 million to build the Wexner Center for the Performing Arts at Ohio University. He has also contributed to the Heritage House, a Jewish retirement home, and funded the education of Israeli civil servants at Harvard's Kennedy School.

FAST FACTS:
- No South African operations.
- No defense-related contracts.
- As of late 1989 The Limited employed 50,000.
- Responded with limited information.
- Columbus, OH.

LITTON INDUSTRIES

Litton is a high-tech corporation that derived 47% of FY89 (July) sales from the U.S. government. The company ranked 38th among the top 50 nuclear weapons contractors, with $133,605,000 worth of prime Department of Defense and Department of Energy contracts in this area, according to Nuclear Free America. The company is working on the guidance system for the Air Force's new short-range attack missile and an upgrade of the Navy's EA-6B Prowler aircraft.

As have many defense contractors, Litton has been involved in its share of lawsuits and controversies. In 1986 Litton's Clifton Precision Special Devices division pleaded guilty to making false claims with respect to procurement and contracting matters. More recently, in 1988 its Data Systems division was one of a number of defense contractors whose premises were searched; it received a grand jury subpoena in connection with a well-publicized government investigation of defense-contractor marketing practices known as Operation Ill Wind. Federal authorities have subsequently informed Litton that the company is not a target of the investigation, according to a spokesperson.

FAST FACTS:
- No South African operations.
- 50,700 employees.
- One woman on 10-person board of directors.
- Responded with printed information.
- Beverly Hills, CA.

MCI COMMUNICATIONS

This company, best known for having broken up AT&T's long-distance monopoly, is generally considered an ethical investment. MCI is not in South Africa (although service to South Africa is provided through European links), has no arms-related contracts, and poses no major threat to the environment. As of early 1989 the company was on *GOOD MONEY*'s buy list.

At the same time, MCI does not believe that providing services for employees is the role of a corporation. Unlike most companies, which boast about promote-from-within policies, MCI's "official goal is to fill at least half of all job openings from outside," says the December 1989 issue of *Business Month* magazine, which selected MCI as one of the five best-managed companies in 1989. In *The Big Boys* Ralph Nader and William Taylor write "The corporation is not a family, McGowan [founder] emphasized time and again. MCI does not guarantee job security. MCI does not provide for 'human needs' beyond what is required to run a successful business. There are no exercise facilities or counselling services. MCI did not even establish a retirement program until April, 1981."[85]

As the company grows, some of this is changing. Human Resources is reviewing work/family options to see if programs need to be established, and the company recently instituted an alcohol and drug counseling program. MCI declined to reveal the size of its charitable giving program, which heavily emphasizes training programs for disadvantaged youth in its funding. As a high-tech concern, MCI is "feeling the pinch" of a shortage of talented applicants and is therefore offering scholarships and internships for engineering students.

MCI is purely a service company and therefore is confronted with few serious environmental challenges. Where these challenges do exist, it strives to meet them responsibly. For instance, MCI is careful not to disturb natural habitats as it installs fiber optic cable lines.

FAST FACTS:
- One woman on eight-person board of directors.
- Around 5% of workforce unionized, from an acquisition.
- 17,500 employees, most of whom are in the U.S.
- Responded with information.
- Washington, DC.

McDONALD'S

The makers of the Big Mac serve up a mixed record on social issues. McDonald's is criticized by environmentalists for contributing to the landfill shortage by packaging its burgers in nonbiodegradable styrofoam containers. For this reason McDonald's was named one of the 10 worst corporations of 1988 by the December 1988 *Multinational Monitor*. The Citizens Clearinghouse for Hazardous Wastes points out that the use of styrofoam is unnecessary because paper packaging is a viable alternative, and competitors such as Wendy's International package their meals in paper.[86]

However, McDonald's is making some efforts on environmental issues. In 1987 it stopped using polystyrene puffed up with CFCs and it is using recycled paper for its kids' Happy Meal packaging and recycled plastic for some of its trays.[87] Increasing pressure might lead to further change. The Council for Solid Waste Solutions said that six states and 31 localities had taken measures to restrict polystyrene, putting pressure on this fast food chain to offer an alternative. In the fall of 1989 McDonald's announced a pilot program for 100 of its New England restaurants to provide separate disposal bins for recyclable plastics.[88] And it plans by year-end 1990 to have recycling bins for foam containers at 2000 of its 8000 U.S. restaurants.[89]

McDonald's has also been questioned about the nutritional value of its menu. McDonald's launched an ad campaign promoting "good nutrition," but when threatened with legal action over these claims, pulled the ads.[90] Just the same, McDonald's discloses the nutritional content of its products in a booklet it produces, "McDonald's Food...The Facts." Meanwhile, Volksmund, a West German organization, declared a boycott of fast food restaurants on October 15, 1988. Volksmund charged that McDonald's imported Costa Rican rain forest beef for use in its European franchises.[91]

Nonetheless, McDonald's has taken some laudable social positions. It was selected as one of 35 "best of the best" companies for blacks in *Black Enterprise*'s survey. And McDonald's has signed an NAACP Fair Share agreement to promote minority development. Of nearly 120,000 employees, 25.9% are black, and 16.8% of 9453 managers are black, including two regional VPs and four regional managers. In addition, McDonald's ranked No. 1 on the BE Franchise 50 roster in 1987 for having 365 black-owned franchises, and again in 1988 for 395 franchises.[92]

McDonald's was left out of *The 100 Best Companies to Work for in America* because, while working at this fast food chain offered opportunities for some, too many young people considered the experience dehumanizing.[93]

Complete charitable information for McDonald's was unavailable. According to the *Taft Corporate Giving Directory*, the company gave more than an estimated $1 million in 1988, a figure that is likely understated, given that Ronald McDonald's Children's Charities has made more than $21 million in grants since 1984.

In an interesting footnote to McDonald's corporate history, Joan

Kroc, widow of founder Ray Kroc, has become a powerful force in the Democratic party and has funded projects she says her husband would never have supported. For example, she gave $12 million to Notre Dame University to establish a research center devoted to world peace and $5 million for AIDS research.[94]

FAST FACTS:
- Part of *GOOD MONEY* index in early 1989.
- McDonald's printed its 1988 proxy statement on recycled paper.[95]
- Around 54% of people training to be owners/operators are minorities or women.
- Responded with annual report.
- Oak Brook, IL.

MERCK

Merck's compassionate distribution of Ivermectin, the drug that brings relief to sufferers of river blindness, is a vivid example of this company's social commitment. Nor have its programs gone unrecognized: Merck was elected the most admired of 305 large U.S. companies for the fourth time running in *Fortune*'s January 1990 survey of corporate reputations.

Certainly one of the most impressive aspects of Merck is its outstanding programs on work/family issues and employee welfare. Merck was counted among the top ten companies in *Working Mother*'s 1989 survey, "The 60 Best Companies for Working Mothers." The article praised Merck for supporting a new child care center near its headquarters complex that accommodates 150 children. The center is run by parents and they, rather than the corporation, maintain control over the quality of the care. However, at the highest corporate ranks women are still not very well represented—only 4.3% of top executives are female.[96] Both flextime and flexplace are options, helping out two-career families. Merck was also profiled as one of 35 "best of the best" companies in *Black Enterprise*'s February 1989 survey, "The 50 Best Places for Blacks to Work." That article attributes the company's workforce diversity to incentive payouts rewarding managers who meet minority recruitment and hiring goals. It says 9.7% of total employees are black, as are 4.0% of the company's 3200 managers. There is one black on the board of directors.

As befits a health-care company, Merck tends to the well-being of its employees. In 1989 the company became totally "smokeless," and Merck offers to foot the bill for any employee kicking the habit by enrolling in the SMOKELESS program. Since 1985 it has had an active employee assistance program prepared to tackle problems ranging from drug abuse to marital difficulties. On the other hand, Merck was left out of *The 100 Best Companies to Work for in America* because of a five-month strike by around 4000 workers in the mid-1980s. That Merck paid top dollar was not in dispute, but employees did not feel that a wage freeze was warranted in light of the company's profitability. The 1988 negotiations were much smoother, and there was no strike.

FAST FACTS:

- Sold off South African operations and now has no ties whatsoever.
- No defense contracting.
- Charitable giving in cash and in-kind contributions topped $36 million in 1988, nearly 2% of that year's pretax income.
- Does do animal testing; has reduced the number of live animals used, although it would not back this up with figures.
- Its PAC contributions for the 1987–1988 election cycle were $50,650, with Republicans receiving $29,350 and Democrats $21,300.
- Responded to questionnaire.
- Rahway, NJ.

MERRILL LYNCH & CO.

Merrill Lynch & Co. has so far steered clear of the insider trading violations in which many large securities firms have been implicated. It has also made some responsible social moves. Merrill placed a blanket ban on all dealings with South Africa in November 1989, a step that went well beyond the policies of other major securities firms. Since 1987 the company has had a policy against conducting business in South Africa, making markets in South African commodities, and engaging in transactions that would result in paying taxes to the South African government. However, its new policy is considerably stricter—Merrill ceased researching and trading all South African stocks and no longer executes orders in these securities for itself or clients other than to liquidate holdings.[97]

In 1988 Merrill gave $8,987,252 to charitable organizations through the corporation, its subsidiaries, and the foundation; this represents 1.4% of that year's pretax income. Education and cultural arts each received 34% of the funds, civic 11%, community services 8%, health 7%, and United Way 7%. Employee contributions to education and the arts are matched dollar for dollar, up to $1,000. One of several innovative activities the company engages in is its annual Christmas Calls program; each year roughly 9000 senior citizens are invited to over 100 offices around the world to use the firm's telephones free-of-charge to call family and friends around the world. In 1988 the company was awarded a President's Private Sector Initiative Commendation for this program, and in 1989, a Presidential Award for Private Sector Initiatives for its scholarship program.

There was one woman on Merrill's 16-member board of directors as of year-end 1988, and domestically, of the company's 1240 officials and managers, 190 are women. Of over 36,000 domestic employees, 6779 are minorities and 15,893 women. The Merrill Lynch Child Care Resource Referral Program provides information and referrals for employees.

CEO William Schreyer has addressed the issue of ethics in the financial marketplace and has spoken out in favor of tougher penalties for insider trading violations. A January 14, 1990, *New York Times* article entitled, "A Blue-Chip Name Is Not Enough," awarded Merrill its highest four-star ranking for its disciplinary track record, based on the number of disciplinary actions and pending cases against the firm or its brokers as a percent of the average number of retail brokers employed by the firm during the 1980s.

In April 1990 Merrill announced the creation of the Eco-Logical Trust, a unit trust that will invest in companies with commitments to responsible environmental practices. ML will lead a syndicate of investment houses in stock selection.

FAST FACTS:
- No arms-related businesses.
- In 1988 its PAC contributed $97,254 to federal candidates.
- Has an employee stock purchase plan.
- Responded with information.
- New York, NY.

MINNESOTA MINING & MANUFACTURING

Known for innovation, 3M is considered an excellent place to work. The company encourages ideas, and does not cringe at bad ones. All employees can spend 15% of their day pursuing projects of their own choosing—one well-known product to come out of this is Post-it brand notes. 3M ranked fifth most admired of the 305 companies surveyed in *Fortune*'s article "America's Most Admired Corporations" on January 29, 1990.

And 3M has turned some of its innovative genius toward social problems. In 1975 it initiated its 3P program: Pollution Prevention Pays. This is an effort to identify potentially costly pollution problems before they become serious. Its new program, 3P-Plus, is an even more ambitious environmental project that consists of the 3Rs— reduce, reuse, and recycle—and looks at waste as an overlooked asset with both cash and environmental potential.[98] In the early 1970s the company installed a fleet of vans to ferry employees to and from work—another way to cut down on pollution.[99]

3M has adopted a benefits program designed to meet the needs of working parents and dual career couples, and it keeps in tune with employee needs through biannual polls and advisory committees. *Working Mother* praises it for its benefits, which include flextime, part-time, and flexible benefits options. 3M also stages a Working Parent Resource Fair, and has a full-time child care administrator on staff. Only one woman holds the title of vice president or above at 3M; however, there are two women on the 15-member board of directors. There are 16,852 women out of 48,860 U.S. employees.[100] Minorities make up 4.9% of the company's officials and managers. 3M recruits at campuses historically important for minority students and has a minority employee advisory program.

In 1988 3M gave $13.296 million in cash grants and $15.793 million worth of in-kind gifts, relative to $1.882 billion in pretax income.

3M has two South African units and employs around 850 people there, roughly half of whom are nonwhite. The company was one of the original signatories of the Statement of Principles and received the highest (Making Good Progress) compliance rating for the three years through June 1989. It also has a multiracial social responsibility board that meets monthly to identify worthy projects and activities and to monitor progress.

3M does perform live-animal testing but is accredited by the American Association for Accreditation of Laboratory Animal Care and favors nonanimal in vitro systems whenever possible.

FAST FACTS:
- Does in excess of $20 million a year in business with the government, well under half of which involves military contracts.
- Responded with information.
- St. Paul, MN.

MOBIL

Long a defender of the rights of corporations to stay in South Africa, Mobil itself left in April 1989 after a change in U.S. tax law prevented corporations from deducting taxes paid to South Africa from U.S. returns. Mobil sold its assets to General Mining Union Corp. for $155 million, and the South African company agreed to maintain Mobil's equal opportunity employment programs and to fund Mobil's work on behalf of blacks for the five years following the sale.

Black Enterprise called Mobil one of "fifteen companies to watch" in its February 1989 survey, "The 50 Best Workplaces for Blacks," praising its initiative of setting five-year growth targets for women and minorities in management, professional, and sales positions. In 1989 Mobil filled 51.7% of its college-student summer job and internship slots with minorities and 42.2% with women. On Mobil's 17-person board of directors sit one minority member and two women; women and minorities fill 8.9% and 8.8%, respectively, of all management positions, a figure that has climbed steadily since the mid-1970s. Mobil is becoming more flexible in order to accommodate female employees. In 1989 it began a nationwide child care referral service, a spousal relocation service, and a reduced workweek program to meet the needs of working parents. These changes are in response to a turnover rate two-and-a-half times as high for high-potential women as among comparable men. One-third of new hires over the past five years have been women, but retention has been tougher for this oil giant.[101]

In terms of the environment, Mobil has made vital product safety data available worldwide through an advanced computerized system. Mobil Chemical Company was the first plastics producer to recycle foam polystyrene packaging, collected mostly from food service facilities, through its Plastics Again joint venture with Genpak Corp. Mobil is also one of eight companies that formed the National Polystyrene Recycling Company to provide a steady source of recycled plastic. On the negative side, Mobil is being sued by the state of Alaska for its partial ownership of the Alyeska Pipeline Service, which was responsible for responding to the Exxon *Valdez* disaster. And the EPA estimates Mobil shares responsibility in the cleanup of 25 toxic waste sites in urgent need of attention.[102]

In 1987 Mobil devoted a below-industry-average 0.5% of pretax income to charitable donations, according to Franklin's *insight*. Employee gifts to the arts, education, and hospitals have been matched on a generous two-for-one basis since 1979.

FAST FACTS:
- An active PAC.
- 20% of total U.S. workforce is unionized.
- In February 1988 about 1800 union employees struck three Mobil refineries, primarily over the company's intention to designate some 120 refinery control-room operators as management employees, eliminating some senior union jobs. After three months the union accepted the wage package, losing on this issue.[103]
- Responded with information.
- New York, NY.

MONSANTO

Although involved in several potent controversies over the years, Monsanto has recently taken some admirable steps. Monsanto became involved in manufacturing polychlorinated biphenyls (PCBs) when it acquired Swann Chemical in 1935 and announced it would pull the carcinogenic chemical only in 1977, two years before PCBs were banned by the U.S. Congress. Monsanto was one of the makers of the chemical defoliant known as Agent Orange, which Vietnam War veterans later blamed for health problems. The validity of these claims has been hotly debated.

Parnassus told the *Chicago Tribune* that Monsanto was on its "worst company" list in part for environmental negligence.[104] The EPA has said Monsanto is a potentially responsible party at 42 toxic waste sites designated as in urgent need of attention.[105] At some sites its responsibility is small. The Natural Resources Defense Council named Monsanto one of the 11 largest emitters of carcinogenic chemicals not regulated by the Clean Air Act for cadmium emissions at its Soda Springs, Idaho, plant. After this NRDC report the plant voluntarily installed pollution-control equipment to cut cadmium emissions from 100,250 pounds per year to less than 6000 pounds.

On the positive side, in 1988 Monsanto publicly set a goal for reducing toxic air emissions worldwide by 90% by the end of 1992, with an ultimate goal of zero emissions. In 1983 Monsanto established a fund sufficient to clean up the portion of liability at waste sites attributed to the company. And Monsanto was the first corporation to print public material-safety data sheets for each product it handles or manufactures.

The company restructured in 1985, moving away from commodity chemicals and toward high value-added performance materials and biotechnology. In 1986 it announced it would not renew its DoE contract to operate its Miamisburg, Ohio, Mound site where it manufactured nuclear weapon components. In 1988, Monsanto still ranked as the 35th largest nuclear weapons contractor, with $156,352,000 worth of DoE and DoD contracts, although it is now no longer in the business. Meanwhile, its first biotech product, bovine somatropin (BST), which both it and Eli Lilly are manufacturing, is controversial. BST is a genetically engineered milk-production hormone that increases a cow's milk output as much as 25% and is being refused by several grocery chains and Ben & Jerry's. Sale of this milk has been approved by the FDA.

G. D. Searle, which Monsanto acquired in ·1985, has been the defendant in several lawsuits launched by women who claim to have been injured and in some instances made infertile by the company's Copper-7 intrauterine contraceptive. Unlike the Dalkon Shield, Searle's IUD is actually a prescription drug, approved by the FDA in 1974. The company pulled the drug from the market in 1986 because it couldn't get product liability insurance for it, although it maintains that the CU-7 is safe. One plaintiff in 1988 was awarded $8.15 million by a St. Paul federal jury, but upon appeal an undisclosed settlement was reached. As of late 1989, more than 300 lawsuits had been filed, and of 19 court cases 15 had been found in Searle's favor. The company said it expected many cases to be dropped.

Meanwhile, Searle was honored by the White House in December 1989 for its Patients in Need program. Its first program, begun in 1987, makes all of Searle's potentially lifesaving drugs available free of charge to indigent patients. As of year-end 1989, around 300,000 free prescriptions had been provided. Under the initiation of Searle's chairman, Dr. Sheldon Gilgore, the company also began refunding patients for all drugs they cannot use. Its most recent program, Patients in the Know, distributes easy-to-understand instructions and information on all drugs prescribed.

Both Monsanto and Searle have South African operations, and received the highest rating, Making Good Progress, for compliance with the Statement of Principles for the three years through June 1989.

Monsanto purchased a Cray supercomputer in 1989, which allows for a reduction in animals used in product screening. However, the chemical concern points out that animal testing is a necessary part of developing its products. Veterinarians are employed by the company to supervise all phases of animal testing.

FAST FACTS:
- ■ Monsanto contributed an estimated $11.5 million in 1989 through its foundation; the company ranks 51st in size of the *Fortune* 500, and 34th in terms of philanthropic giving.
- ■ Responded with information.
- ■ St. Louis, MO.

NCR

NCR, which develops, manufactures, markets, installs, and services business information systems, is a generous corporate contributor. The company targets an above-average 2% of its domestic pretax income averaged over the prior three years. Half of these funds go to higher education, and the remainder is divided among United Way chapters and civic, arts, health, and welfare projects. Employee gifts to higher education are matched dollar for dollar. In 1989 employees at the South Carolina plant used NCR trucks to carry supplies to areas that had been hard hit by Hurricane Hugo.

There was one woman on NCR's 12-person board of directors in 1989. The company supports the Dayton-based Childcare Clearinghouse, an information and referral service open to employees. At other locations employees can turn to affiliates of the organization.

In 1989 NCR sold its South African operations, which employed around 500, to Fintech. The company signed a distribution agreement so that most of its principal products continue to be sold in South Africa.

FAST FACTS:
- ■ Not one of top 500 DoD contractors for 1988.
- ■ 60,000 employees worldwide, 30,000 in the U.S.
- ■ Responded with information.
- ■ Dayton, OH.

NATIONAL SEMICONDUCTOR

Few social initiatives could be found for National Semiconductor, a leading semiconductor manufacturer. The company did not respond for this book, and it does not publish information about these issues in its annual report.

The semiconductor industry is highly cyclical, and FY89 (May) was a rough year—the company posted a loss. In response to this, it reduced its workforce by 2000. As of late 1989, it employed around 37,000.

National Semi has several overseas manufacturing plants—something that has excited criticism because it is regarded as a way of shipping out work to places with lower wage scales.

FAST FACTS:
- No South African operations.
- No women on the seven-member board of directors.
- Did not respond.
- Santa Clara, CA.

NORFOLK SOUTHERN

Norfolk Southern, a holding company that owns two major railroads and a motor carrier, describes its 1988 performance as "thoroughbred" in its annual report, yet its social initiatives are uninspiring. The company gives an annual $1–1.5 million in charitable contributions, a well-below-average 0.1–0.15% of pretax earnings. Areas of emphasis are cultural programs and education, much of it funded through United Way chapters. In its headquarters city of Norfolk the railroad sponsors opera, symphony concerts, and the children's hospital.

As of January 1, 1990, employees were able to set aside pretax dollars for child care. There are no women and no minorities on the company's 13-person board of directors.

Norfolk Southern has prime contracts with the Department of Defense for the shipping of military hardware. The company says it meets environmental regulations, and is currently working to make sure that fuel doesn't pollute the groundwater.

The majority of its 31,000 employees are unionized.

FAST FACTS:
- No South African operations.
- Responded with information.
- Norfolk, VA.

NORTHERN TELECOM LTD.

Northern Telecom Ltd., 52% owned by BCE Inc., is the largest telecommunications equipment manufacturer in Canada, and second only to AT&T in the U.S. In 1988 the company's annual charitable contributions were more than 5% of pretax earnings and 0.5% of pretax revenues; it funds projects in the arts, health and welfare, and education. Much of this giving is through traditional outlets such as United Way chapters. The U.S. branch of Northern Telecom worked with the Committee for Economic Development to study what factors lead to children missing out on public education. As a result of the study, it put together a television program on the problem, *Children in Need*. The company also matches employee gifts to higher education dollar for dollar.

VP Margaret Kerr, the company's on-staff environmentalist, handles health and safety issues. One impressive step the company has taken is to announce that it will eliminate CFCs from its operations by the end of 1990, well ahead of most other companies. Northern Telecom explained that while it is convenient to use a solvent that contains CFCs in the soldering process, it is possible to change the process and eliminate the CFCs.

Canadian headquarters provides a referral service on child care assistance and sick-child programs. Meanwhile, Northern Telecom's Nashville office has a cooperative agreement with a local day care center—it helped the center start in exchange for pledged spots.

FAST FACTS:
■ No South African operations.
■ One woman on 20-person board of directors.
■ 50,000 employees worldwide, 22,000 in the U.S.
■ Responded with information.
■ Mississauga, Canada.

OCCIDENTAL PETROLEUM

Occidental's reputation has been badly bruised by several environmental and safety problems, although it has recently taken steps to improve its record in these areas.

In part Oxy's negative image rests on Hooker Chemical, which it acquired in 1968. In the 1940s Hooker bought the strip of land off the Niagara River in upstate New York that later became known as Love Canal, used it as a dump site for toxic chemicals, filled it in, and sold it to the Board of Education in 1953 for a dollar. The School Board was informed of the chemicals buried there and advised against selling the land for construction, a warning the school board disregarded.[106] In the late 1970s chemicals began leaching into people's basements and 200 families had to be evacuated in what was declared a health emergency. Oxy never took responsibility for Love Canal, arguing that the dumping took place long before it owned Hooker, but there is evidence that Occidental tried to dissociate itself from the landfill to avoid later blame.[107] In 1989 Oxy was one of four companies whose waste-hauling records were under investigation for the presence of compounds suspected to be carcinogenic near Niagara Falls.[108] Occidental's OxyChem division's internal search turned up no evidence of having ever used these compounds.

Even without Love Canal, other controversies remain. The Natural Resources Defense Council called Occidental one of the 11 largest emitters of carcinogenic chemicals unregulated under the Clean Air Act for emissions of a chromium compound at its Castel Hayne, North Carolina, plant.[109] The company says current emissions of the chromium compound have decreased. And OxyChem's Lathrop, California, plant was one of the manufacturers of dibromochloropropane (DBCP), a chemical used to control nematode worms, which was found to cause male sterility.[110] The company stopped selling DBCP in the later 1970s. Meanwhile it ranked second least admired of ten in the Food category of the January 29, 1990, *Fortune* survey.

Throughout the 1980s, Oxy took some positive environmental and safety steps. It has a sophisticated environmental computer monitoring system that keeps facilities in touch with headquarters, and the system has been so successful that Oxy markets it commercially under the name OXY-EAS. In 1988 it increased environmental safety-related expenditures 20%, and reported 38% fewer environmental incidents that year. It has also re-examined safety programs since the explosion of the Piper Alpha oil platform in the North Sea in July 1988, which claimed 167 lives and cost the company an estimated $1 billion, most of which was covered by the company's insurance.[111]

OSHA has levied several violations on Oxy subsidiaries, the largest of which went to its IBP meat-packing division. The Dakota City division was fined $3,133,100 in May 1988, and the year before IBP was given a record-keeping fine of more than $2.5 million. IBP did not admit liability, and ultimately settled all claims for significantly less—$975,000.

Armand Hammer, Oxy's colorful leader, is known for generous charitable giving, although the company's contributions are modest for a company with $548 million in pretax operating profits in 1988. In 1987 Oxy donated $1.2 million, half of which went to arts and humanities, according to the *Taft Corporate Giving Directory*.

FAST FACTS:

- IPB, which had been fiercely antiunion, made an about-face and recognized the United Food and Commercial Workers (UFCW) at its Joslin, Illinois, plant.[112]
- One woman on 18-person board of directors.

■ Responded with information.
■ Los Angeles, CA.

PARAMOUNT COMMUNICATIONS

A name change for this company, formerly Gulf & Western, emphasizes its motion-picture and television production and distribution businesses as well as stressing its other communications operations, including the publisher, Simon & Schuster.

In its brochure on equal employment opportunity, Paramount says that creating and maintaining diversity among its 12,000 employees worldwide is "essential to our company's continuing success." Unlike most other companies, Paramount specifically comments on sexual harassment in its brochure. To meet its EEO goals, Paramount recruits at colleges with higher concentrations of minorities and women and, when practical, advertises in minority news media. At Paramount there's a script-submission program for women and minorities in conjunction with the Writer's Guild of America, and there's an associate producers' program specifically designed to give minorities experience. Paramount funds scholarship programs for minorities through the National Achievement Scholarship Program for Outstanding Negro Students, the National Hispanic Scholarship Fund, and the United Negro College Fund. At the end of 1988 there was one woman on Paramount's 15-person board of directors.

Paramount says it participates in the New York City Summer Jobs Program, Reading Is Fundamental, the Reading Reform Foundation, and the Barbara Bush Foundation for Family Literacy.

FAST FACTS:
■ The company does "not have direct business operations, investments or employees" in South Africa, a spokesperson responded.
■ No military contracts.
■ Roughly 10% of workforce is unionized.
■ Responded with information.
■ New York, NY.

PEPSICO

Women and minorities are treated well at PepsiCo. The company has a black managers association and extensively recruits at black universities and minority career expos—two examples of why it was one of 50 companies selected in *Black Enterprise*'s survey of the best workplaces for blacks. According to *The Best Companies for Women*: "We talked to 11 women at PepsiCo, and not one of them said a woman couldn't go just as far as she was able, regardless of the fact that there are no women in the executive suite on the third floor as yet. To these women, it was only a matter of time."[113] Pepsi has several well-documented affirmative action programs, although its divisions are fairly autonomous, making the whole sometimes difficult to evaluate. The company calls its Minority Business Enterprise (MBE) program a "win-win situation"; in 1987 the company purchased $149.3 million from minority-owned businesses, up from $4 million in 1982, and it plans to purchase $800 million through this program between 1988 and 1993.

In the soft-drink business packaging is the major environmental question. Pepsi is helping fund a solid-waste division at the National Soft Drink Association to assist communities in developing solid-waste programs and supports the Plastic Recycling Foundation at Rutgers University. Its Frito-Lay division operates five primary waste-water treatment systems and has updated systems to minimize air emissions from its facilities.

FAST FACTS:

- PepsiCo tied for sixth out of 305 in *Fortune*'s January 29, 1990, survey of "America's Most Admired Corporations."
- Pepsi disposed of properties in South Africa acquired along with Kentucky Fried Chicken, but says "We have no legal right to terminate licenses with those who purchased the operations."
- 30% unionized corporatewide.
- More than 1% of annual pretax earnings goes to charitable contributions.
- In 1988 PepsiCo contributed $182,442 to PACs.
- Responded to questionnaire.
- Purchase, NY.

POLAROID

An early proponent of equal employment opportunity, Polaroid took a pioneering stance in severing its ties to South Africa. In 1970 the company's founder, Edwin Land, heard that Polaroid's distributor, Frank & Hirsch Pty. Ltd., was supporting apartheid by selling its products to the government and by paying black employees less than whites. The company rectified these inequities and halted sales to the

South African government. When Polaroid found out that its South African distributor was violating this agreement, it cut off all ties.[114]

Although Polaroid has demonstrated its good intentions, the follow-through has been hampered by economic woes. The shrinking amateur photography market has hurt its bottom line and the company has been a takeover target. Still, the inventor of instant photography was named one of "The 60 Best Companies for Working Mothers." One woman sits on Polaroid's 15-member board of directors, and women make up 28% of the company's U.S. workforce. Polaroid picks up the tab for up to 80% of a family's child care costs, depending on the employee's ability to pay. This program, established in 1970, was the first of its kind in this country.

Of U.S. employees 82.9% are white, 14.4% black, 1.4% Hispanic, 1.1% Asian, and 0.2% native American. Polaroid boasts a strong benefits package, with a profit-sharing and pretax savings program, and a stock equity plan through which employees hold a 19% stake of company stock.

In 1968 Polaroid launched Inner City, a wholly owned and financially self-sufficient subsidiary that trains the unemployed in classroom and manufacturing skills. Trainees are paid for their work and prepared for finding jobs.

The Community Relations Report says that Polaroid has often implemented environmental protection processes years ahead of regulatory requirements.[115]

FAST FACTS:

■ Teaches basic reading and arithmetic skills classes for employees.[116]
■ Included in *The 100 Best Companies to Work for in America*.
■ Polaroid Foundation is run by employee volunteers.
■ Employs 7900 in the U.S. and 3125 overseas.
■ Responded with information.
■ Cambridge, MA.

RALSTON PURINA

Headquartered at Checkerboard Square in St. Louis, Ralston Purina is involved with more than just pet food—the company owns Wonder bread, Hostess cakes, Eveready batteries, Chex cereal, and acquired Beech-Nut baby food in October 1989. Well before the acquisition, Beech-Nut was at the center of a widely publicized fraud when it labeled a mixture of sugar, water, and flavoring as apple juice. The case resulted in the indictment of Beech-Nut and two high-level executives who were handed down jail sentences but are appealing the decision.[117] Ralston Purina points out that none of the offenders remain at Beech-Nut.

Ralston described its charitable contributions as in the range of 1% annually. The focus of giving is on St. Louis projects involving low-income neighborhoods and youth-oriented organizations. The pet food maker also favors animal groups and makes donations to individual humane societies.

Some of Ralston Purina's plants are unionized, and the company is one of the largest employers of Teamsters, who drive its Continental Baking trucks. Although there are no women or minorities on the company's 16-person board of directors, two women and two blacks are corporate VPs. Flextime and job sharing can be arranged with supervisors, but the company makes no provisions for child care. The company has an employee assistance program for substance abuse and psychiatric counseling.

FAST FACTS:
- ▪ No South African operations.
- ▪ Employs 37,000 in the U.S. and 19,000 more worldwide.
- ▪ No weapons-related businesses.
- ▪ Responded with information.
- ▪ St. Louis, MO.

RAYTHEON

Raytheon was the 13th largest nuclear weapons contractor for 1988, according to Nuclear Free America. Its prime Department of Defense and Department of Energy nuclear weapons contracts totaled $831,539,000 for that year, while total sales to the DoD topped $4.5 billion. Raytheon's businesses are electronics, aircraft, major appliances, and energy services; its largest defense program is the Patriot surface-to-air missile system. Raytheon also makes major appliances through Amana, which it acquired in 1965. Prior to the acquisition, Amana was primarily owned by the Amana Society, a communal corporation known for corporate commitment.[118]

Although Raytheon publishes information on corporate programs in its annual report, it does not disclose the extent of its giving. Recipients of this funding include a new engineering/research facility at Northeastern University, the Hospice Federation, and the Bristol Rehabilitation Center, which serves the disabled in Tennessee.

Stockholder proposals to cease doing business with South Africa were defeated "by wide margins" at the 1989 annual meeting. The company is an endorser of the Statement of Principles, which means it has fewer than 25 employees there (if any at all) and gives an annual donation to the program.

Raytheon is involved in several environmental cleanup projects or disputes. In 1985 Raytheon and two other companies voluntarily agreed to perform a remedial investigation/feasibility study about possible soil and groundwater contamination at Mountain View, California. Meanwhile, in 1986 the town of Bedford, Massachusetts, named Raytheon as a defendant in a suit over chemical contamination of the town's well field. The suit will be tried by the United States District Court for the District of Massachusetts, and the defendants include the Massachusetts Port Authority, the U.S. Air Force, and the Navy.

FAST FACTS:
- One woman on 15-person board of directors.
- Responded with information.
- Lexington, MA.

ROCKWELL INTERNATIONAL

Rockwell International, maker of the space shuttle and the plutonium triggers for thermonuclear bombs, ranked ninth largest nuclear weapons manufacturer in 1988, according to Nuclear Free America. Its prime nuclear weapons DoD and DoE contracts totaled $1,542,835,000. However, Rockwell will no longer be operating the Rocky Flats, Colorado, plant, which makes the plutonium triggers that detonate warheads, so its exposure will likely drop in the future. Overall, only a quarter of its total $12.5 billion in business is derived from Pentagon contracts.[119] Rockwell was handed a criminal indictment for overbilling the Air Force, charging it in both 1982 and 1983 for the same work.[120] Yet, Rockwell has an active ethics program and has an extensive minority-business purchasing program.

In 1989 the Department of Energy and Rockwell reached an agreement to end the company's operation of the Rocky Flats plant. The previous year the Energy Department charged that there was a breakdown in management, and internal 1986 DoE memos criticized the plant for being in poor condition in terms of environmental compliance, calling its waste facilities "patently illegal."[121] Further, in June 1988 the FBI alleged that Rockwell had dumped cancer-causing chemicals into streams; this investigation is continuing.[122] If Rockwell is found guilty of misconduct at Rocky Flats, it could mean a suspension of DoE contracts. The contractor threatened to close down the weapons plant unless granted immunity from criminal and civil prosecution of laws governing waste disposal.[123] On September 15, 1989, Rockwell and the Energy Department decided to turn the facility over to a new contractor, EG&G.

Rocky Flats has also been questioned for its operation of Hanford, a complex in southeast Washington state, where it had ignored safety hazards, according to former employees and House Energy and Commerce Committee investigators in *The Wall Street Journal*'s August 30, 1989, article, "Rockwell Bomb Plant is Repeatedly Accused of Poor Safety Record." Rockwell has not operated the Hanford complex since 1987. These controversies come from a company that has a far-reaching ethics sensitivity training program in which all employees participate. In 1989 85,000 employees attended refresher ethics courses.

In 1989 Rockwell made $12.4 million in charitable contributions, around 1.03% of that year's pretax income. The company emphasizes education, encouraging high school students to pursue higher education, and offers a graduate fellowship program for science and engineering.

Rockwell has also made substantial efforts to hire women and minorities and has published its results. For the ten years through June 1989, 21% of Rockwell's 10,538 new college graduates hired were members of minority groups and 22% women. The company purchased more than $100 million in products and services from around 800 minority suppliers in FY89 (Sept.). There is one woman but no minority individuals on its 14-person board of directors.

FAST FACTS:
- Around 109,000 employees.
- Three pages devoted to corporate citizenship in 1989 annual report.
- Did not respond.
- Pittsburgh, PA.

SCHLUMBERGER

This oil-drilling and equipment company derives only 30–40% of its annual revenues from the U.S.—the rest comes from the more than 100 countries it operates in worldwide. Not surprisingly, a corporation with such far-flung operations has a presence in South Africa, employing 30–40 workers there. Schlumberger has decided against signing the Statement of Principles; the board of directors says if it were to evaluate all the political systems of the countries it operates in, it would have to rethink many other operations as well. Schlumberger also says its small corporate staff was unwilling to take on the paperwork that yearly evaluations would generate. Its South African operations are service-oriented and there are no capital assets there.

Schlumberger has a VP of safety, who applies technology to making safer and more environmentally sound products.

The company has no women on its board of directors or among the top-ranking officials of the company. However, many of its highest officers are from foreign countries and are of different ethnic backgrounds. Of the company's 45,000 employees, only one-third work in the U.S.

The company has a charitable giving trust, the Schlumberger Foundation, but would not release charitable giving numbers. However, in 1986 the company contributed $1.432 million, 81% of which funded education projects, according to the *Taft Corporate Giving Directory*.

FAST FACTS:
- Employee benefits vary by location.
- Responded with limited information.
- New York, NY.

SEARS, ROEBUCK AND CO.

Not only can Sears, Roebuck demonstrate affirmative action progress, but it's also willing to do so—the company earns high marks for social disclosure as one of only a few companies that publishes its equal opportunity numbers in its annual report. Having implemented a formal affirmative action program in 1968, Sears aggressively recruits women, minorities, and the disabled at colleges and universities as well as involving itself in organizations and conferences targeting these groups. There are one black woman and two white women on the company's 16-person board of directors. In 1988, 39.6% of Sears' 26,000 officials and managers were women, up from 38.7% in 1987. Meanwhile, 7.8% of officials and managers were black, 4.2% Hispanic, 0.6% Asian/Pacific Islander, and 0.4% American Indian/Alaskan Natives. The company was included in *Black Enterprise*'s February 1989 survey of "The 50 Best Places for Blacks to Work."

Buying American goods has been a policy of the Sears Merchandise Group for more than 30 years; in 1988 nine out of ten merchandise dollars wound up with domestic suppliers. The Sears, Roebuck Foundation and company business groups made more than $25 million in charitable contributions in 1988, an above-average 2.3% of that year's pretax income. Corporate philanthropy at Sears is oriented toward education, one example of which is its more than 20 years of support for *Mister Rogers' Neighborhood.*

FAST FACTS:

■ No South African operations.

■ In addition to retailing, Sears owns Allstate Insurance Group, Dean Witter Financial Services Group, and Coldwell Banker Real Estate Group.

■ Ranked least admired of ten in Retailing category of *Fortune's* January 29, 1990, survey of corporate reputations.

■ No defense-related businesses.

■ Very small percentage of 520,000 employees worldwide are unionized.

■ In 1988 Sears Merchandise Group purchased $97,923,496 from minority-owned businesses and $155,899,803 from women-owned businesses.

■ Maintains deposits in a consortium of 60 recognized minority- or women-owned banks nationwide.

■ Responded with information.

■ Chicago, IL.

SKYLINE CORP.

Skyline Corp., a maker of manufactured homes and recreational vehicles, provides affordable housing, thereby fulfilling a societal need. Beyond its basic business, few social initiatives could be located for the company, although this could be because of its limited disclosure. A spokesman for Skyline questioned this enterprise, and declined to respond to the questionnaire. In a letter dated December 5, 1989, he wrote: "Unfortunately, the questionnaire does not address a fundamental aspect of corporate social responsibility—the necessity of achieving a level of success that sustains the production of goods or services and creates continuing employment opportunities. For example, a company might be able to cite the existence of progressive policies for dealing with many or all of your questions. But if the company's future is jeopardized by inadequate profits, are society's long-term interests served?" Skyline's prompt, effective service was cited as a "moral obligation" the company meets.

FAST FACTS:
- No South African operations.
- No women on Skyline's nine-person board of directors.
- Did not respond.
- Elkhart, IN.

SOUTHERN COMPANY

Southern Company is an electric utility holding company, operating in the southeastern U.S. Although its main energy sources are coal (76%), nuclear power (17%), hydroelectric (6%), and oil and gas (1%), it has launched several demonstration projects using alternative forms of energy. These projects, commissioned by the Department of Energy, involve clean coal technology and solar energy.

One widely discussed bill to curb acid rain would cost the Southern electric system as much as $2.1 billion by the year 2001, by its own calculations. The company has collected data for and contributed to studies on the effects of acid rain. It also played a leading role in establishing the nonprofit Living Lakes organization, which treats lakes and streams to reduce their acidity. Since 1985, when the program began, it has treated 40 bodies of water in eight states and has restocked some waters with native species of fish.

In October 1989 Southern's Pensacola, Florida-based Gulf Power Co. unit pleaded guilty to two felony charges: making illegal political contributions and tax evasion. The company paid a $500,000 fine. (Federal law prohibits utility holding companies from making political contributions.) At the time of this writing, a federal grand jury was investigating other aspects of Southern's accounting practices and pension fund transactions, according to *The Wall Street Journal* on April 24, 1990.

There are two women on Southern's 21-person board of directors.

FAST FACTS:
- No South African operations.
- Ranked tenth of ten in Utilities category of *Fortune*'s January 29, 1990, survey of America's most admired corporations.
- No Department of Defense prime contracts.
- Some of the 30,000 employees are unionized, frequently line crew workers.
- No overseas operations.
- Did not release charitable giving numbers.
- Responded with information.
- Atlanta, GA.

SQUIBB CORP.

During the writing of this book, Squibb merged with Bristol-Myers and is profiled under Bristol-Myers Squibb.

TANDY CORPORATION

Founder Charles Tandy took a chain of bankrupt electronics shops and turned them into one of the nation's biggest retailing success stories: the Radio Shack chain. This consumer electronics manufacturer and technology retailer has taken some moderate social initiatives. Tandy Corp. was profiled in *The 100 Best Companies to Work for in America*, which noted that Charles Tandy set the tone for the company's easygoing relations by answering his own phone.

One minority member and one woman sat on Tandy's 14-person board of directors at midyear 1989. The company recruits women and minorities on campuses and through women- and minority-oriented outreach programs and organizations. Tandy also identifies high-potential minority individuals and women and monitors their progress in the company. Meanwhile, Tandy has a minority- and women-owned vendor program.

Charitable contributions are geared toward nonprofit organizations in Fort Worth, where corporate offices are located. The remaining funds go to education, health and human services, and the arts. The company matches annual employee gifts of up to $500 on a two-for-one basis, and beyond that matches gifts of up to $7500 dollar for dollar. The Tandy Technology Scholars Program awards cash stipends and scholarships to outstanding teachers and students in math, science, or computer science.

FAST FACTS:
- No South African operations.
- Plants are not unionized.
- Responded with information.
- Fort Worth, TX.

TEKTRONIX

A leading manufacturer of electronic equipment, Tektronix, a.k.a. Tek, is considered a good place to work. Named in *The 100 Best Companies to Work for in America* and praised in *A Great Place to Work: What Makes Some Employers So Good (And Most So Bad)*, Tek maintains informal communications with its employees, and each year the president makes two State of the Company addresses, fielding tough questions from employees.[124] Other meetings between senior management and employees are often aired on the company's internal TV network. Another plus is Tek's extensive profit-sharing plan—35% of pretax profits are paid out to employees, half of it advanced monthly and half at six-month intervals. Tek's communication with its shareholders is informal and refreshingly candid. "Emotionally bumpy, financially flat, the year we leave behind is the kind of year you like to leave behind," says its FY89 (May 27) annual report.

Although known as "one of the sleepiest of high-tech companies" before its turnaround efforts,[125] Tek has long been wide-awake to its environmental responsibility. Tek has a corporate environmental and safety manager, and managers' performance reviews include an environmental category. Oregon environmentalists have praised the company, according to *Electronic Business*, highlighting these five positives: Tek has had a waste minimization program since the mid-1970s, which saves more than $3 million per year in recovered materials; it takes an active role in toxics-use reduction legislation; it participates aggressively in local toxics-handling councils; it makes all levels accountable for chemical use; and it established an action-oriented, seven-person environmental team.[126]

FAST FACTS:
- No South African operations; however, Tek does sell products to an independent company, Protea Technology, which sells to other South African firms.
- Does not release equal employment numbers for its 15,469 employees; of 15 officers, three are women and none minorities.
- In FY89 Tek made $4.542 million in charitable contributions.
- Pretax dollars can be deducted for child care costs.
- Responded to questionnaire.
- Beaverton, OR.

TELEDYNE

Deriving 25% of its sales from the U.S. government, not all defense-related, Teledyne ranked 39th in terms of prime Department of Defense contracts for research, development, testing, and evaluation in 1988. These contracts were worth around $96,492,000. Although Nuclear Free America ranked the company 44th among the top 50 nuclear weapons contractors, quoting over $83 million worth of DoD and DoE prime contracts in this area for 1988, Teledyne protested that it was not directly involved in manufacturing nuclear weapons. It does, however, make zirconium and hafnium, which are used in nuclear reactors, and Teledyne Energy Systems makes thermonuclear power systems.

Charitable giving is funneled through the Teledyne Charitable Trust Foundation. In 1986 Teledyne gave around $1.63 million to charitable organizations, according to the *Taft Corporate Giving Directory*. It also runs the Teledyne Research Assistance Program, which funds projects of interest to the company and universities. The company matches employee gifts to education on a generous two-for-one basis.

Each of the 120 companies within Teledyne designates a member of its management staff to be in charge of environmental and safety issues.

No minorities or women sit on Teledyne's five-person board of directors although one woman is counted among the company's six officers.

FAST FACTS:
- No South African operations.
- 45,000 employees, some unionized.
- Responded with information.
- Los Angeles, CA.

TEXAS INSTRUMENTS

Texas Instruments, an electronics company credited with the invention of the integrated circuit, is also a major defense contractor through its manufacturing of electronic defense systems. Its Department of Defense contracts for FY88 were worth $1,220,053,000, making it the 19th largest DoD contractor that year.

Globalization has been a key ingredient in TI's recipe for success. Of 73,000 employees worldwide, approximately 50,000 work in the U.S. The company made its move to Asia early, establishing Texas Instruments Asia Ltd. in 1964. Many socially responsible investors are concerned that relocating manufacturing sites overseas ultimately costs Americans jobs. On this subject, President and CEO Jerry Junkins has said:"It's too simplistic to say you lose jobs. If you've got a corporation that's not competitive on a world-wide basis, then you've got a company that's probably going to have problems maintaining its job base in its home territory."[127]

In 1988 Texas Instruments gave an estimated $8.775 million in charitable contributions, a generous 1.7% of that year's pretax income. These gifts were, however, valued at more than $12.7 million, according to the company. Around 48% of the funds went to social services (mainly through United Funds), 27% to arts and humanities, 19% to education, 4% to health, and 2% to other, according to the *Taft Corporate Giving Directory*.

TI is one of several defense contractors subject to U.S. government investigations concerning procurement of contracts. It is also a potentially responsible party for its disposal of waste materials and, following EPA investigations, may share in cleanup costs for certain sites.

Pretax dollars can be put toward benefits at Texas Instruments, including child care expenses.

FAST FACTS:
■ No South African operations.
■ No unionized employees.
■ Responded with information.
■ Dallas, TX.

TOYS "R" US

Toys "R" Us, the world's largest toy specialty retailer and a presence in the children's clothing market through Kids "R" Us, signed on with the NAACP's Operation Fair Share in the fall of 1988. The company is working with the NAACP to strengthen its minority purchasing program, to increase the number of minority members in its workforce, and to hike its advertising in minority media. At this time, there is one minority officer, Vice Chairman Robert Nakasone, but no women on the 11-person board of directors. There are three women at the officer level, which includes some 50 professionals. The toy-store operator was exploring child care options at this writing; it had abandoned an earlier subsidy program because most employees were not using it. The January 1990 issue of *Clean Yield* profiled the company and said: "In an industry notorious for low pay and stingy benefits, Toys has built up a loyal workforce by treating its employees well."

Toys "R" Us is involved in some innovative charitable programs, although the company declined to disclose the extent of donations. Its emphasis is on the health-care needs of children, and it supports Easter Seals and the Sloan Kettering Memorial Hospital. Its Hospital

Playroom Program is an ambitious attempt to see that there are playrooms in all hospitals that treat children.

In October 1987 the toy retailer was given an award by the Illinois Council Against Handgun Violence for responding to the problem of look-alike guns.

FAST FACTS:

■ No South African operations.
■ No arms-related work.
■ 30,000 U.S. employees.
■ No unionized employees.
■ Responded with limited information.
■ Rochelle Park, NJ.

UAL

Who should own UAL? In late 1989 several corporate raiders had staked claims, Coniston Partners was trying to oust the present board of directors, and the pilots wanted to try their hand at running the company. Mere word that financing for a UAL takeover couldn't be put together drove the market down 190 points on October 13, 1989. But management hadn't given up. CEO Stephen Wolf was trying to make himself accessible to employees, answering their questions and pressing them to follow in archrival American Airlines' footsteps and make concessions that would allow the company to get ahead.[128] For these reasons UAL poses a unique challenge to evaluate. As of April 1990 a $4.38 billion buyout of UAL Corp. by its unions had been approved by UAL directors.

United Airlines, the main business of UAL, has experienced labor unrest before but does not have the checkered past other airlines do. Out of 70,000 employees, around 45,000 belong to a union. Its most recent strike was a pilot strike in 1985. Prior to that was the machinists' strike in 1979.

There is one black man and one woman on UAL's 15-person board of directors. Women and minorities are actively recruited—the company uses job fairs, university programs, and an internship program to meet affirmative action goals. UAL would not release EEO statistics.

FAST FACTS:

■ No South African operations.
■ United Airlines gave $1.57 million in charitable contributions in 1987, according to the *Taft Corporate Giving Directory.* (UAL

posted a loss that year.) 63% of the funds went to social services, 16% to education, 12% to arts and humanities, 6% to civic and public affairs, and 2% to health.
- No military work.
- Responded with information.
- Chicago, IL.

UNISYS

This information services and defense electronics concern ranked 19th in Nuclear Free America's 1988 list "The Top 50 Nuclear Weapons Contractors," with DoD and DoE prime contracts totaling more than $418 million. Unisys is one of the top ten national suppliers of defense electronics, a business that accounts for 25% of its revenues.

Unisys, the company formed out of the 1986 Sperry and Burroughs merger, has already experienced controversy. In 1988 a few former managers of the Defense Systems business acquired from Sperry were found to be involved in unethical procurement activities. The company is believed to have obtained several contracts through insider information and is involved in the federal Ill Wind investigation. In response Unisys overhauled its surveillance unit, changed its system of hiring managers, placed some employees on leave pending investigation, and agreed to cooperate fully with the government.[129] It also developed an internal ethics program and a formal code of conduct for its Defense Systems group.

Although Unisys sold its South African marketing and sales subsidiary in 1988, its products continue to be sold there through a subdistributor arrangement, and it had continued to endorse the Statement of Principles as of June 1989.

In a restructuring announced the summer of 1989, Unisys expected to restore the company to profitability by scaling back on growth plans. To accomplish this it announced it would trim 7000–8000 of its 88,000 total employees through layoffs and attrition.

FAST FACTS:
- One woman on 15-person board of directors.
- About 46% of Unisys revenues derived overseas.
- Responded with information.
- Blue Bell, PA.

UNITED TECHNOLOGIES

One of the country's top military contractors, United Technologies derived 53% of 1988 revenues from aerospace and defense. The company puts strong emphasis on charitable giving and made $12.23 million in total domestic contributions in 1988, 1.05% of that year's pretax income. Half of UT's contributions went to education; health and human services, cultural arts, and civic projects are other areas of emphasis. United Technologies has selected 21 "focus schools" to support because of their quality engineering programs and has played a major role in teacher enrichment programs.

United Technologies ranked as one of the largest arms contractors for 1988, with Department of Defense and Department of Energy prime contracts worth around $2.099 billion, according to Nuclear Free America. Pratt & Whitney, its largest defense unit, captured the lion's share of the U.S. Air Force's fighter-engine requirements for the second consecutive year in 1988, and won its Big "Q" Quality Award. UT noted that it has been designated a potentially responsible party for liabilities under the Comprehensive Environmental Response, Compensation and Liability Act (CERCLA), for which authorities will seek expenditures and damages for the release of environmental pollutants.

UT's Otis Elevator Company installs and services products in over 160 countries. It is therefore not surprising to find Otis in South Africa, where it has a manufacturing facility in Wadeville. Otis is a signatory of the Statement of Principles, and received the middle rating, Making Progress, for the three years through June 1989.

FAST FACTS:
- Two women on 12-person board of directors.
- Responded with information.
- Hartford, CT.

UPJOHN COMPANY

Upjohn, a multinational pharmaceutical and health-care-product concern, has demonstrated commitment to its headquarters community of Kalamazoo, Michigan, where it has approximately 8000 employees. In October 1988 the drug company announced it would provide $2 million a year for a five-year program to assist Greater Kalamazoo in "upgrading community infrastructure and to encourage greater intergovernmental cooperation." Upjohn underscored its commitment to Kalamazoo by announcing that it would build a new $122-million research facility there.

Upjohn is one of several drug companies named defendant in suits for alleged injuries to the children of pregnant women who took diethylstilbestrol (DES), a drug prescribed to prevent miscarriages. Upjohn discontinued marketing DES ten years prior to the FDA's recommendation against its use.

In 1987 the company spent nearly $17.2 million to reduce chemical air and water emissions at its main manufacturing plant in Michigan. It has pledged to halve air emissions of the solvent methylene chloride over a two-year period. However, actions have also been brought against Upjohn by the EPA for the cleanup of roughly 30 Superfund sites for which it is one of several potentially responsible parties.

Upjohn has two South African subsidiaries and is a signatory of the Statement of Principles. Its products are not strategic, and it received the highest rating, Making Good Progress, for the year ending June 1989. As of mid-1989 Upjohn employed 261 people in South Africa, 47% of whom are nonwhite.

FAST FACTS:
- One woman and no minority members on Upjohn's 14-person board of directors as of year-end 1988.
- Upjohn made cash, product, and equipment contributions totaling $7,069,472, or 1.38% of 1988 pretax income.
- No weapons-making businesses.
- Roughly 21,000 employees worldwide.
- Responded with limited information.
- Kalamazoo, MI.

WAL-MART STORES

Wal-Mart, one of the nation's largest discount chains, is offering a good corporate image along with its merchandise. It has taken the unusual step of "green-product labeling," indicating which goods are manufactured by environmentally progressive companies.[130] And since 1985 Wal-Mart has had a "Buy American" program, which it claimed had created or retained more than 41,000 jobs for U.S. workers.

Profit-sharing and stock purchase programs include employees in the success of the company, which was exceptional throughout the 1980s. Wal-Mart was included in *The 100 Best Companies to Work for in America*; the authors liken the company to a family and describe its spirit as "rah-rah." Every operating unit has a safety committee to assure a safe environment for employees and customers. And Wal-Mart boasts employee perks such as a health hotline and Resources for Living, a personal-needs counseling service. That a "people greeter" meets customers at the front door is indicative of this company's spirit.

Employee grants to charitable organizations are matched dollar for dollar. The company handed out more than $1.2 million in Wal-Mart Scholarships for the year ending January 1989.

Wal-Mart tied for sixth most admired out of a field of 305 major companies in *Fortune*'s January 29, 1990, survey of corporate reputations. It was also a Franklin's *insight* social recommendation in 1989.

FAST FACTS:
■ No South African operations.
■ No arms-related businesses.
■ Employed 223,000 in January 1989.
■ Responded with printed materials.
■ Bentonville, AR.

WEYERHAEUSER

Forest- and paper-product companies are not known for scoring points with environmentalists, but Weyerhaeuser generally rates a little higher than its peers. The company has a long-standing practice of planting more trees than it harvests and in 1986 celebrated the planting of the two-billionth seedling in 20 years of its High Yield Forestry program. In 1989 its environmental capital costs were expected to be $45.9 million. Weyerhaeuser was also given the 1988 Arbor Day Foundation Education Award. And it publishes a booklet on its environmental policy and statement of corporate values, which emphasizes disclosure of its policies. That William Ruckelshaus, two-time administrator of the EPA, was on the payroll in the late 1970s speaks well of its environmental record. Weyerhaeuser was also a social pick of Franklin's *insight* as of the fall of 1989.

Weyerhaeuser earmarked an estimated $4.441 million for charitable giving in 1988, according to the *Taft Corporate Giving Directory*, a well-below-average 0.58% of that year's pretax earnings. However, Weyerhaeuser's charitable program is growing—in 1989 the company donated $5.2 million and $6.2 million for 1990. Its funding emphasis is on basic human services.

Weyerhaeuser employs 9600 women and 7800 minorities among

its 42,000 employees. No women sit on its 11-member board of directors, although the company does help employees solve child care problems by contracting with the Northwest Family Network, an information and referral service. And it has issued an explicit statement against sexual harassment that outlines the complaint procedure.

FAST FACTS:
- No South African operations, although a small amount of its wood pulp is sometimes sold there by an independent sales agency.
- In *The 100 Best Companies to Work for in America*.
- Profit-sharing plans for employees.
- About 40% of employees are unionized.
- Has a minority-business purchasing program.
- Operates two PACs—one for managers and one for major shareholders.
- Responded to questionnaire.
- Tacoma, WA.

WILLIAMS COMPANIES

Few outstanding social initiatives could be located for Williams Companies, a pipeline transmission and telecommunications corporation, and yet it has avoided many controversies, neither having operations or agreements with South Africa nor manufacturing weapons.

Environmental issues affect the company. Natural gas, which Williams gathers and transports, is environmentally important because it burns more cleanly than many other fuels. Its Northwest Pipeline Corp. has been cleaning up potentially carcinogenic PCBs in waste-disposal facilities at some field locations, for which the company will be reimbursed by a former owner. Minor PCB contamination was also found in its natural gas company's air-compressor systems and disposal pits.

Williams has between 4000 and 5000 employees, less than half of whom are unionized.

Employee gifts to United Way, education, the arts, and several nonprofit organizations are matched on a one-for-one basis.

Pretax dollars can be put toward child care expenses, and flextime is available on an informal basis. However, there are neither women nor members of minority groups on the company's 14-person board of directors.

FAST FACTS:
■ No minority- or women-owned business purchasing program.
■ Responded with limited information.
■ Tulsa, OK.

XEROX

Xerox is not just a carbon copy of other companies. Many of its policies are innovative, and it has a long history of social responsibility. The company emphasizes volunteering, and has offered a social service leave program since the early 1970s. Employees propose projects and their requests are reviewed by a committee; leave is granted for up to a year at full Xerox pay, and approximately 10 to 15 employees generally take advantage of this opportunity each year. Working with AIDS patients and counseling drug addicts are examples of what leavetakers have done.

Xerox also has a comprehensive ethics policy in place. All executives are required to read and sign the company's ethics policy each year and make certain that their employees do so. Anyone knowing of an ethical infringement is expected to inform management.

Xerox has taken a firm stand on affirmative action and has received recognition from both *Black Enterprise* and *Working Mother* for its efforts. *Black Enterprise* credits CEO David T. Kearns with the company's commitment to affirmative action. Kearns has often stated that although "national trends may fluctuate, this company's stance is unwavering" on EEO issues, according to the February 1989 issue of *BE*. Basing 20% of a manager's performance review on success with human resources management, including affirmative action, was another part of Xerox's effort, according to a November 15, 1989, *Wall Street Journal* article entitled, "A new push to break the 'glass ceiling'". And these good intentions translate into solid results. Xerox has a black president, A. Barry Rand, who heads the company's largest domestic marketing division, and around 12 black VPs out of roughly 90. *BE* notes that this is more than any other major U.S. industrial company. On the 17-person board of directors sits a black man, Vernon Jordan, former president of the National Urban League. Blacks make up 13.8% of the overall workforce and 11.4% of officials and managers.

Women fare well at Xerox, too. Forty percent of sales workers are women, and women account for 31.8% of officials, managers, and professionals. One woman sits on the board of directors. Pretax dollars can be set aside for child care costs, and flextime, part-time, and job-sharing options are available.

The company gives around $18 million a year to charitable projects, a well-above-average 3.8% of 1988 pretax income. Education, culture, arts, and social programs are areas emphasized.

FAST FACTS:

■ Sold its South African operations in mid-1980s; still has a trade agreement there.

■ Ranked 288th for Department of Defense prime contracts in 1988; contracts are not weapons-related.

■ Approximately 110,000 employees, about half of whom work overseas.

■ Around 5% of employees are unionized.

■ Received one of two National Quality Awards for 1989.

■ Responded with information.

■ Stamford, CT.

■ 9 ■
PROFILES
OF 100
COMPANIES
ETHICAL
INVESTORS
SHOULD KNOW

This chapter examines companies culled from the news, ethical investors' best and worst company lists, and industries of interest to social investors. These are points of departure rather than destinations; some stories are amusing, some inspiring. However, unlike the companies in the S&P 100, these companies cannot readily be compared against each other. It's clear that a giant would be prone to have more problems and offer a wider range of benefits and programs than a company which only recently went public.

AMR CORP.

AMR, owner of American Airlines, has known fewer employee conflicts than most other major airlines. *Fortune*'s January 29, 1990, survey of corporate reputations ranked it second most admired of ten in the airline category, and Shearson's socially responsible investment account manager recently rated the company a buy.

Black Enterprise profiled AMR in its February 1989 compilation "The 50 Best Places for Blacks to Work," noting that its EEO policies are enforced by coordinators and the corporate affirmative action staff. AMR identifies talented minority candidates to receive special assignments in order to gain promotions. Of the company's 65,154 employees, 8.86% are black, and blacks comprise 2.5% of its 840 managers. One black man—Christopher Edley, CEO of the United Negro College Fund—sits on the 14-member board of directors, but no women are represented.

To succeed in the competitive airline business, AMR convinced its employees to accept short-term wage concessions. Around 21,000 of its employees belong to the Transport Workers Union, and the company has an active profit-sharing and stock purchase plan.

AMR is involved in a lawsuit to liberalize the weight restrictions and appearance checks for flight attendants, according to *The Wall Street Journal*.

FAST FACTS:
- An endorser of the Statement of Principles, which entails an annual contribution to the program.
- Did not respond.
- Dallas, TX.

ABBOTT LABORATORIES

Abbott Labs, a worldwide health-care concern, fulfills many social needs through its products and charitable contributions. At the same time, it remains in South Africa, where it manufactures and sells its full, albeit nonstrategic, product line.

In 1988 Abbott gave $7.6 million in charitable contributions (0.72% of 1988 pretax earnings), with a heavy emphasis on support for medical disasters. Donating supplies to victims of the Armenian earthquake was one major philanthropic project; it is also active in local drug and alcohol abuse programs. Environmental projects are also favored by Abbott, which demonstrated its commitment to conserving natural resources by outfitting its Puerto Rico site with a $6-million wastewater treatment and reclamation plant.

Abbott has one woman but no minority members on its board of directors. Meanwhile, there is one Hispanic but no women among its 60–70 VPs. Throughout the U.S. Abbott offers employees the Child Care Solution, an information and referral service, and a flexible benefits program, enabling employees to put pretax dollars toward child care costs.

Free of charge Abbott will send out informational pamphlets on subjects such as AIDS, sexually transmitted diseases, and mosquito control.

Just the same, Abbott is one of several companies named in a group of product liability cases for injuries alleged to have resulted from the use of certain synthetic estrogen drugs, including diethylstilbestrol (DES), during pregnancy. And FDA inspectors recently turned up quality-control problems in Abbott's North Chicago injectable-drug facility. The FDA cited 56 violations, some of which concerned microbial growth and faulty sterilization.[1] Abbott notes that the problems are technical regulatory issues it is working to resolve with the FDA. Meanwhile, the FDA has taken no action against the company.

Abbott's South African operation employs 155 workers, over 40% of whom are nonwhite. It has signed the Statement of Principles and received the middle rating, Making Progress, for the year ending June 1989. This is a move in the wrong direction; the year before, Abbott had received the highest rating.

FAST FACTS:

∎ Roughly 41,000 employees worldwide, around 30,000 of whom work in the U.S.
∎ Company has an AIDS diagnostic test.
∎ Very small percentage of workforce is unionized.
∎ Responded with information.
∎ North Chicago, IL.

ADVANCED MICRO DEVICES

This integrated circuit maker is known for treating its employees well. Much of its corporate culture revolves around profit-sharing: It's believed at AMD that hard work should be rewarded. These attitudes earned AMD a place in *The 100 Best Companies to Work for in America*, in which the authors praised CEO Jerry Sanders for promising no layoffs in the business downturn of 1981–1983. This record was later broken when AMD laid off 2400 employees worldwide in response to a precipitous decline in sales. It now employs around 13,500 total.

Although AMD does not provide on-site day care, it offers a referral service for working parents. There are no women on its seven-person board of directors.

AMD earmarks around 1% of pretax profits annually for charitable contributions; however, it scales this back in years when the corporation posts a loss. AMD matches employee gifts of up to $500 to universities on a dollar-for-dollar basis and will contribute $10,000 worth of parts for courses or research to selected universities.

Parnassus counted AMD among its picks in 1989.

FAST FACTS:
- No South African operations.
- No unionized employees.
- Not one of top 500 Department of Defense contractors.
- Responded with information.
- Sunnyvale, CA.

AETNA LIFE & CASUALTY

One of several socially attractive aspects of Aetna is its Corporate Responsibility Investment Committee (CRIC), which develops policies for Aetna's community investment program, acts as a finance committee for proposed investments, and monitors company performance in this area. Through this program, Aetna sets aside around $30 million annually for social investments that do not meet traditional financial criteria. Typically, these funds are loaned to low-income housing projects and minority- or women-owned businesses. Parnassus and Franklin's *insight* both counted it as a social pick in 1989. However, the company is not without its share of controversies.

Aetna was listed among "The 60 Best Companies for Working Mothers" in *Working Mother*'s October 1989 survey. This article praised Aetna for decreasing the hours per week a part-timer must work and still qualify for benefits to 15—the reverse of a trend to exclude part-time employees from coverage. Provisions for women with family commitments include flextime, part-time, job-sharing, paid leave to care for a sick family member, and a child care and elder care referral service. Nearly 17% of the company's 2400 officers are women.

Black Enterprise profiled Aetna as one of the 50 best workplaces for blacks. The insurer sponsors Minorities in Corporate America seminars and has encouraged its Minority Managers and Supervisors employee group to work with senior management on EEO issues.[2] Blacks account for 5% of all officers at Aetna. There are one black and one woman on the 11-person board.

Aetna donates over $13 million annually to nonprofit education, youth, employment and urban revitalization, civil justice, and social services organizations. For 1988 this came to just over 1.6% of pretax income. Qualifying employee gifts are matched dollar for dollar. The National Society for Fundraising Executives honored Aetna for its charitable work in 1989. Aetna also has a three-part program called Stepping Up, which tackles educational problems that cause disadvantaged groups to have trouble finding employment. The American Society for Training and Development singled out Aetna for its 1989 Corporate Award.

Due to slowing growth in the workforce, in 1989 Aetna launched a project to recruit 130 slots each year, or 6% of its entry-level positions, from Hartford's inner city. Aetna spends between $7,000 and $10,000 on training each candidate, including salary. A *Wall Street Journal* article says "supervisors are happy because the program graduates are better prepared than previous hires."[3]

However, not everyone would give Aetna the same glowing report. Named among "The Ten Worst Corporations of 1988" in the *Multinational Monitor*, Aetna was criticized for tort reform, which the article claimed was a campaign to impose caps on pain and suffering awards and limits on punitive damage awards. Consumer advocate Ralph Nader called this "one of the most unprincipled public relations scams in the history of American industry."[4] Aetna said its purpose was not to impose caps on awards but to get the public thinking about the high cost of "frivolous lawsuits." The insurer is not suggesting tort reform for "life-changing accidents" in which the victim was disfigured or handicapped.

Aetna was named co-defendant with A. H. Robins Company in more than 100 product liability suits involving the Dalkon Shield IUD. In general, these suits claim that Aetna acted with Robins not to disclose the alleged dangers of the device.[5] Under the settlement for the Breland class suit, Aetna must pay $75 million to the trust to compensate claimants. Around 2400 women excluded themselves from settlement of the trust and could therefore still launch suits against Aetna.

FAST FACTS:
- No South African ties.
- No arms-related businesses.
- Around 43,000 employees.
- No unionized employees.
- Responded with information.
- Hartford, CT.

ALLWASTE

Allwaste's main business is cleaning up the environment; this environmental services concern provides air-moving, asbestos abatement, tank cleaning and resource recovery services. The company uses a heavy-duty vacuum system to remove asbestos and other contaminants from industrial sites. Allwaste has grown quickly through acquisition and has expanded into the glass-recycling business. Through its acquired Guzzler line it manufactures the air-moving equipment it uses and also sells this equipment to other companies. Having only gone public in late 1986, Allwaste has demonstrated impressive growth. It was selected as the second-best small company in America in *Forbes'* November 1989 survey and ranked 16th in *Business Week's* May 22, 1989, article "Hot Growth Companies."

Allwaste has few established employee programs but some good intentions. It rolled out a charitable contribution program in the summer of 1989 and plans to build slowly to its goal of donating 1% of annual pretax earnings. The company is reviewing its maternity, paternity, and adoption benefits.

FAST FACTS:
- There are no women or minorities on the eight-person board of directors.
- No South African operations.
- A buy on Franklin's list as of October 1989.
- 5% unionized from a division that had organized before it was acquired by Allwaste.
- Roughly 2000 employees.
- Responded to questionnaire.
- Houston, TX.

AMERICAN BRANDS

American Brands is a worldwide consumer-products holding company with three core businesses: tobacco, alcohol, and life insurance. Each of its well-over-400 companies has a fairly autonomous management, making the company a challenge to evaluate. However, substantial social initiatives for the company could not be located. Its product lines, with tobacco accounting for well over half of total revenues ($7.019 billion of $11.98 billion in 1988), are often under attack. The company, along with several other tobacco manufacturers, is a defendant in various lawsuits based on allegations that tobacco use has resulted in illness.

American Brands devotes the last page of its annual report to social responsibility, a fairly unusual step for a corporation. Its programs feature direct contributions to the community, matching gifts, and personal involvement; unfortunately, these worthy aims aren't backed up generously. The company's charitable giving was an estimated $2 million in 1988, according to the *Taft Corporate Giving Directory*—a well-below-average 0.2% of its pretax earnings for that year. (The company did not confirm the number and it could be understated.) Philanthropic projects it funds include helping a Connecticut hospital build a proposed center for continuing care and providing work projects for retarded citizens in Connecticut and Illinois.

FAST FACTS:
■ No South African ties.
■ One woman and no minorities on 16-person board of directors at year-end 1988.
■ Not among the top 500 DoD prime contractors for 1988.
■ Responded with limited information.
■ Old Greenwich, CT.

AMERICAN CYANAMID

A biotechnology and chemical company, American Cyanamid has operations in South Africa and was involved in some controversies in the 1970s. Women who worked in the company's lead pigment division of its Willow Island, West Virginia, chemical plant were told that exposure to lead was potentially harmful to the fetus in case of pregnancy. Five women who chose sterilization and later regretted the decision launched a sex discrimination suit against the company, and asked OSHA to ban such sterilizations.[6] In 1983 American Cyanamid settled out of court, but admitted no liability.

American Cyanamid has two South African subsidiaries and is a signatory of the Statement of Principles. It received the highest compliance rating, Making Good Progress, in June 1989.

FAST FACTS:
■ One woman on ten-person board of directors, and one woman out of 14 officers.
■ Instituted a board-level public responsibility committee to review corporate policies in 1979.
■ Responded with limited information.
■ Wayne, NJ.

AMERICAN HOME PRODUCTS

American Home Products, a worldwide manufacturer and marketer of health-care, food, and household products, boasts admirable employee relations but is being boycotted for its aggressive marketing of infant formula to developing nations. This marketing is considered dangerous because it encourages women to give up healthful breast-feeding in countries where the infant formula is often mixed with impure water and can cause disease and even death.[7] AHP says that its marketing is in full compliance with the WHO International Code of Marketing of Breast-Milk Substitutes, and it states that breast-feeding is the healthier alternative on all product literature and labels. Since 1982 AHP asserts that it has only supplied infant formula to hospitals and clinics upon written request or order.

Senator Edward Kennedy of Massachusetts has announced he wants to hold hearings about promotional advertising in the prescription drug industry. Franklin's *insight* lists AHP as one company under examination for using a frequent flier program to sell its high-blood-pressure drug Inderal. For every patient prescribed the drug, the doctor receives 1000 points toward American Airlines travel.[8] AHP explains that through its Ayerst Patient Profile Program, doctors who prescribed Inderal LA were asked to complete and return a questionnaire on new patients; participating doctors were given a customary honorarium of bonus points that could be used for medical books, equipment, or air travel, preferably to medical conventions.

Worldwide, 41% of AHP's employees are unionized, and the company's union relations have been excellent. The January/February 1985 issue of the *OCAW Reporter* and the July/August 1984 issue of *UFCW Action* both describe the company's harmonious union/management relation and encourage union members to buy the company's products. As of June 1989, AHP employed 24,032 people in the U.S., 48.9% of whom were female and 19.49% minorities. In terms of a total 3457 managers, 20.13% were women and 12.32% minority members. Adjusted work schedules are available for parents with child care responsibilities.

AHP makes use of recycled paper, paperboard, and corrugated cartons as well as co-generation, an alternative energy process.

The company asked that a stockholder proposal against live-animal testing that appeared in the 1989 proxy statement be defeated, and it was—by 94.8%. AHP has spent or given $500,000 from 1987 to 1989 for developing alternatives to animal testing.

In 1988 AHP agreed to acquire A. H. Robins for $700 million worth of AHP stock and payment of $2.3 billion to a claimants' trust for settlement of Dalkon Shield cases. Robins, which was under Chapter 11 bankruptcy protection at the time of the purchase agreement, was embroiled in one of the most infamous product liability cases in corporate history—its IUD has been accused of injuring thousands of women, and the company was blamed for not disclosing its dangers. In November 1989 the Supreme Court refused to hear challenges to the settlement plan, thereby clearing the way for Robins to be acquired. AHP is buying a company whose behavior was denounced as "corporate irresponsibility at its meanest" by Federal Judge Miles Lord.[9] AHP's acquisition of Robins is considered a boon for the claimants since it guarantees that they will receive payment.

FAST FACTS:

- AHP recently sold its South African division but continued to endorse the Statement of Principles; it is allowing the new owners to license certain trademarks for a limited period of time.
- Employee gifts are matched one for one, and the company gave $6,997,000 to charitable projects in 1989.
- $43,735 was contributed to AHP Good Government Fund in 1988.
- Responded to questionnaire.
- New York, NY.

AMETEK

Ametek is on several ethical investors' buy lists, primarily because of its renewable energy, environmental conservation, and water purification products. Specifically, it has an ongoing research and development project on photovoltaic cells and solar energy. Its cells achieved 11% efficiency in May 1988, the highest verified by the Solar Energy Research Institute at that time. This is why the New Alternatives fund included the company in its portfolio as of the summer of 1989. It is also working on water purification equipment, another positive environmental story. As of late 1989 its under-the-sink filters were the first ever bought and installed with Superfund money after the EPA tested all point-of-use type filters on the market. Ametek's Microfoam, a low-density polypropylene foam used in packaging and cushioning, is recyclable due to the resins in it. The Microfoam division has a Waste and Recycling Management Committee that is concentrating on developing recycling materials for this product and providing converter/distributors with the recycling equipment. In 1988 Ametek spun off 14 businesses to its shareholders, forming a new company named

Ketema (Ametek backward). Ametek is now tilted predominantly toward technology.

One woman but no minorities sit on Ametek's nine-person board of directors. Of Ametek's 5038 employees 45% are women and 13.4% minorities, excluding its Aerospace Products and Weston divisions, for which statistics were unavailable.

A small percentage of its business is in aircraft, some of which are sold to the Defense Department. This accounts for between 1 and 5% of the company's overall business.

Ametek was a recent pick of Calvert and of Franklin's *insight*.

FAST FACTS:
■ No South African operations.
■ Ametek Foundation gave $1 million last year to education, hospitals and medical research, general welfare, and youth projects, a generous 1.8% of pretax income.
■ Some divisions are unionized.
■ Flextime available for some factory workers.
■ Responded with information.
■ New York, NY.

ANHEUSER-BUSCH

Anheuser-Busch (BUD on the ticker) ranks high in most categories of corporate responsibility. Its detractors argue that the beer-brewing business can't be considered socially responsible because abuse of its product leads to drunk-driving accidents and alcoholism. The company's business, however, is broader than beer—it includes a major baking company (Campbell-Taggart), Eagle Snacks, and family entertainment theme parks.

Anheuser-Busch is a generous corporate contributor. In 1989 the brewer and its foundation donated an estimated 2.6% of its pretax income to charitable causes. After the 1989 San Francisco earthquake, BUD handed the Red Cross and Salvation Army $1 million each for victims, and is donating $250,000 to help rebuild historic neighborhoods that were damaged. The company has taken an interest in funding wildlife conservation; in 1989, it donated $400,000 to Ducks Unlimited's Wetlands America Fund. Another environmental plus is its Container Recovery Corp., one of the nation's largest recyclers of aluminum cans; it purchases and processes over 200 million pounds of used containers each year.

Anheuser-Busch reached an agreement with Reverend Jesse Jackson's

Operation PUSH in 1983 after PUSH threatened to boycott the company's products. The brewer maintained its 18% minority representation was a record to be proud of, something which Jackson ultimately acknowledged, saying his earlier criticism "may have been attributable to a failure of communication."[10] For its part, Anheuser-Busch made an even stronger commitment to the minority community. It was selected as one of the 35 best workplaces for blacks in *Black Enterprise*'s survey. Around 22% of Anheuser-Busch's 41,000 employees are minorities, and minorities account for 11% of its 6000 managers. The *BE* article noted that in the past few years, approximately 30% of all new positions were filled by minority applicants.

Two women, one of whom is black and one Hispanic, sit on the company's 14-person board of directors.

Anheuser-Busch signed a three-year contract with the International Brotherhood of Teamsters in March 1988 that spells out benefits such as profit-sharing. The company offers counseling services for employee problems, including alcoholism.

Anheuser-Busch has been attacked for its aggressive marketing of alcoholic beverages and for glamorizing drinking. The company asserts that it is very much concerned about alcohol-abuse problems and demonstrates this concern by contributing to Students Against Driving Drunk (SADD), a not-for-profit group that sponsors educational programs. The brewer made an interactive videotape available for free loan called *Your Alcohol IQ* and enhanced its advertising and grass-roots education programs by forming a Department of Consumer Awareness in June 1989.

FAST FACTS:

▪ No South African operations.
▪ No defense-related contracts.
▪ Its Partners in Economic Progress program awarded an estimated $80 million worth of contracts to minority-owned businesses in 1989.
▪ In *The 100 Best Companies to Work for in America*.
▪ Ranked ninth most admired of 305 major U.S. companies in *Fortune*'s January 29, 1990, survey of corporate reputations.
▪ Responded with information.
▪ St. Louis, MO.

APPLE COMPUTER

Apple is a pick of many ethical investors. At Apple the making and selling of personal computers takes on the aspect of a social crusade. Its corporate literature speaks of "empowering the individual," and most of its varied social initiatives incorporate this notion. For example, Apple has granted millions of dollars worth of computer systems to schools and community groups, and all levels of employees are first loaned and then given a computer through the company's Loan to Own program. The Apple Child Care Center, which opened in 1989, uses computers to create a learning experience, and Apple worked on a project to link 50 California organizations for the homeless and the hungry by computer. The company gave an estimated $3.4 million to charitable organizations in 1987, 0.83% of that year's pretax income.

These projects have won the company applause from ethical investors and corporate critics. Apple is included in *The 100 Best Companies to Work for in America*, named one of the ten best companies in the *Working Mother* survey, and one of 15 to watch in *Black Enterprise*'s "The 50 Best Places for Blacks to Work." There's one woman on the seven-person board of directors, and women account for 41% of the professional staff, according to the October 1989 *WM* article. The company created a Multicultural Advisory Board to sensitize upper management to workforce diversity issues.[11] Apple is a Parnassus pick, and Hugh Kelley of the Socially Responsible Investment Group praises it for having taken environmentally positive steps, even though Silicon Valley has many polluting by-products.

Apple is in *Clean Yield*'s portfolio, although the October 1989 issue cautioned that the company had "raised the eyebrows of SRI investors when it disclosed that the company won a multi-year contract to supply the Air Force with Macintoshes." Although well below its exclusion rate of 2% of sales to the military, the newsletter says this raises the specter of Apple becoming a large defense contractor in the future.

FAST FACTS:
- New employees receive a brochure entitled "There's More to Life Than Work," and volunteering is encouraged.[12]
- Up to six months of unpaid leave is available for some in addition to standard maternity leave.
- Flextime, part-time, and job-sharing options exist.
- Did not respond.
- Cupertino, CA.

ARCHER DANIELS MIDLAND

Archer Daniels Midland, an agricultural products company, has an environmentally interesting twist to its business. Its cornstarch has been used in the production of patented degradable plastic products, according to *Clean Yield*, which recommends the stock. In the November 6, 1989, "Heard on the Street" column, *The Wall Street Journal* describes ADM's developing of its cornstarch-based compound this way: "It's as if a sod farmer suddenly discovered diamonds in the dirt."

Although compelling, breaking down plastic is not ADM's only environmental story. The company also manufactures ethanol, a gasoline substitute and additive that burns more cleanly than conventional fuels and is made from corn. Ethanol reduces carbon monoxide emissions, and ethanol blends can be used safely by U.S. cars without any adjustment. ADM also has five fully operational co-generation plants, which burn high-sulfur coal with virtually no sulfur dioxide emissions and therefore no acid rain-causing pollutants. In 1988 it received *Power* magazine's Energy Conservation award for these plants.

Clean Yield says the company has put most of the problems of the early 1970s behind it. At that time ADM was convicted of manipulating prices in the Food for Peace program. Its chairman, Dwayne Andreas, was criticized for being too close to many politicians, but is now "applauded as one of the most avid spokespersons and participants in bringing the East and West together through trading partnerships."[13] ADM is a pick of New Alternatives and one of the top ten holdings of the Fidelity Select Environmental Services Portfolio as of the fall of 1989.

FAST FACTS:

■ No presence in South Africa or Northern Ireland.
■ Made $1,894,268 in charitable contributions in 1987—roughly 0.4% of that year's pretax income—according to the *Taft Corporate Giving Directory.*
■ 10,214 employees.
■ One woman, Mrs. Nelson A. Rockefeller, on the 15-person board of directors as of June 1989.
■ Responded with annual report.
■ Decatur, IL.

BAY STATE GAS

This natural gas utility is environmentally attractive because its product burns more cleanly than most other fuels. Bay State stock was a pick of both Pax and New Alternatives in 1989.

Bay State has no women or minorities on its 11-person board of directors. However, flextime and part-time schedules are available, and employees can establish dependent care accounts through which they can earmark pretax dollars for child or elder care expenses.

This company's charitable giving is very small, in part because contributions are disallowed from rate charges. But what contributions Bay State does make are subject to employee input. Employees have formed a council, operating on company time, to determine where corporate funds should go. The company also participates in Crime Watch programs by providing training materials so that its employees can phone in trouble from their radio-equipped cars and trucks.

FAST FACTS:
- No South African operations.
- No defense contracting, although natural gas is provided to DoD.
- Over 1000 employees.
- 60% unionized.
- Responded with information.
- Canton, MA.

BEN & JERRY'S HOMEMADE

Ben & Jerry's is one company with which even the most demanding ethical investor would be hard-pressed to find fault. From christening its products with progressive names like Peace Pops and Rainforest Crunch to its capping top salaries at five times that of the lowest, this company is testing the limits of what a company can accomplish on social issues. Right off the bat, an investor can tell what Ben & Jerry's is doing—its 1988 annual report was printed on recycled paper and its three-pronged Statement of Mission was published on the inside front cover. Its social mission is printed before its economic one and reads: "To operate the company in a way that actively recognizes the central role that business plays in the structure of society by initiating innovative ways to improve the quality of life of a broad community: local, national and international." The company has been a financial success and is a media darling, proving that social responsibility in itself can be a drawing point.

In 1978 best friends Ben Cohen and Jerry Greenfield opened an ice-cream parlor in a converted gas station in Burlington, Vermont. From the start the venture succeeded despite its founders' conflicts about corporate success. When Ben took the company public, he turned it into a force for social change, a corporation held in trust for the community. Much of this is accomplished through the Ben & Jerry's Foundation, which receives 7.5% of the company's pretax income, by far the highest giving level of any company profiled in this book. With this it funds "projects and organizations that are models for social change, enhance people's quality of life, exhibit creative problem solving, and are infused with a spirit of generosity." One project supported is 1% for Peace, a nonprofit organization that encourages cultural exchange between the U.S. and the Soviet Union; another is the Burlington, Vermont, Community Land Trust, a transitional housing project for women and mother-led families.

The company "recycles" waste ice cream by giving it to a local farmer to feed pigs. And Ben & Jerry's made headlines in 1989 by refusing to accept any milk from cows given bST (bovine somatropin), an experimental growth hormone that boosts milk production as much as 25%. The cooperative dairy from which it purchases all its cream has agreed to supply Ben & Jerry's from cows not receiving the hormone. The company contends that people are uncomfortable with this milk and that the hormone will hurt smaller family-owned ventures by driving down milk prices.

In its 1988 annual report Ben & Jerry's candidly addresses having no women on its five-member board of directors, saying it hopes to change this. Because of the company's mission, its social disclosure is excellent—its own account of operations is more instructive than many news sources. One controversial move Ben & Jerry's made was taking Pillsbury to court over its use of exclusive distribution arrangements, forcing independent distributors to sell only Haagen-Dazs. In 1984 the company won an out-of-court settlement limiting Haagen-Dazs' practice of exclusive arrangements, but Ben & Jerry's mode of attack raised some eyebrows and the company was accused of using attention-grabbing tactics to sell ice cream. Slogans such as "Haagen, your Dazs are numbered" were prohibited by the settlement.

FAST FACTS:
■ No South African operations.
■ No weapons-related businesses.
■ Responded with information.
■ Waterbury, VT.

BORDEN

Not only a food giant but also a major producer of wall coverings, packaging films, and consumer and industrial adhesives, Borden took a positive stand on minority purchasing programs in the late 1970s. Borden's former chairman, Augustine Marusi, initiated one of the earlier minority buying programs and chaired the National Minority Supplier Development Council from 1976 to 1980. In 1989 the company purchased goods and services worth $77 million through its minority purchasing program. Women and minorities are well represented on Borden's board of directors, with one black man and two women out of 11 members. Out of 32,700 U.S. employees, 25.2% are women and 24.0% minorities, and among the 3770 officials and managers, 10.7% are women and 7.9% minorities.

Within the 1984–1988 period Borden gave on average 0.51% of pretax earnings in annual cash contributions and around 2.03% in noncash contributions to charitable organizations. It currently emphasizes disadvantaged children and the homeless in its cash giving. Borden recently received the Second Harvest Partnership Award for financial and product contributions. Eligible employee gifts are matched dollar for dollar.

Borden has one South African subsidiary which, the company notes, distributes whole milk powder as a child nutrient. The company is a signatory of the Statement of Principles and has received the highest (Making Good Progress) compliance rating since the ratings began. Two-thirds of Borden's 314 South African employees are black, as are 40% of managerial, professional, and sales people there.

Borden has taken steps in waste minimization and has three plants that have achieved nearly 100% recycling. Overall, 10–25% of the materials Borden uses are recyled. And it has won awards for its co-generation project at the Borden Chemicals and Plastics plant in Geismar, Louisiana.

FAST FACTS:
- 46,230 employees as of year-end 1989.
- Around 45% of domestic workforce is unionized.
- 15.8% of 1989 sales came from snack foods.
- Borden Good Government Committee has received on average $15,000 in recent years.
- No live-animal testing.
- Responded to questionnaire.
- New York, NY.

THE BRAND COMPANIES

As the nation's leader in the removal of asbestos, the Brand Companies performs a socially and environmentally necessary task. The EPA estimates that there are 733,000 public and commercial buildings and an additional 30,000 schools with some asbestos in them. Asbestos has been linked to the lung disease asbestosis, and to cancer.[14] The Brand Companies is 49% owned by Chemical Waste Management; the rest of the stock is traded over the counter. Brand's relationship with Chemical Waste Management and its parent, Waste Management, enables the company to perform a wider range of functions than it could alone.

Brand is primarily a specialty contractor. It began by applying thermal insulation to power plants, including nuclear ones, but by 1987 asbestos abatement accounted for 50% of revenues. Brand also offers a counseling service to present information to affected groups.

Approximately 4500 people work for the Brand Companies, over half of whom are minorities, but this figure fluctuates according to the size and number of projects the company has undertaken. There are no women or minorities on the company's nine-person board of directors, although one of five executive officers is a woman.

FAST FACTS:
- ∎ No South African operations.
- ∎ No weapons-related businesses.
- ∎ 50–60% of workforce is unionized.
- ∎ Responded with information.
- ∎ Park Ridge, IL.

BROOKLYN UNION GAS

Natural gas is a boon to the environment because it burns much more cleanly than oil or coal. That's why Brooklyn Union Gas, primarily a natural gas distribution company, is attractive to socially responsible investors and was a recent pick of Pax. In addition to selling natural gas, the company has built two natural-gas-powered demonstration buses. The cost of operating these buses is competitive with other vehicles, yet the pollution is minimal compared to diesel-powered bus emissions. In 1989 the company was saluted by the American Lung Association for this clean air project.

Brooklyn Union also operates a natural gas co-generation plant on Long Island, New York. Energy is generated from natural gas, and extra electricity is sold off to the Long Island Lighting Co. In 1990 Brooklyn Union will give out its first $25,000 annual fellowship to a graduate student working on a project to improve the urban environment.

Cleaner energy already qualified the company as a good community member, but it has taken further steps to secure this distinction. Around 25 years ago Brooklyn Union Gas embarked on its Cinderella program to restore deteriorating houses in neighborhoods where it operates. Many of these buildings had become eyesores, but the company bought, renovated, and sold them as a way of revitalizing communities that had fallen upon hard times. The company's charitable giving is limited because funds come from stockholders and ratepayers. However, its new area-development fund is supporting affordable housing and an innovative project to put the city's pool of unskilled labor to work making traffic cones and street barricades from recycled plastic.

Starting in January 1990, employees will be able to reserve pretax dollars for child care costs. The company considered starting a child care center but was advised against it by a women's group that pointed out that rush-hour city subways and buses were no place for small children. That it so carefully researched these options illustrates its commitment to employees.

FAST FACTS:
- No South African operations.
- One woman and one black on the ten-person board of directors.
- Most of the 3500 employees are unionized.
- Responded with information.
- Brooklyn, NY.

BROWNING-FERRIS INDUSTRIES

Browning-Ferris, a leader in waste collection, treatment, and transport, performs an environmentally essential task and yet it has been criticized for regulatory problems and charged with price-fixing. In the past few years it has taken steps to enhance its image. It is chaired by an environmental specialist—William Ruckelshaus, two time administrator for the EPA—and has approximately 100 environmental specialists on staff. The lion's share of Browning-Ferris' business is waste collection, but around 11% is landfill. In 1990 the company announced it would exit the hazardous waste business.

BFI recently established a nature habitat at its newest landfill in

Shelby County, Tennessee, in conjunction with State Fish and Game and a nature conservancy organization. And an environmentally interesting business BFI engages in is the collection of recyclable materials, a service it provides to more than a million homes through 130 programs.

Browning-Ferris, like other large players in this area, has had its share of regulatory problems. Many of the larger problems were worked out in the late 1970s to early 1980s, a spokesperson asserted.

More recently, the former operations manager of BFI's CECOS hazardous waste subsidiary, John Stirnkorb, was found guilty of eight felony and two misdemeanor counts in Williamsburg, Ohio, for violating state environmental regulations at that site. The incident occurred in 1984; contaminated rainwater was discharged from a partially closed waste-disposal cell into a ditch that drained offsite in violation of environmental regulations. Since then CECOS has made an effort to involve the community in oversight of the site.

Lawsuits have been filed against BFI and Waste Management, alleging that the two competitors engaged in a nationwide conspiracy to fix prices for containerized waste services. These suits have been combined as a class action by the U.S. District Court in Philadelphia. The trial was still to be scheduled as of February 1990.

The company supports organizations such as the Nature Conservancy, the United Way, and the Special Olympics. Early in 1989 the corporate offices began a paper-recycling drive the proceeds of which are funneled to its Cares About People internal volunteer organization that does charitable community work. BFI is recycling around 14 tons of paper a month and in the first six months raised $4000–$5000 this way.

FAST FACTS:
- No South African operations.
- One of the top ten holdings in the Fidelity Select Environmental Services Portfolio as of October 1989.
- No arms-related businesses.
- 22,000 employees, predominantly in the U.S.
- No women or minorities on the 16-person board of directors.
- "Well below half" of the employees are unionized said a spokesperson.
- No child care, although flextime is sometimes informally available.
- Responded with information.
- Houston, TX.

CPC INTERNATIONAL

CPC International, a multinational consumer food and corn-refining company, derives 57% of its revenues from operations in 46 foreign countries, and roughly 70% of its 32,000 employees work outside the U.S. This makes evaluation tricky, although the company does have some aspects over which an ethical investor can sigh with relief—it has no ties to defense, sold off its South African operations to a consortium of investors in April 1987, and ended its license agreement with its former subsidiary on October 11, 1989. Many of CPC's brand names are immediately recognizable: among them Skippy, Hellmann's, and Mazola.

Of 1491 high-ranking U.S. corporate positions, 16.7% are filled by women and 8.8% by minorities. In addition, CPC boasts it is "one of only about 50 U.S. corporations with at least two women on its Board of Directors." Although the company does have numerous unions at various plants, "There have been essentially no work stoppages of consequence for many years," said a spokesperson.

CPC is working on reducing packaging tonnage, focusing on recycled paper and corrugated board.

FAST FACTS:
- Donated about 2% of its $494.2-million pretax income in FY88 in cash and food to charitable organizations.
- Matches U.S. employees' contributions to nonprofit organizations on a two-for-one basis.
- Responded with information.
- Englewood Cliffs, NJ.

CRSS INC.

CRSS Inc. stakes two good claims to being a socially responsible company: first, it treats its employees well; second, its engineering and construction work has positive environmental applications. As a diversified design and construction services company, CRSS is committed to financing power and co-generation plants, specialty-program insurance underwriting, and the acid rain pollution-control market. It was selected as one of five "likely winners" from the growing emphasis on the environment by the June 1989 issue of *Money* for its systems that reduce the pollutants that cause acid rain. It plans to offer a low-cost system for reducing these emissions by injecting baking soda mixed with certain proprietary materials into smokestacks through NaTec Resources, Inc., of which CRSS owns roughly a 45% stake. Shares of NaTec can be purchased directly on the over-the-counter market. NaTec's system is expected to reduce sulfur dioxide emissions by 20–80%, and to reduce nitrous oxide by up to 40%. CRSS's co-generation efforts are also environmentally attractive. The company uses its engineering expertise to design power plants that work through co-generation—the production of electricity and steam from a single fuel source, often clean-burning natural gas.

The company is known for its entrepreneurial spirit. *The 100 Best Companies to Work for in America* praises CRSS for handing over responsibility to employees and for being a pioneer of flexible benefits in its industry. CRSS was also featured in a 1989–1990 PBS series based on Tom Peters' bestseller, *Thriving on Chaos*. Peters emphasized CRSS' commitment to client service and its success in building a "performance culture" among its employees.

CRSS recently donated more than $300,000 to civic, arts, and charitable organizations, roughly 1.2% of its pretax income.

FAST FACTS:
- No South African operations.
- No women on ten-person board of directors as of June 1989.
- Approximately 3200 employees.
- Responded with information.
- Houston, TX.

CAMPBELL SOUP

In addition to soup, Campbell serves up a square deal for its women employees. Perhaps this food company's most impressive initiative is an on-site child care center at its Camden, New Jersey, headquarters, which accommodates 110 children. Campbell covers a portion of weekly fees, lightening the burden for parents. And Campbell, which was picked as one of 60 top companies by *Working Mother*'s survey, began offering job-sharing and flextime options in the mid-1980s. There are two women at the VP level, and 18% of officials and managers are women. Within the U.S. there are 14,466 women out of 32,300 employees.[15] Meanwhile, minorities account for 31% of total U.S. employees, and in FY89 (July) Campbell purchased $61 million from minority-owned businesses. There are four women, one of whom is black, on the 15-person board.

To boost sluggish performance, Campbell's restructuring plan calls for closing at least nine plants and eliminating about 2800 jobs.[16]

Before closing down a plant the company likes to give workers six to nine months' notice.[17] Campbell was praised for its strong support of revitalization efforts for its headquarters city of Camden in *Rating America's Corporate Conscience*. However, in the early 1980s it was criticized by the Farm Labor Organizing Committee (FLOC) for the living conditions of migrant workers who harvested tomatoes for the company's products. Although the migrant workers were not Campbell employees, the company was believed to have influence over the farmers who hired them and eventually signed a joint agreement that won better contracts for these workers.[18]

For FY89 Campbell made a very generous $4.825-million outlay in charitable contributions, more than 4% of the company's pretax income. Education received 30% of the funds. One innovative project Campbell funds is FITNESSGRAM, which gives young people a report card on health and fitness.

Campbell's shipping cartons are partially made of recycled paper and its frozen dinner trays carry a code so that they can be easily sorted for recycling.

In May 1989 Campbell reached a settlement with ten states, agreeing not to run ads for its soups that made broad claims of high fiber and calcium content.[19]

FAST FACTS:
- No South African operations.
- Has on-site health facilities and an employee assistance program.
- Responded with information.
- Camden, NJ.

CHAMBERS DEVELOPMENT

Described as "the nation's major waste collection company with fewest landfill problems" by the June 1989 issue of *Money*, Chambers Development is one of five "likely winners" pinpointed by the magazine for an expected emphasis on the environment. Public since 1985, Chambers is actually the country's third largest waste disposal company, and yet it has run into few environmental flaps and has never been cited for groundwater pollution—a frequent complaint against other waste disposal companies. The company attributes this to the foresight of CEO and founder John Rangos, who implemented safety measures well beyond regulations, thereby allowing the company to meet today's tougher standards. For example, Chambers installed clay liners and built leachate treatment facilities before they were mandated.

Chambers has instituted recycling programs that reduce overall solid waste and preserve valuable landfill space. Chambers operates ten landfills and employs 2800.

Chambers is one of the top ten holdings of The Fidelity Select Environmental Services Portfolio as of October 1989, and a pick of Franklin's *insight*. *Business Week* called it the "fastest growing solid waste disposal company" in the country.[20]

FAST FACTS:
- No South African ties (no overseas operations at all).
- No DoD work.
- No women or minorities on the board of directors.
- Participates in community functions such as cleanup days.
- Responded with information.
- Penn Hills, PA.

CHEMICAL WASTE MANAGEMENT

Chemical Waste Management is the largest company in the U.S. catering exclusively to the treatment and disposal of hazardous waste. Waste Management owns a 79% stake in the company, but Chemical Waste has been publicly listed on the New York Stock Exchange since late 1986. As regulations for the disposal of hazardous waste become more stringent, many waste generators are hiring outside specialists to take care of this situation—a positive for the company. In 1988 Chemical Waste purchased a 49% stake in The Brand Companies, gaining exposure to asbestos abatement, and holds an option to hike its ownership to 55%.

Chemical Waste employs environmental compliance officers; however, all facility general managers are directly responsible for complying with regulatory requirements and taking speedy action on problems. The company has a formal environmental policy statement. Its Chem-Nuclear Systems subsidiary manages low-level nuclear waste. Meanwhile, its contract services operations division, when appropriate, instructs companies on complying with waste regulations, posts on-site descriptions of hazardous materials, and explains record-keeping for this area. It provides extensive remediation services to clean up contaminated sites. One high-profile bid Chemical Waste won was the cleanup of residuals and debris after the Exxon *Valdez* catastrophe.

Chemical Waste would not disclose its charitable giving numbers, but its emphasis is on environmental and health-related causes. For example, the company contributes to the Sierra Club, the National Wildlife Association, and Keep America Beautiful. Employee gifts are matched on a one-for-one basis except to educational institutions, which are matched two for one.

FAST FACTS:
- No South African operations.
- Approximately 4000 employees.
- Provides cleanup services to the government.
- Has a minority purchasing program, run through Waste Management (size not available).
- Small percentage of hourly employees are union-affiliated.
- No women or minorities on eight-person board of directors.
- One woman of 12 corporate officers.
- Responded with information.
- Oak Brook, IL.

CHEVRON

Oil giant Chevron has demonstrated a firm commitment to affirmative action goals and to both funding and initiating environmental programs. This is a departure from its reputation for entrenched conservatism; Rating America's Corporate Conscience, published in 1986, accused the company of a "reluctance to address environmental and fair hiring issues."[21] The company still has critics, especially antiapartheid activists who condemn its presence in South Africa through its joint ownership of Caltex.

Chevron appeared on Black Enterprise's "The 50 Best Places for Blacks to Work" list. It boasts 78 affirmative action programs to ensure that minorities and women gain fair representation in the workplace. To accomplish its goals, Chevron identifies minorities for internships and scholarships and recruits at predominantly black colleges. Around 8.5% of overall employees and 3.3% of 6000 managers are black.[22]

In 1987 Chevron established its Save Money and Reduce Toxics (SMART) program. Its ambitious goal is a 65% reduction in hazardous wastes across the board by 1992. Disposal of this waste is costly; reduction makes financial as well as environmental sense. In 1987 Chevron cut hazardous waste disposal from 135,000 to 76,000 tons and saved $3.8 million in disposal costs. In 1981 Chevron initiated its Tank Integrity Program to spot and prevent leaks in older underground storage tanks at its service stations across the country.

In 1988 Chevron contributed $19.5 million, around 0.6% of pretax income, to charitable organizations. One unique aspect of its giving program is that 19% of the funds were directed to conservation and wildlife preservation programs, primarily in California. The remainder was donated to education (29%), health and human services (22%), arts and culture (15%), civic (9%), and international relations (7%).

Since Mobil's 1989 exit from South Africa, Chevron and Texaco, through their joint ownership of Caltex, are the only major U.S. oil companies to maintain a presence there. Caltex is a signatory of the Statement of Principles, and received the highest, Making Good Progress, compliance rating for the year ending June 1989, up from the middle rating the previous year. The General Assembly of the Episcopal Church of the United States is boycotting Chevron for its South African operations.

FAST FACTS:
- Roughly 51,000 employees.
- Publishes a booklet on business conduct.
- Responded with information.
- San Francisco, CA.

CHRONAR

Chronar is one company whose very business—solar energy—is deemed socially responsible. The company is an international leader in the development and commercial production of amorphous silicon thin-film photovoltaic panels, which convert light directly into electricity. While photovoltaic (solar) cells have existed for many years, as the cells have improved they've become more feasible as alternative sources of energy. New Alternatives, which invests in Chronar, calls these cells the most exciting story in alternative energy, although it cautions that they have not always made the best investments because of the steep learning curve that means one company is always topping the next.

Because of its size Chronar has fewer benefits and programs than many others in this book. Chronar's equal employment numbers look good. Of 265 employees, 100 are women and 100 minorities. There are four women and three minorities among the 30 employees considered upper management.

FAST FACTS:
- No South African ties.
- One-third of workforce is unionized.
- In 1988 Chronar gave $10,000 to United Way and local charities.
- Responded to questionnaire.
- Princeton, NJ.

CHRYSLER

Chrysler has taken several bold moves in employee relations. When Lee Iacocca took the helm in 1979, bringing the company back from near-bankruptcy, he exchanged employee programs for wage and benefit concessions. Pluses for employees were the Employee Stock Ownership Program and a profit-sharing plan.

Chrysler credits its operating and labor agreements for its success in the marketplace. The company was one of the first to give a union leader a seat on its board of directors. Currently, Owen Bieber, president of the United Automobile, Aerospace, and Agricultural Implement Workers of America, industrial union, sits on the 19-person board.

Chrysler has placed recruiting and promoting women and minorities high on its agenda for the 1990s, said *Black Enterprise*, which listed the company as one of 35 "best of the best" places for blacks to work. To accomplish this, EEO goals and timetables are reviewed quarterly. Of Chrysler's estimated 90,000 employees, 26% are minorities and 11.4% of managers are minorities. There is one black and one woman on the board. The company is becoming involved in the NAACP Fair Share program. In 1988 Chrysler Motors approved a $500,000 loan to the National Minority Business Development Council to foster growth in minority businesses.

Although regarded as the Big Three manufacturer with the best record for meeting gas efficiency and air emission standards, Chrysler is facing some environmental and safety problems. OSHA levied a $1,576,100 penalty to its Newark, Delaware, site in July 1987 for violations under the Occupational Safety and Health Act. Likewise, its Belvidere, Illinois, facility was fined $910,000 by OSHA. Meanwhile, Chrysler shares responsibility for 64 toxic waste sites the EPA has designated as in urgent need of attention.[23]

Chrysler gave an estimated $8.5 million in 1988 in charitable contributions, according to the *Taft Corporate Giving Directory*. This represents a below-average 0.5% of that year's pretax income.

Education received more than half of Chrysler's charitable funds, and around 30% went to health and human service organizations.

FAST FACTS:
■ No South African operations.
■ Chrysler's Physically Challenged Resource Center offers information and rebates on driving aids and equipment for the physically handicapped.
■ Responded with limited information.
■ Highland Park, MI.

CITIZENS UTILITIES

A "no nuke" utility offering natural gas, wastewater treatment, telecommunications, co-generation, electricity and water services, Citizens Utilities avoids most of the don'ts about which socially responsible investors are concerned. Its stock has been highlighted by both *Clean Yield* and *GOOD MONEY*.

Citizens boasts a strong financial record of 44 consecutive years of earnings growth, something it is not shy about advertising. Following a description of its achievements, the 1988 annual report asserts: "There is no other company comparable to Citizens Utilities." Retiring CEO Richard Rosenthal used the annual report as a forum for airing opinions on industry, politics, and society.

Citizens assigns personnel to local schools to teach children how to dial for help and give proper information in emergencies. Meanwhile, its Colorado gas operations have "adopted" a mile-long stretch along the highway to keep clear of litter.

Clean Yield says the company's overall labor relations appear to be "very good." However, there were no women and no minorities on the company's seven-person board of directors.

FAST FACTS:
■ No South African involvement.
■ Charitable giving numbers not released.
■ No weapons production.
■ Responded with annual report.
■ Stamford, CT.

CLOROX

Clorox is considered a good corporate citizen, something it has demonstrated through its community action projects and emphasis on underprivileged youth. In FY89 (June), the company made $2.4 million in charitable contributions, around 1.05% of that year's pretax income. Clorox's giving has been innovative; the company has tackled tough problems like improving child care, helping the homeless, and battling crime and drug abuse. Its Community Development Program, run by plant managers and their employee advisory teams, identifies and supports youth projects. Clorox also helped purchase a building which is a center for programs that help Hispanic youth with addictions. In 1989 Clorox was praised by the President's Citation Program for Private Sector Initiatives for its Drug Abuse Prevention Program. And it was one of 50 companies to be awarded the Private Sector Initiatives award in 1986, which it received for creating job opportunities for youth in its East Oakland Youth Development Center.

Calvert, which included Clorox in its portfolio holdings as of June 1989, praised the company for developing emergency response devices to protect against the accidental release of chlorine gas. These electronic systems sample the air around the clock to detect even minute leaks and automatically shut down chlorine tank cars and chlorine lines.

Clorox does perform live-animal testing, although it has no in-house facilities. Its tests are performed by labs accredited by the American Association for the Accreditation of Laboratory Animal Care. For the first half of 1988 the numbers of rats and rabbits used decreased 38% from 1983, although the number of guinea pigs, which is very small, increased over that time period.

Clorox took a stand on maintaining quality television shows and adopted a policy against advertising on programs that "contain gratuitous displays of violence or sex, offend prevailing community standards, engage in ethnic or religious slurs, demean human dignity, or encourage drug usage or alcohol consumption," according to a brochure it publishes on the subject.

FAST FACTS:
- No South African operations or agreements.
- Approximately 4800 employees.
- No weapons-related businesses.
- Around half of plants are unionized.
- One woman on 14-person board of directors.
- Responded with information.
- Oakland, CA.

COMMUNITY PSYCHIATRIC CENTERS

Community Psychiatric Centers is the oldest, and one of the largest, publicly held companies in its area: treating mental health and alcohol abuse problems. The business itself is socially useful, and it was a recent pick of both Pax and *Clean Yield*.

In August 1989, the company restructured, spinning off its dialysis and home health lines to shareholders as a new, publicly traded corporation named Vivra. Community Psychiatric owns 49 psychiatric hospitals, six of which are in the U.K.[24]

The company has no women or minorities on its six-person board of directors, although two of 11 VPs are women.

FAST FACTS:
■ No South African operations.
■ "Minimal" charitable donations, according to a spokesperson.
■ No DoD work.
■ Profit-sharing plan.
■ Around 5000 employees.
■ Responded with information.
■ Laguna Hills, CA.

CONSOLIDATED NATURAL GAS

Consolidated Natural Gas stands to gain from the antipollution laws that could boost sales of its relatively cleanly burning natural gas. That's why the company was selected as one of five "likely winners" from the growing interest in environmental matters in the June 1989 *Money* article. CNG is also the industry leader in co-firing. When combined with other technologies, co-firing can halve acid rain-causing pollutants. By the end of 1988 the company had six co-firing projects in operation. One other plus for CNG is that its service fleet consists of 1500 natural-gas-powered cars and trucks, the largest fleet of its kind.

CNG has donated roughly $3 million annually to charitable organizations for the past four years. Its contributions support educational facilities, economic development, and cultural activities in the communities it serves. CNG has given funding to small liberal arts colleges in its areas, a project for which it earned the Council of Independent Colleges' Award for Corporate Philanthropy in January 1990. Employee gifts are matched on a dollar-for-dollar basis.

At CNG women occupy several key posts—specifically, two of the

11 corporate VPs are women, and among five corporate officers there is one woman. On CNG's board of directors sit one woman and one minority member. Companywide, women make up 24% and minorities 12% of the total workforce. Several subsidiaries recruit from black universities and professional organizations, and individual divisions have minority business purchasing programs. Similarly, some divisions have child care referral provisions.

FAST FACTS:
- CNG was a social pick of Franklin's *insight* in 1989.
- No South African operations (no operations outside the U.S. and Canada).
- No weapons-related businesses.
- 55% of the 7500 employees are unionized.
- Responded with information.
- Pittsburgh, PA.

ADOLPH COORS COMPANY

Coors has been in the center of several controversies but over the past few years has turned some of these negatives into positives. It survived a ten-year AFL–CIO boycott, which ended in 1987, as well as protests by minority groups, homosexuals, and those angry about the company's funding of the anti-Nicaraguan contras.[25] Over the past few years, Coors has earned kudos; one example is its being named the country's top manufacturer for providing opportunities to minorities and women at the 1989 NAACP award ceremonies.

The AFL–CIO boycott ended when the brewer agreed to put union representation to a vote. Coors' workers voted the union down two to one; many prounion employees called the end of the boycott short-sighted, according to the *National Boycott News*. Other groups have continued to boycott the company. Gay and lesbian activists contend that Coors' use of a lie detector test in employment weeded out those with labor sympathies and allowed the company to discriminate against homosexuals and minorities. Coors stopped subjecting interviewees to a lie detector test in 1986.[26]

In 1984 the NAACP called for a boycott of Coors after CEO William Coors made a disparaging comment about the intellectual capacity of blacks.[27] Following that, Coors signed an agreement with the National Black Economics Development Coalition to recruit and hire more blacks and to bring its purchasing from black-owned businesses in line with its 10% of sales to blacks. A similar agreement was reached with the Coalition of Hispanic Organizations. These steps have won the company praise; in fact, Coors was selected as one of the 35 best workplaces for blacks in the *Black Enterprise* February 1989 survey. Of 6400 Coors employees, 21.8% are women and 14.5% minorities; in upper management, it's 2.1% and 1.3% respectively.

Vice Chairman Joe Coors, a "long-time Republican rainmaker," was linked to the federal Housing and Urban Development scandal when his letter to HUD Secretary Samuel R. Pierce, Jr., became public, according to a *Business Week* article on which he would not comment.[28]

The company has taken a stance on several social problems. It has launched campaigns advertising the perils of drinking and driving. Coors is a sponsor of High Priority, the AMC Cancer Research Center's national breast cancer education project. For advocating employee wellness, Coors was awarded the $25,000 1989 Health Action Leadership Award. Coors took first place in four categories: best corporate values, prenatal care, seat belt safety, and fitness program. The prize money will be used to develop pilot community wellness programs for Coors distributors and small businesses.

FAST FACTS:

- No South African operations.
- Not one of top 500 DoD contractors.
- Since 1970 its Cash for Cans program redeemed over 20 billion cans.
- Made $3,097,000 in charitable contributions in 1988, relative to $76.975 million in pretax earnings that year.
- Second least admired of eight in Beverages category of January 29, 1990, *Fortune* survey of corporate reputations.
- Responded to questionnaire.
- Golden, CO.

CORNING

"As makers of glass, our base technology ought to give us the key not only to making glass ceilings, but also to breaking them," said Corning's Chairman James R. Houghton in a May 1988 address. This frank admission that glass ceilings for women and minorities exist is rare in the corporate world, but not unusual for Corning.

On completing an internal study, Corning found that while only one in 14 white male professionals left the company between 1980 and 1987, about one in six blacks and one in seven women with comparable positions exited over that same time period. Since the study Houghton has been candid about turning this situation around. "We do a good job at hiring [women and blacks], but a lousy job at retention and promotion. And it's not good enough just to bring them through the front door."[29] Houghton set specific goals—by 1991 he wants the executive payroll to include ten women rather than only four in early 1989, and five minority members instead of two. To accomplish this he told male executives that their own promotions would in part hinge on how well they worked toward these goals. Corning, which was included in "The 60 Best Companies for Working Mothers," has introduced a wide variety of work options like flextime and part-time schedules to accommodate women with family commitments.

The glass manufacturer introduced a unique philanthropic program, its Corning Crafts Project, which grants loans of up to $25,000 at 2 percent interest to local artists. In exchange the artists must establish an "open" studio or shop near the main shopping district in Corning. This project benefits both the arts and the community. Corning's charitable giving was an estimated $2.3 million in 1988, according to the *Taft Corporate Giving Directory*; that represents around 0.85% of pretax income.

FAST FACTS:
- No South African operations.
- No defense contracting.
- The Corning Cookware and Corelle Cookware divisions are on the AFL–CIO's September–October 1989 "Do Buy List" because products are made by the Aluminum Brick & Glass Workers International Union.
- A social pick of Franklin's *insight* in 1989.
- Most admired of ten in Building Materials category of *Fortune*'s January 29, 1990, survey.
- Responded with information.
- Corning, NY.

CUMMINS ENGINE

Widely acknowledged as a good corporate citizen, Cummins is a generous charitable contributor and has made efforts to recruit and promote minorities. These are a few of the strengths cited by *The 100 Best Companies to Work for in America* in its Cummins profile. One reason Parnassus likes the diesel engine manufacturer is that Cummins has supported its hometown of Columbus, Indiana, by offering to pay architectural fees for public buildings there.[30] The town boasts a school by Harry Weese, fire station by Venturi & Rauch, and city hall by Edward Charles Bassett, for all of which Cummins Engine Foundation paid the fees. In 1988 Cummins gave an estimated $4 million in charitable contributions, according to the *Taft Corporate Giving Directory*. The company posted an earnings loss that year. Despite its financial woes, Cummins gave more to charity in 1988 than all but 95 of the *Fortune* 500 companies.[31]

Cummins is known for paying above-average wages and for producing a quality product. In fact, the rejection rate for engines that have to be reworked at the end of its assembly line is around 1%—one-third of the industry average. However, foreign competition has created a much tougher market, and the company slashed 4000 jobs at headquarters during the 1980s in order to compete. *The Wall Street Journal* published a December 13, 1989, feature article on Cummins, calling it "a model of capitalist benevolence" that is struggling due to "forces largely outside the company's control."

Cummins does do work with the DoD and ranked 183rd for prime defense contracts in 1988.

Cummins meets at least one of the *Valdez* Principles: it has an environmental expert, William Ruckelshaus, on its board.

FAST FACTS:

- Cummins is an endorser of the Statement of Principles, which means that it makes an annual contribution to support the program.
- The Diesel Workers Union represents about 3850 Cummins production employees.
- A social pick of Franklin's *insight* in 1989.
- Responded with limited information.
- Columbus, IN.

DAYTON HUDSON CORP.

One of the nation's largest general merchandise retailers, Dayton Hudson Corp. enjoys a well-deserved reputation as a good corporate citizen. Its policy of donating 5% of annual pretax profits to charitable causes inspired and encouraged other companies to follow suit and it is one of the forces behind the Minnesota Keystone Awards Program. How it divvies up its charitable funds is also unique—a full 40% is given to social action projects and another 40% to the arts. Programs recently supported include JobPlus, an on-the-job training partnership that has assisted young women at risk of long-term dependency, substance abuse prevention programs, The Storytellers, an international cultural arts program, and AIDS and the Arts Task Force. The company is not afraid to fund causes that are not traditional and has supported Planned Parenthood education programs.

At Dayton Hudson and its operating companies there are 168 women and 71 minorities in management. The Dayton Hudson department store division is reviewing some of its key benefit policies to see how it could better meet work/family needs and is piloting parent support groups at several locations. It is also launching a Valuing Diversity Program.

The company minimizes solid waste from packaging by recycling. Its Target division recycles about 80% of each store's waste, and its Mervyn's stores are recycling plastic hangers and styrofoam packaging materials.

As can be expected, Dayton Hudson graced many social investors' buy lists in 1989, including *GOOD MONEY*, Pax, and Franklin's *insight*. It was listed in *The 100 Best Companies to Work for in America* and was picked as the most socially responsible of ten retailers in the January 29, 1990, *Fortune* survey. In 1989 Dayton Hudson won the Council on Economic Priorities' award for charitable giving. It also received the 1989 National Medal of Arts Award, established by Congress in 1984 to honor individuals and groups that enhance the availability of the arts.

In what *Business Week* called an apparent first for a large corporation, Dayton Hudson told its pension funds to stay away from hostile dealmaking. The company itself was the object of a never-carried-through corporate raid in 1987.[32]

FAST FACTS:
- No South African operations.
- No weapons-related businesses.
- Responded with information.
- Minneapolis, MN.

R. R. DONNELLEY & SONS COMPANY

R. R. Donnelley, the world's largest commercial printer, is a responsible corporate citizen, delivering a high-quality product, according to Calvert, which counted it among its investments as of the summer of 1989. Donnelley prints magazines like *Time, Business Week*, and *The New Yorker* as well as books, catalogs and directories.

The printer is in the process of hiking corporate contributions to charity; over the next five years, it is raising the 0.5% of pretax income earmarked for charitable causes to a full 1%. It also matches employee contributions of up to $2000 to education and arts and culture on a one-and-a-half-to-one basis. The company gave an estimated $2 million in 1988, according to the *Taft Corporate Giving Directory*.

In the fall of 1989, Donnelley introduced a program to allow employees to set aside pretax dollars for child care expenses. However, it has no formal flextime or part-time programs.

Six or seven Donnelley employees were involved in an insider trading scandal for purchasing stocks written up in *Business Week*'s "Inside Wall Street" column prior to the magazine's publication. The company has not been charged in this case and has dismissed the employees involved.

FAST FACTS:
- No South African operations.
- No weapons-related businesses.
- Supports environmental groups like Nature Conservancy.
- None of the 22,000 domestic employees of 24,000 total are unionized, although the U.K. division is unionized.
- Responded with information.
- Chicago, IL.

DUN & BRADSTREET

Dun & Bradstreet, a leading provider of business information services, boasts an exceptionally generous matching gifts program—the company donates four dollars to every employee's one given to education. This funding emphasizes employee input to the decision-making process. D&B gave an estimated $3.022 million in 1988, according to the *Taft Corporate Giving Directory*. This represents a below-average 0.38% of that year's pretax income.

Calvert, which counts D&B among its investments, praises the company for making a clean break from South Africa once it sold its operations there, rather than maintaining indirect ties such as licensing, franchising, or marketing agreements.

In late 1989 *The Wall Street Journal* published a feature article charging that D&B's ubiquitous credit reports are frequently off the mark. Since the decision to extend credit to a business may very well hinge on its D&B report, these inaccuracies can have serious consequences. The reporting problems seemed to stem from overly ambitious goals set for employees. "Former D&B credit reporters tell how they were expected to meet unrealistic production quotas that made the preparation of accurate reports extremely difficult."[33] In early 1990 D&B announced it would restructure this division, but the outcome of this has yet to be determined.

Earlier in the year, *The Wall Street Journal* reported on complaints and lawsuits against D&B's Credit Services division from customers alleging that they had been misled into buying larger credit-data packages than they needed. D&B vigorously denied this, except for a few cases it had already addressed.[34] In late 1989, D&B announced an overhaul of its Credit Services operation, according to a November 16, 1989, article in *The Wall Street Journal*.

FAST FACTS:

- No women on 14-person board of directors.
- No arms-related businesses.
- No minority- and women-owned-business purchasing program.
- No unionized employees.
- Around 70,000 employees.
- Responded with limited information.
- New York, NY.

ENSR CORP.

Toxic waste and air quality problems are ENSR's business. This specialist in the assessing and remediation of hazardous wastes takes on the environmentally necessary task of tackling industrial problems that if left unchecked pose risks to the public health. It has worked on more than 75 Superfund sites. ENSR is one of the companies *Business Week* highlighted in its October 16, 1989, article, "Cleaning up on the Coming Cleanup."

ENSR, which has been publicly listed since 1987, has emphasized technology to remove and get rid of PCBs, which were banned by Congress as carcinogenic in the 1970s. ENSR's Health Sciences division can provide information and consulting on the health risks of exposure to hazardous substances, and the company has researched acid rain for the EPA, the Canadian government, and the electric utility industry.

There are no women and no minorities on ENSR's seven-person board of directors; however, one of seven corporate officers is a woman. In ENSR's largest division there are four women and two minorities among 24 officers.

As of April 1990, an offer had been made to acquire ENSR.

FAST FACTS:
- No South African operations.
- Around 1500 employees.
- Responded with limited information.
- Houston, TX.

H. B. FULLER COMPANY

"Enlightened self-interest" is one of the practices H. B. Fuller's President Tony Andersen preaches.[35] More than preaching, the company lives it through its unique charitable contribution program. Not only does H. B. Fuller give just over 2% of worldwide pretax earnings to charitable activities, but it lets its employees determine how the money is spent. Overseas employees have a say in distributing the funds, too, and this makes for diverse projects. Recent recipients include a day care center for children of low-income working mothers in Brazil and a foundation for handicapped children in Chile. For these efforts the company won the 1987 Wien Award for Corporate Social Responsibility from Columbia University.

Although chemical concerns like Fuller are notorious for poor environmental records, Fuller's record is better than most. It won the Environmental Responsibility Award from the Council on Economic Priorities in 1988. The company turned the 95 acres of land surrounding its headquarters into a wildlife preserve and is in the process of eliminating underground storage tanks as well as reducing and monitoring waste and reworking/recycling wastewater at plants whenever possible.

One social problem Fuller is now grappling with is that Latin Americans are sniffing its glue, Resistol, and becoming addicted to it. To combat this problem, Fuller realizes it must go beyond warnings and educational programs that would work in the U.S. Fuller is working with local social service organizations on educational and prevention programs.

FAST FACTS:
- No South African ties.
- Recent pick of New Alternatives and a social pick of Franklin in 1989.
- Included in *The 100 Best Companies to Work for in America.*
- Of 1872 U.S. employees 548 are women and 295 minorities; there are one woman and one minority among the 25 considered upper management.

- Formal sexual harassment program included in supervisory training.
- 1% unionized, from a company Fuller acquired.
- Responded to questionnaire.
- Saint Paul, MN.

GTE

GTE boasts an innovative corporate giving program and publishes its EEO numbers in its annual report. It also is a maker of electronic defense and intelligence systems which it sells to the government. This telecommunications company is working on an advanced mobile communications system for the army and is providing engineering services and equipment for the launch control facilities of the air force's Peacekeeper intercontinental ballistic missile system.

In 1988 GTE gave an estimated $19.5 million in charitable contributions, according to the *Taft Corporate Giving Directory*; this represents around 0.63% of that year's pretax earnings. The company teamed up with the National PTA to develop an educational program to fight drug and alcohol abuse among schoolchildren between the ages of nine and 14. It has also awarded grants to colleges for developing programs to recruit minorities in math and science at the undergraduate level.

One of 52 profiled in *The Best Companies for Women*, GTE has a high percentage of female employees, especially in its Yellow Page division. In 1988 women accounted for 43% of total employees and minorities 18%. Women held 22% and minorities 10% of management-level positions.

FAST FACTS:
- Around 160,000 employees.
- Responded with annual report.
- Stamford, CT.

GANNETT

"For Gannett, equal employment is not just the right thing to do—it is the smart thing to do," stated chairman and CEO John Curley in the company's EEO statement. The statement acknowledges that speaking out against discrimination is not good enough; therefore the company's Partners in Progress programs link executive bonuses to the meeting of the company's goals of ensuring that the make-up of Gannett's workforce is as diverse as America itself. Gannett even has a Public Responsibility Committee that meets annually to review corporate responsibility progress.

The company's EEO numbers are excellent: There are two minority members and four women (including former First Lady Rosalynn Carter) on Gannett's 17-person board of directors. And of 38,191 full- and part-time employees, 15,286 are women and 8041 minorities. It was cited as one of 35 "best of the best" in the *Black Enterprise* survey of corporations, one of "The 60 Best Companies for Working Mothers," and included in *The Best Companies for Women*.

Gannett left the Genesee Valley Club in Rochester, New York, because it did not admit women—the club subsequently reversed the policy and Gannett rejoined.[36] Gannett's Open Door policy encompasses more groups than most, prohibiting "discrimination or harassment because of sex, age, race, creed, color, religion, marital status, sexual orientation, national origin, disability or veteran status." The company provides child care referral services at corporate headquarters and at *USA Today*, while some subsidiaries have nearby or on-site child care facilities.

FAST FACTS:

- A Franklin's *insight* social pick in 1989.
- About 20% of the workforce is unionized.
- Company won first Pulitzer Gold Medal for Public Service awarded to a wire service.
- Recent pick by Calvert.
- No South African ties.
- Through Match Maker Program, company will match gifts of $25 to $12,000 dollar for dollar to eligible nonprofit groups as long as the employee is an active volunteer of that organization.
- In 1988 Gannett Foundation grants and programs totaled about $27.1 million, with local grants receiving the lion's share at 43.1%.
- Responded to questionnaire.
- Arlington, VA.

GENERAL MILLS

General Mills serves up a good reputation for equal employment opportunities as well as a generous charitable giving program. Included in *The Best Companies for Women*, General Mills was praised for having taken a hard line against sexual harassment. Women are well represented in the company's upper management: There are six female VPs out of 33 total, and two women sit on its 17-person board of directors. The new president of the General Mills Foundation is a black woman, Reatha Clark King. The company was included in both *Working Mother*'s survey of the best companies for working parents and *Black Enterprise*'s list of 50 top companies for blacks. General Mills has two black VPs but no minorities on its board.

With annual charitable contributions at 2% of pretax earnings, General Mills not only generously funds philanthropic projects but also distributes these funds to organizations well beyond the traditional, placing a heavy emphasis on the disadvantaged, abused, or handicapped.

Although federal law prohibits the use of recycled materials in packaging that comes in contact with food, General Mills uses recycled newspaper for boxboard in its cereal and baking-mix packages. As a result, it is the single largest user of recycled newspaper in the city of Minneapolis. To simplify the task of separating plastic containers for recycling, General Mills codes the plastics it uses. And nearly all employees at the Minneapolis headquarters have recycling files at their desks for the disposal of office paper.

However, as have other cereal makers, General Mills has come under FDA scrutiny, because of the use of psyllium, an Asian grain, in its Benefit cereal. Prior to launching this product in April 1989, General Mills said it funded a University of Minnesota study that found psyllium apparently helped reduce blood cholesterol. The grain is not considered a health hazard.[37]

FAST FACTS:
- No South African operations or agreements.
- No weapons contracts.
- 8% of roughly 84,000 employees are unionized.
- Responded with information.
- Minneapolis, MN.

GEORGIA-PACIFIC

One of the world's largest manufacturers of forest products, Georgia-Pacific turned itself around in the mid-1980s. As of early 1990 Georgia-Pacific was acquiring Great Northern Nekoosa in the industry's first uninvited takeover bid, making it difficult to evaluate.

Georgia-Pacific was involved in several environmental controversies, including a $625,000 civil penalty it paid in 1986 in Louisiana to settle a lawsuit over air pollution violations at one of its facilities, according to *Rating America's Corporate Conscience*. That business has since been spun off, and is no longer part of the corporation. *Everybody's Business* says G-P was regarded as "the tough guy of the forest products industry" for blaming conservationists and government for timber shortages.[38]

On the plus side, the company has exposure to recycling—13 of its 28 mills use some recycled fiber.[39] G-P plants around 35 million seedlings each year, and has donated generous tracts of land to wildlife refuges. In 1986 it gave Mendocino, California, 7000 acres of redwood timberlands, and made two large gifts in 1985—28,000 acres to the Louisiana Department of Wildlife and Fisheries and 1000 acres to the Department of Wildlife Conservation in Mississippi.

G-P has a Management Incentive Plan and in 1988 instituted a Long-Term Incentive Plan that awards shares of common stock to executives and key managers if these shares double in value over a five-year period.

FAST FACTS:
■ No South African operations.
■ No military-contracting businesses.
■ One woman but no minority members on the 13-member board of directors.
■ Responded with limited information.
■ Atlanta, GA.

GERBER PRODUCTS

Gerber does not stop with feeding babies—through its toy line it entertains them, and through the Gerber Apparel Group clothes them. The company has also taken several steps to be environmentally responsible. It employs a full-time environmentalist who helps design equipment and procedures to save energy and lower emissions. For example, Gerber uses the steam from processing to power other activities, gives waste products from its food production to farms for livestock, and recycles cardboard for its shipping boxes. Gerber has also taken several admirable steps in corporate safety, reducing accidents by around 53% and slashing injury-related costs by 60% over the past five years. For these efforts it was awarded the National Safety Council's Distinguished Service to Safety Award.

Gerber makes charitable gifts through the Gerber Foundation but would not release the size of contributions. Projects supported by Gerber include educational grants, baby food shipments to disaster sites, research into baby nutrition, and guidelines for appropriate infant diets.

The marketing of Gerber Baby Formula directly to the public raised an outcry from the American Academy of Pediatrics and some doctors, who fear that the ads will discourage women from breast-feeding.[40] A Gerber spokesman noted that the product, launched in October 1989, has a 90% distribution rate to supermarkets.

In 1984, Gerber recalled two lots of baby food when customers claimed to have found glass shards in it. Two years later, there were around 300 highly publicized but never substantiated claims of glass in its baby food. The company did not recall the product, and no proof was ever found that the claims were true.

FAST FACTS:
- Gerber has a licensing agreement with the South African company Reckett & Coleman.
- No animal testing.
- "Well over half" of 14,691 employees are unionized, according to a spokesperson.
- Responded with information.
- Fremont, MI.

THE GILLETTE COMPANY

Gillette emphasizes safety in its products and in its workplace and has been up-front about publishing numbers of women and minorities employed at the company. It also notes that all corrugated box trays, liners, and intermediate packaging materials are recyclable. At the same time, it has been criticized for its presence in South Africa, albeit a nonstrategic one, and is the target of highly publicized protests by animal-rights activists for its live-animal product testing.

Gillette has an entire department devoted to product integrity as well as a director of environmental affairs.

The company publishes its progress in meeting EEO goals; it employs 29,600 worldwide, of whom 7767 work in the U.S. Of its domestic employees, 3693 are women and 1769 minorities. In the U.S. Gillette considers 1205 employees upper management, and within that group there are 263 women and 94 minority members. Gillette has contracted with the Child Care Information and Referral Service to offer free employee assistance in making child care decisions.

Gillette donates approximately 1% of pretax earnings to charitable projects, many of which are nontraditional. Some representative grants for 1988 were the Asian Community Development Corp., Freedom from Chemical Dependency, the Boston Food Bank, and Literacy Volunteers for Massachusetts.

Animal-rights activists began boycotting the company when a Gillette animal caretaker, Leslie Fain, released filmed and taped information about the alleged suffering of its laboratory animals. The company denied that the film footage was of its lab. According to the *National Boycott News*, Gillette was reportedly issued a warning notice from the USDA Animal and Plant Health Inspection Agency regarding violations of the federal Animal Welfare Act, but the company closed its internal testing facility in Rockville, Maryland, in March 1987, before further action could be taken.[41] Gillette emphasized that it was not found in violation of regulations. It now contracts with outside testing facilities accredited by the American Association for Accreditation of Laboratory Animal Care. The boycott against Gillette, called by Ark II, persists because the company still commissions live-animal testing even though it is conducted off-site. Much of the debate hinges on whether effective alternatives to animal testing exist. In one of its reports, Gillette quotes Dr. Frank Young, Commissioner of the FDA, who when asked if any nonanimal alternatives to acute toxicity tests such as the Draize eye-irritancy test existed, answered: "At the present time and in the foreseeable future, the answer is no."

Gillette has two South African subsidiaries, employing 130 workers. It has been a signatory of the Statement of Principles since 1977 and received the highest rating, Making Good Progress, for the two years ending June 1989. In February 1985 Gillette became South Africa's first private-sector sponsor of a legal aid clinic, a program it continues to support.

FAST FACTS:

■ No arms-related businesses.

■ Approximately 7% of the U.S. workforce is unionized.

■ Purchased more than $12 million in goods and services from minority-owned businesses in 1988.

■ Granted the Coalition for the Homeless 1989 Award of the Year.

■ Audubon A Award for Water Conservation efforts.

■ Reached an agreement with California's attorney general and environmental groups to remove trichloroethylene, a potentially cancer-causing chemical, from its Liquid Paper in California; company maintains the product is safe.

■ Responded to questionnaire.

■ Boston, MA.

GOODYEAR TIRE & RUBBER

Goodyear was a vocal proponent of corporations' maintaining South African operations until it sold off its own subsidiary there to Consol Ltd., part of the South African conglomerate Anlovaal Ltd., in 1989. The sale was prompted by a change in U.S. tax law that prevented corporations from deducting taxes paid to the South African government from their U.S. returns. Goodyear's exit has been criticized because it signed a technical and assistance agreement with Consol.

Goodyear is no stranger to controversy. In the early 1970s it was fined for making illegal contributions to Richard Nixon's reelection fund.[42] In Federal court proceedings in Washington, D.C. in May 1989 it pleaded guilty to charges that it violated the Foreign Corrupt Practices Act by participating in an international bribery scam. Goodyear admitted paying nearly $1 million in bribes to Iraqi middlemen in exchange for $19 million worth of tire sales from the Iraq government between 1979 and 1983.[43]

Goodyear is one of four companies whose waste-hauling records are under investigation because toxic chemical waste, associated with rubber production and believed to be carcinogenic, has been found near Niagara Falls.[44]

FAST FACTS:

- Employee gifts to higher education are matched on a dollar-for-dollar basis.
- Responded with limited information.
- Akron, OH.

GREEN MOUNTAIN POWER

This investor-owned, independent electric utility emphasizes environmentally attractive conservation programs through its Energy Action Plan. For example, in the summer of 1989 it installed insulation jackets on electric water heaters. GMP serves retail customers in Vermont and offers rates lower than those of state-regulated utilities. Eight of its plants are powered by hydroelectric energy, a clean and renewable energy source, and GMP is diversifying into propane gas. Meanwhile, the company is taking its conservation message to the communities where it operates—it is working with the Vermont Department of Agriculture and the University of Vermont on a project to help farmers use electricity more efficiently. One caveat: A portion of GMP's electric generation is nuclear, through an 18% interest in the Vermont Yankee nuclear power plant.

GMP is aware of its environmental responsibility. The company voluntarily regulated water levels at one of its hydroelectric ponds to protect fragile loon-nesting areas. It also worked with the Vermont Fish and Wildlife Department to install pole-mounted breeding platforms for endangered ospreys on its wetland properties. These two projects earned it a Take Pride in America Award from Vermont.

Charitable contributions are shaved off shareholders' returns, with 1.25 cents per share the minimum annual contribution. This totals around $47,000 per year. In strong financial years, giving is hiked to 1.5 cents per share. Green Mountain emphasized environmental projects in 1989 giving, and has selected human services for its 1990 funding project.

Green Mountain has 410 employees, about 150 of whom are unionized. Of total employees, 109 are women and three minorities; there is one woman but no minority members on the 11-person board of directors. Pretax dollars can be set aside for child care, and the company is exploring other work/family options.

GMP revised its safety program in 1988, shifting primary responsibility to immediate supervisors. This resulted in a 37% drop in disability illness and injuries for 1988 over the preceding year, as well as a 64% decline in lost day accidents.

FAST FACTS:
- No South African operations.
- No Department of Defense contracts.
- Responded with information.
- South Burlington, VT.

JOHN HARLAND

John Harland, one of the nation's leading check printers, is generally considered a good corporate citizen. *Clean Yield* recommended the stock during 1989. The company has none of the major don'ts that ethical investors often shy away from—it has no South African operations, no ties to the defense industry, and has not been the target of product liability suits, boycotts, or scandal. The company, however, did not respond for this book, and few social initiatives could be located for it.

There are no women or minorities on Harland's 13-person board of directors, and among 15 corporate officers only one is a woman.

FAST FACTS:
■ An employee stock purchase program.
■ 5600 employees.
■ Atlanta, GA.

HARTMARX

Hartmarx, an apparel manufacturer and retailer, is considered a good corporate citizen and was part of the *GOOD MONEY* index as of early 1989. Hartmarx operates 468 U.S. apparel stores and has 32 brands; it also has licensing agreements in 13 countries.

There is one woman on Hartmarx's 12-person board of directors. The company often reserves a number of spots for employees' children through local schools with child care programs.

FAST FACTS:
■ No South African operations.
■ No arms-related businesses.
■ Around 20,000 employees; most of the men's apparel manufacturing employees are affiliated with the Amalgamated Clothing and Textile Workers Union, while various other employees also belong to unions.
■ Responded with limited information.
■ Chicago, IL.

HECHINGER

Hechinger, an operator of building supply stores, has strong women's employment numbers in an industry not traditionally known for it. The statistics are exceptional—three out of 13 board members are women, one of them black, and of 29 corporate officers, eight are women. Just under half of all employees are women, or 7060 out of 15,000. The company was cited among the 60 best in the *Working Mother* survey.[45]

Clean Yield, which recommends Hechinger, calls the company "all around socially responsible." Benefits include flextime, part-time, job-sharing, and profit-sharing. A very generous 12-month unpaid parental leave is available, and employees can take time off to care for a sick dependent.

In 1988 Hechinger gave an estimated $1.6 million in charitable contributions, a generous 2.5% of FY89 (Jan.) pretax income. The distribution of funds was tilted toward social services (51%); the rest is shared among arts and humanities (23%), education (12%), civic and public affairs (8%), health (3%), and other (2%), according to the *Taft Corporate Giving Directory*.

Hechinger's close relationship with the arts is evident from its FY89 (Jan.) annual report, which also serves as the catalogue for a public exhibit of the John W. Hechinger Collection. The exhibit, generally displayed at headquarters, is called "Tools as Art" and links the company's products to the art world.

FAST FACTS:
- No South African operations.
- No unionized employees.
- Responded with information.
- Landover, MD.

HERSHEY FOODS

Hershey Foods is dedicated to social causes, a path founder Milton Hershey established in the company's early days. The Milton Hershey School, founded in 1909, is perhaps the greatest monument to Hershey's largesse and was endowed with his fortune. Through the Hershey Trust Company, the school owns 42% of Hershey Foods' common stock. At first the school was strictly for orphaned boys, but it now admits girls and children without adequate parental care. About 1150 students attend this school.

The Hershey Trust Company, through the Milton S. Hershey Foundation, also funded the Milton S. Hershey Medical Center of The Pennsylvania State University in 1964 with a $50 million start-up grant. The Milton S. Hershey Foundation was established as a non-profit foundation to administer several cultural and educational activities in the community. From public gardens to the Hershey Theater, Hershey's community has been shaped by the company's founder.

The company supports the United Way and The Children's Miracle Network. Another project—Hershey's National Track & Field Youth Program—introduces children to physical fitness through track and field events, and the company hosts the National Final each August in Hershey, Pennsylvania.

Hershey initiated an equal opportunity monitoring system in 1970, requiring upper management to file periodic reports on placing and promoting women and minorities within the corporation. Hershey is a corporate sponsor of the National Minority Supplier Development Council. It did not reveal the size of this effort or its EEO numbers.

GOOD MONEY included Hershey in its portfolio in 1989.

FAST FACTS:
- Since 1973 the company has provided nutritional labeling on most of its products.
- One black woman, Dr. Sybil Mobley, and one white woman, Francine Neff, sit on the 11-person board of directors.
- Responded with information.
- Hershey, PA.

HUNT MANUFACTURING

Attractive for its community responsiveness and fair employment practices, Hunt, maker of office and art/craft products, was on the buy lists of both *Clean Yield* and Calvert in 1989.

Hunt has contributed an extremely generous 2.5–4.0% of pretax income to nonprofit organizations since 1982, donating on average 3.1%. Its charitable giving goes well beyond the traditional. For example, the Hunt Manufacturing Co. Foundation makes grants to less-established performing groups, artists, and writers. It also funds projects exposing children from low-income neighborhoods to creative endeavors. Hunt was given the 1988 Philadelphia Business Committee for the Arts Award for its corporate support.

Clean Yield notes that employee productivity is encouraged by stock-bonus and profit-sharing plans, and benefits such as an employee assistance plan.

More than half of Hunt's employees are women, and one woman sits on the 11-person board of directors.

FAST FACTS:
- No South African operations.
- No military contracts.
- No history of environmental problems, according to *Clean Yield*.
- Responded with limited information.
- Philadelphia, PA.

IMCO RECYCLING

Born on October 3, 1988, out of the merger of Frontier Texas Corp. and its subsidiary International Metal Co., IMCO Recycling is ideal for the investor looking for an environmentally beneficial company given that its primary business is recycling aluminum cans and their by-products. About 55% of the record 79 billion cans manufactured in

1988 were recycled, and *Clean Yield*, which includes IMCO in its model portfolio, predicts that this should increase to 75% within the next five years. Many state legislatures are enforcing tougher recycling laws, and business has found that aluminum is cheap to recycle. Aluminum recycling also saves tremendous amounts of energy—another plus.[46] What's more, IMCO has opted for less-polluting natural gas as fuel.

IMCO is small—its employees number only around 325, but its equal employment record is none too encouraging. Only around 15 employees are women and the company said no figures were available for minorities. Four employees are considered upper management, all of them white males. Partially due to the company's age and size, there are no child care benefits or minority-purchasing programs in place.

FAST FACTS:
■ No South African ties.
■ 20% of the workforce is unionized under previous ownership.
■ A Franklin *insight* buy as of October 1989.
■ Has air emissions controls and an injection well for waste water.
■ Responded to questionnaire.
■ Dallas, TX.

INTEL

Intel, a maker of microprocessors and microcomputers, passes most social screens. The company was a recent pick of Parnassus, has no South African operations, and is considered a good place to work. Listed in *The 100 Best Companies to Work for in America*, Intel has a sabbatical program—every seven years an employee is eligible to take off eight weeks at full pay on top of the regular three-week vacation. Employees may also apply at that time to take off up to six months without salary to pursue public service, teaching, and/or exceptional educational opportunities.[47]

The company stresses keeping communications "open" between employees and therefore has shoulder-high cubicles instead of individual offices.

FAST FACTS:
■ Responded with limited information.
■ Santa Clara, CA.

KELLOGG COMPANY

Kellogg has been singled out for its equal employment progress. It was one of 35 "best of the best" companies in *Black Enterprise*'s February 1989 survey, which cited its decentralized affirmative action program, annual meetings to assess progress in reaching EEO goals, and mandatory affirmative action training for all managers. In 1987 the company awarded $7.1 million in contracts to minority vendors. And on its 13-person board of directors, sit one black and two women. Approximately 8% of the company's more than 800 managers are black and 20% women.

Kellogg has taken several nutritionally positive steps, including removing coconut oil from its Cracklin' Oat Bran cereal in late 1988 in response to concerns that tropical oils were linked to heart trouble.[48] Kellogg's new cereal, Heartwise, has been in the center of another debate over the health properties of psyllium, a grain reputedly beneficial in lowering blood cholesterol. For cereals to make health claims, some argue that they should then be registered as drugs with the FDA. Research on psyllium thus far has been very positive, noted the company.

Kellogg has used recycled paper in its cereal boxes since 1906 when the company was founded. In recent years 100% of its cereal boxes have been made from recycled paper. The company received one of five Corporate Conscience awards from the Council on Economic Priorities in 1990.

Kellogg has a South African operation that employs around 300 workers, 200 of whom are black. Less than 0.5% of Kellogg's earnings are derived from this operation, and Kellogg supports education for blacks and the black trade union movement in South Africa. It is a signatory of the Statement of Principles, and received the highest rating, Making Good Progress, for the three years through June 1989.

Kellogg was taken to task for a recent Nut 'N' Honey cereal commercial in which a group of cowboys ask the cook what's for breakast, and he responds "Nut 'N' Honey." The cowboys then point their guns at him and the screen goes dark. The Coalition Against Media and Marketing Prejudice accused Kellogg of a homophobic double entendre that promoted anti-gay violence. Kellogg maintained that the cowboys did not raise their guns because of a perceived come-on, but in response to being told there's nothing for breakfast. The commercial has not been on the air since 1988.

FAST FACTS:
- No defense-related businesses.
- In 1988 Kellogg announced a $1.5-million gift to underwrite three years of new programs for the public television children's series *Reading Rainbow*.
- Responded with information.
- Battle Creek, MI.

KIMBERLY-CLARK

Kimberly-Clark has taken several attractive employee initiatives, including its comprehensive health management program. Designed to achieve a higher level of wellness, to reduce absenteeism, and to control escalating health care costs, this program has four parts—health screening, athletic facilities and exercise programs, nursing services, and an employee assistance program. This paper-products concern was the most admired of ten in the Forest Products category of *Fortune*'s January 29, 1990, ranking. Although primarily a consumer-products company, Kimberly-Clark also has a commercial airline subsidiary, Midwest Express Airlines.

The company generally donates around 1% of annual domestic pretax earnings to charitable contributions. Total 1988 grants topped $3 million, two-thirds of which went to social welfare, medicine, and health. The company forsook its generous two-for-one matching gifts program, which gave employees a say in the company's charitable giving, to boost its contribution to the United Way.

Kimberly-Clark has a minority interest in a South African corporation; however, it stopped signing the Statement of Principles when Reverend Sullivan renounced them.

FAST FACTS:
- Around 37,000 employees, 20,000 of whom are in the U.S.
- Has a department devoted exclusively to environmental affairs.
- Responded with limited information.
- Dallas, TX.

KIMMINS ENVIRONMENTAL SERVICE CORP.

Kimmins operates within the socially necessary area of environmental cleanup services. It went public in May 1987 and provides services ranging from the management of hazardous and nonhazardous waste to asbestos removal and abatement to mobile incineration (the burning of hazardous waste and contaminated soil at the problem site). In July 1989 the company added solid-waste management services, focusing on landfill development and operation, recycling, and transportation. It had been planning to reenter this area after the expiration of CEO Francis Williams' no-compete agreement with Browning-Ferris Industries, which Williams had signed five years earlier when he sold BFI a waste company.

About one-third of Kimmins' work is with the federal government.[49] Specifically, it has contracts with the DoD for demolition and asbestos abatement, although it has no weapons-related businesses. The company's first federally funded remediation project was the Love Canal in 1978.

Kimmins also has an insurance arm and posts surety bonds for, among other things, environmental cleanup projects.

FAST FACTS:
- No South African operations.
- No women among five directors and executive officers.
- Not a union shop, although does contract with unionized help.
- 850 employees.
- Ranked 46th for *Business Week*'s May 22, 1989, survey of small growth companies.
- Responded with information.
- Tampa, FL.

KINDER-CARE LEARNING CENTERS

Operator of the largest child care chain in the nation, Kinder-Care Learning Centers helps working parents juggle their career and family responsibilities. With child care centers at 1240 locations, the company accounts for 2.5% of the $15-billion child care industry. A *New York Times Magazine* article addressed concerns about the professionalizing of parenthood through child care corporations. "But though a few experts still fear that for-profit child care may be marked more by concern for money than for children, most have come to agree that there is no inherent reason why a publicly traded corporation cannot care for children as well as, or better than, the lady next door or the local YMCA."[50]

Kinder-Care Learning Centers, once part of Kinder-Care Inc., was spun off in 1989, and is now a pure investment in child care.

Each center's curriculum is prepared at corporate headquarters, but the centers tailor activities and even meals to their regions.

Teacher/child ratios are determined by individual state licensing regulations, but each center accommodates between 90 and 150 children. Employees receive discounts on child care for their own children. One woman sits on the seven-person board of directors, and out of 17,000 employees, more than half are women.

Kinder-Care's national corporate charity is the Muscular Dystrophy Association, for which its centers raised $1 million in 1988. Meanwhile, some local centers fund specific community projects, and corporate headquarters makes contributions to hometown attractions such as the Children's Museum, the Children's Zoo, and the Shakespeare Theatre.

FAST FACTS:
- No South African operations.
- No DoD contracts.
- No unionized employees.
- Responded with information.
- Montgomery, AL.

LOTUS DEVELOPMENT

This software company was recently highlighted by two social investment experts, *Clean Yield* and Franklin's *insight*. Lotus is known for having strong employee relations and for its fair treatment of women, who account for more than half of its 2743 employees. And *The Best Companies for Women* praises Lotus for its commitment to rectifying inequities in pay between men and women.[51] Lotus began offering on-site day care in early 1990; parents are billed according to household income. The company also offers afternoon aerobics classes and a workout facility. There is a profit-sharing plan and an employee stock purchasing program.

Lotus generally donates 1% of its international pretax profits to charitable organizations. That was nearly $3 million in 1988, $2.25 million of which was in software donations. Projects funded include the AIDS Action Committee and inner-city projects. Employees' gifts are matched two for one, and volunteering is encouraged through the Lotus Volunteer Alliance. The National Philanthropy Day Committee of Massachusetts gave Lotus the 1989 Wizard Award for its fund-raising efforts.

FAST FACTS:
- No sales to South Africa.
- No unionized employees.

■ Responded with information.
■ Cambridge, MA.

MARRIOTT CORP.

With 230,000 employees in 1989, Marriott ranks as the nation's eighth largest employer. *Everybody's Business* points out that the company has been shaped by its founding family's hard-working Mormon heritage. At the same time, the authors note: "Marriott fights against any increases in the minimum wage and is no friend of unions."[52] Some of this might be changing. *Working Mother* magazine named Marriott as one of seven companies to watch in its article on the best opportunities for working mothers. The company opened a pilot child care center at its Princeton (N.J.) Marriott in the fall of 1989, and half of its total employees are women. On its eight-person board of directors sits one woman, co-founder Alice Marriott.

Marriott is moving into a new area as it develops 150 senior living communities at a cost of around $1 billion.[53]

FAST FACTS:

■ Half of charitable contributions goes to health and human services and 30% to education, according to the *Taft Corporate Giving Directory*.
■ Did not respond.
■ Washington, D.C.

MAYTAG CORPORATION

Maytag Corporation is known for its quality products and strong employee relations, which are its primary social strengths. Calvert praised Maytag Corp. for its "good union-management relations" and for offering wages and benefits at or above industry and regional norms. Recent buy lists that Maytag has graced read like a rollcall of socially responsible investors: Pax, *GOOD MONEY*, Shearson Lehman Hutton's individual accounts, Franklin's *insight*, and New Alternatives all recommended this stock in 1989. New Alternatives pointed out that the superiority of Maytag brand machines (making for lonely repairmen) is also environmentally sound since these appliances require only half the energy they did a few years ago. Maytag publishes technical bulletins on energy conservation for its appliances.

Maytag Company, a division of Maytag Corp., has been hailed for its "work simplification" plan. In effect since 1947, the plan puts employees through a training program to learn how to make constructive suggestions. Employees are then qualified to submit time- or money-saving ideas after reviewing and improving them with their supervisors. If the idea is implemented, the employee receives half of what has been saved for the first six months, up to $7500.

FAST FACTS:

- Maytag Corp. has a policy prohibiting South African relationships; however, it gained a distribution agreement to provide parts and services there when it acquired Hoover's British subsidiary.[54]
- 45% of workforce is unionized.
- One woman and no minorities on 17-member board of directors.
- In 1988, the company gave 0.95% of pretax income to charitable organizations.
- Responded with information.
- Newton, IA.

McCORMICK & COMPANY

The Power of People, the title of former chairman Charles P. McCormick's book on management, sums up an important attitude of this company. When McCormick took the helm of this spice-manufacturing company in the midst of the Depression he reduced the number of hours employees worked, increased wages 10%, and instituted the Multiple Management system. The core of this system is boards that meet every other week to devise projects, around 80% of which are then implemented by senior management.

The company gives a generous 2% of pretax profits to charity; to encourage employee participation in charitable contributions, it designates one Saturday a year C (for Charity) Day. Participating employees work a full day and donate their paychecks, which are matched dollar for dollar by McCormick, to the charity of their choice. Nearly $660,000 was given out on C-Day 1987.

The company was highlighted in *The 100 Best Companies to Work for in America* and was a pick of the Ariel Growth Fund in 1988.

FAST FACTS:

- No South African operations or assets, although small (less than $2000 annually) sales there.
- Only Gilroy, CA, plant is unionized.
- Company considers 11% of its 7626 employees upper management; of that group 19% are women and 12% minority members.

- Recycles plastic waste.
- Co-generation facility in Gilroy.
- Responded to questionnaire.
- Hunt Valley, MD.

NATURE'S SUNSHINE PRODUCTS, INC.

Described as "the Mary Kay of the herb industry," Nature's Sunshine manufactures nutritional and personal care products, including encapsulated herbs, food supplements, and water-treatment systems.[55] These products are sold directly to consumers through a part-time sales force of roughly 45,000. The company, which began with the simple idea of putting nutritionally valuable herbs into capsules to make them easier to eat, profited from the health and fitness craze of the 1970s and 1980s.

Another unique aspect of Nature's Sunshine is that its chairman and founder is a woman—Kristine Hughes. And as of late 1988 two out of the six board members were women. However, since President Kerry Osay left the company in late 1989, this could change.

Clean Yield recommended the stock in 1989.

FAST FACTS:
- No South African operations.
- No military businesses.
- Did not respond.
- Spanish Fork, UT.

NYNEX

NYNEX was embroiled in a strike from August to early December 1989, which ended when the company dropped its demand that nonmanagement employees assume responsibility for part of their weekly health-care premiums.[56] The striking unions were the Communications Workers of America, with around 40,000 NYNEX workers, and the International Brotherhood of Electrical Workers, with 20,000 workers. Totally, around 60% of employees are represented by unions. Prior to the strike Calvert, which counted the stock among its picks, had praised NYNEX for its high level of union representation. It was also a Pax pick as of the summer of 1989.

In many ways, NYNEX is attractive for socially responsible investors; it does no defense contracting, has established some praiseworthy programs, and has no South African operations. A NYNEX subsidiary, the BIS Group, does have contracts with two South African banks, which it cannot legally terminate. NYNEX receives no revenues from these and has dissolved all other ties.

NYNEX's charitable contributions are generally divided among education, health and welfare, and culture, and it matches employee contributions on a dollar-for-dollar basis. In 1989 NYNEX made an estimated $3.8 million in contributions, according to the *Taft Corporate Giving Directory*. New England Telephone is part of the New England Corporate Consortium, which is preparing AIDS-education packages for the workplace. And in 1988 NYNEX spent $106.5 million with minority- and women-owned businesses.

In 1988 the Yellow Page division of NYNEX created a flap by refusing to list Heritage of Pride, a New York gay and lesbian group, in its phone books, saying there was no suitable heading for the organization.[57] In January 1989, the New York City Commission on Human Rights ruled that the organization should be listed in the directories. The Yellow and White Page divisions of NYNEX subsequently became the first company to provide separate listings for gay and lesbian organizations under an overall heading of Social and Human Services in its directories.

FAST FACTS:
- Contributes to NYNEX Federal PAC.
- Responded with information.
- New York, NY.

OGDEN CORP.

Ogden is interesting to many socially responsible investors because of its 90%-owned subsidiary, Ogden Projects, a leader in the waste-to-energy business. Ogden Projects operates 13 waste-to-energy facilities and was constructing seven more as of September 1989 (see below). A *Business Week* article describes these operations as "the engine behind Ogden's revived profits."[58] Over the next two to four years Ogden Corp. plans to spin off its major businesses to its shareholders. As of late 1989 it had already handed shareholders a 2.5% share in Ogden Projects as a supplemental dividend.

Ogden's other major subsidiary is Ogden Allied Services, which provides services to entertainment events, airports, and industry. In early 1988 it began an asbestos abatement and decontamination service.

Ogden has three women and one minority on its 17-person board.

The CEO of Ogden Financial Services is a woman, Maria Monet, who also serves as Ogden Corp.'s chief financial officer.

FAST FACTS:
- No South African operations.
- Responded with printed information.
- New York, NY.

OGDEN PROJECTS INC.

Ogden Projects Inc., which went public in August 1989, is one of the leaders in the waste-to-energy industry. Its business is environmentally interesting: With landfills facing space shortages, the alternative of burning waste while generating energy that can be sold to local utilities is very appealing. Ogden Corp. owns 90% of Ogden Projects' stock, but the remainder is traded on the New York Stock Exchange.

Although 90% of Ogden Projects' business is solid-waste management, its Ogden Environmental Services subsidiary specializes in cleaning up sites contaminated by hazardous wastes. Ogden is processing soil contaminated by coal-tar residue in Sacramento, California, and cleaning up PCB-contaminated soil at the Kenai Wildlife Reserve in Alaska.

Each site has its own charitable contribution budget, and the total, which exceeded $250,000 in 1988, is growing as the company adds new facilities. Its emphasis is on local community needs.

FAST FACTS:
- No ties to South Africa.
- One minority and three women on the Ogden Corp. board of directors (one woman on Ogden Projects' board as well).
- 450 employees.
- Some sites are unionized.
- Responded with information.
- Fairfield, NJ.

PACIFIC ENTERPRISES

Although Pacific Enterprises operates in three major areas—natural gas distribution, oil and gas production, and retailing—it is the natural gas utility that would catch the eye of an environmentally aware investor. This more cleanly burning fuel not only cuts down on pollution but should also be a financial boon as pollution control laws tighten. The company takes its environmental responsibilities seriously—

it is installing additional emission-control systems on its compressors and actively investigating hazardous waste sites, some of which are over 100 years old, in order to design and carry out remediation programs. The utility has taken steps to promote natural gas as an alternative fuel for motor vehicles and has established an alternative energy division that operates wood waste-to-energy plants. Pacific Enterprises was a pick of Pax as of mid-1989.

Labor relations have posed a problem for the utility. A union was formed in 1938, and Pacific went from open to closed shop in 1971. Currently the union has 8600 members. Although a recent bid by a union leader to win a seat on Pacific Enterprises' board was defeated in a proxy contest, another attempt may be made in the future. The union representative opposed the company's diversification into lines other than natural gas. Despite this friction, the utility hasn't had a strike since the 1950s.

Although Pacific Enterprises does not determine charitable contributions as a fixed percentage of earnings, it worked out to around 1.1% for 1989. This budget allocated approximately $2,750,000 for health and human services, over $900,000 for civic and community affairs, more than $600,000 for education, over $300,000 for arts and culture, and more than $300,000 for in-kind donations. Employee gifts to education, arts, and culture are matched dollar for dollar.

Of Pacific Enterprise's 29,000 employees at year-end 1988, 12,100 were women and 9700 minorities. The company considers 7870 employees upper management, and there are 1980 women and 2000 minority members in this category. The utility has a program to purchase from minority-owned and female-owned vendors.

FAST FACTS:
- No South African operations.
- No weapons-related businesses.
- Two employee funded PACs.
- Responded to questionnaire.
- Los Angeles, CA.

PAN AM

In June 1989 Pan Am shed its Pan Am World Services division, which qualified it as the 34th largest nuclear weapons contractor in 1988, in order to concentrate exclusively on its flight business. The division, which had received $157,282,000 worth of DoD and DoE prime contracts for 1988, was sold to Johnson Controls. Pan Am is no longer involved in defense-related work.

In the summer of 1989 the airline agreed to cease its appearance checks for flight attendants and relax its weight requirements. Flight attendants reported they'd been asked to pirouette in front of supervisors, and the checklist they were subjected to included disproportionate weight or flabbiness and categories such as thighs/hips and figure/physique. This decision settled a discrimination lawsuit pending in the federal appeals court of San Francisco.[59]

Because of Pan Am's recent economic problems, a company spokesperson said charitable contributions are "inappropriate" and have been minimal. The airline has, however, tried to provide transportation for various charities whenever possible.

Women and minorities are well-represented in management at 18% and 14%, respectively. Of nearly 25,000 employees, 2000 are considered management and there is one woman on Pan Am's nine-person board of directors. Flextime is available for flight attendants; however, Pan Am's financial difficulties have prevented it from developing child care and other benefit provisions.

Around 85% of the Pan Am workforce is unionized. Labor agreements made in 1988 were designed to produce total savings of $500 million over the three years these contracts would run.

FAST FACTS:
- No South African operations, and no flights to that country.
- Responded with information.
- New York, NY.

PFIZER

Pfizer, a health-care, specialty chemical, agriculture, and consumer company, operates in a socially useful field and yet has been condemned by some health-care experts for its Bjork-Shiley convexo-concave prosthetic heart valve, which was prone to fracture and failure. Pfizer reported to the FDA that 394 of the 85,000 valves sold worldwide between 1978 and 1986 are known to have failed because of a specific design flaw.[60] Shiley has been faulted with being slow to report the first strut breaks; Shiley heard of the first fracture in August 1979, but didn't notify the FDA until March 1980. More than 200 victims or their families have launched lawsuits against Pfizer over this; alleged deaths from failure of the valve totaled around 252.

The *Multinational Monitor* named Pfizer in its "The Ten Worst

Corporations of 1988" list because of problems with this heart valve. The Public Citizen Health Research Group charged that corporate memos relating to problems with the valve indicate Pfizer was aware of potential dangers. A report from a former employee and inspection of the valve-manufacturing facilities turned up insufficient training of employees about how defects could arise and inadequate product testing, according to Public Citizen. Pfizer points out that the valve has not been manufactured or made available since 1986 and that the percentage of cases of reported strut failure is "very small" given the number of valves that have been implanted worldwide.

Pfizer has also been charged with keeping quiet about adverse reactions by overseas users of its antiarthritis drug, Feldene, until after it received U.S. FDA approval for the drug.[61] Pfizer says that the FDA's most recent review in 1986 concluded that the drug was safe and effective for arthritis patients.

On the other hand, Pfizer has taken the very admirable step of launching an urban renewal project around its manufacturing complex in the East Williamsburg/Bedford Stuyvesant area of Brooklyn, New York. Unlike other companies that have packed up and fled decaying neighborhoods Pfizer chose to stay and has been the cornerstone in the Broadway Triangle Urban Renewal Program to develop commercial properties and low- and middle-income housing.

Pfizer has a South African subsidiary and has signed the Statement of Principles. For the three years through June 1989 Pfizer received the highest, Making Good Progress, rating.

Pfizer's annual corporate contributions for 1988 were $8.37 million for both foundation and direct corporate contributions. That is roughly 0.76% of that year's pretax income. Education received the biggest portion at nearly 30%, followed by health, civic, culture, and international endeavors.

Shopping for a Better World notes that Pfizer has reduced the number of animals used in testing by 40% or more over the past five years.

FAST FACTS:
- No defense contracts.
- One woman on 17-person board.
- Responded with limited information.
- New York, NY.

PHILIP MORRIS COMPANIES INC.

Philip Morris has taken several positive social steps, most notably in equal employment. Not only is Philip Morris one of 35 "best of the best" workplaces for blacks in *Black Enterprise*'s survey, but it is specially highlighted in the article.[62] And it ranked second most admired of 305 major companies in *Fortune*'s January 29, 1990, survey of corporate reputations. At the same time, some investors would avoid this consumer goods giant because, in addition to food, it manufactures cigarettes and alcohol. The *Multinational Monitor* cites Philip Morris as one of the ten worst corporations for 1988 because of its cigarette advertising aimed at young people in the Third World, where the adverse effects of smoking are not well known.[63] The company launched an ad campaign to commemorate the 200th anniversary of the Bill of Rights that has been criticized as "an attempt to bolster its beleaguered image by wrapping itself in the document that is a cornerstone of American democracy."[64]

Black Enterprise attributes Philip Morris' affirmative action initiatives to CEO Hamish Maxwell and says that women and minorities have accounted for 45% of the recent new hires in professional, managerial, and technical positions. The company has one black and four women on its 22-person board of directors. Kraft, which was acquired by Philip Morris in December 1988, has also had a strong affirmative action record. In 1987 PM awarded $216 million worth of contracts to minority-owned firms.

Philip Morris contributed cash and in-kind services valued at more than $40 million, or approximately 1.2% of 1987 pretax earnings, to organizations working in health and welfare, the environment, education, nutrition, and the arts. Projects supported range from a solid-waste recycling center in Georgia to the Brooklyn Academy of Music's Next Wave Festival.

FAST FACTS:
- No South African operations.
- No defense work.
- Miller Beer subsidiary recycles cans.
- More than half of workforce is unionized.
- Responded with information.
- New York, NY.

PHILLIPS PETROLEUM

Phillips Petroleum has taken several moderate social steps, perhaps the most impressive of which is its safety record. Just the same, it has not managed to avoid controversy, including illegal political contributions, concealing funds in the early 1970s, and more recently, a supporting role in the failure to react quickly enough to the Exxon *Valdez* spill as one of several owners of the Alyeska Pipeline (its interest is small—1.36%). Alyeska has been named a defendant in a number of lawsuits concerning this accident.

In 1988 Phillips was honored by the American Petroleum Institute as the safest member of the U.S. oil industry. This was based on its 1987 rate of lost-time injuries. In 1988 recordable injuries dropped 6%, while lost-workday cases remained constant.

In the 1970s Phillips was under scrutiny for illegal contributions to political campaigns, and it pleaded guilty to federal tax charges of concealing funds, according to *Everybody's Business*. Because of this the company was forced to broaden its board of directors to include six outside members.[65] The company points out that since then it has instituted a rigorous code of ethics and is under completely different management.

Phillips spent $49 million to protect and improve the environment in 1988, in addition to $106 million on existing environmental control systems. The company also developed a process for recovering sulfur from natural gas that has been implemented at a Texas facility.

The Labor Department moved to fine Phillips $5.7 million, accusing the company of willful safety violations in connection with explosions at a chemical plant near Houston in October 1989; however, the company said it would contest the citations, according to an April 20, 1990, *Wall Street Journal* article.

Its Participative Action Team program saved $16 million in 1988. The teams meet to solve work-related problems and to encourage innovation. In 1988 around 43,000 shares of common stock were distributed through the Special Stock Award program to recognize outstanding employee performance.

Charitable giving in 1988 was $5.2 million, or a below-average 0.46% of that year's worldwide pretax income.

FAST FACTS:
- 21,000 employees at year-end 1988.
- No South African presence, but Phillips is an endorser of the Statement of Principles, which means it makes an annual contribution to the program.

- Company addresses social responsibility issues in its annual report.
- One black woman, Dolores Wharton, on 13-person board.
- Responded with information.
- Bartlesville, OK.

PITNEY BOWES

Pitney Bowes, a leading maker of office equipment, has demonstrated that it is a responsible employer, especially for typically short-changed groups like minorities and women. CEO George Harvey has mandated that 35% of all new hires and promotions on the professional staff go to women, and 15% to minorities.[66] The company is included in both *The Best Companies for Women* and "The 60 Best Companies for Working Mothers." Of 22,639 U.S. employees, 8373 are women and 4386 minorities. And there are 633 women and 239 minorities among the 2836 employees considered upper management. Pitney Bowes was one of the early proponents of flextime—employees are required to work from 10:00 A.M. to 2:00 P.M., but beyond that the schedule is at the discretion of the employee and supervisor. Women and primary caregivers are allowed 90 days of unpaid leave beyond typical leave, and the company offers a Child Care Resource and Referral Program.

Benefits for all employees are generous. In addition to the annual shareholder meeting, Pitney Bowes holds a jobholder one, at which employees have an opportunity to question upper management. A profit-sharing package is another benefit. Pitney Bowes was one of the top ten companies profiled in *The 100 Best Companies to Work for in America*.

The company has three on-staff positions—director of Corporate Safety and Environmental Affairs, manager of Corporate Environmental Engineering, and Corporate Hygienist—that tend to the company's environmental policies and practices. Pitney Bowes has a waste minimization program with a goal of zero discharge of hazardous pollutants by 1996.

Roughly 1% of Pitney Bowes' pretax earnings are given to charitable causes each year, or around $1.693 million in 1988.

Pitney Bowes was a pick of both *GOOD MONEY* and Franklin's *insight* in 1989.

FAST FACTS:
- No South African operations.
- Not a top 500 DoD contractor.

- No unionized employees.
- Pitney Bowes does not contribute to PACs and has banned the backing of political candidates in its "Business Practice Guidelines."
- Purchased $4.3 million from minority-owned businesses in 1989.
- Given the corporate leadership award from the Stamford branch of the NAACP.
- Responded to questionnaire.
- Stamford, CT.

PROCTER & GAMBLE

Procter & Gamble may be the type of place where "the organization man in the gray flannel suit feels right at home,"[67] but it's also a company that treats its employees well (minorities and women, too!). What's more, the company is rising to the occasion and tackling some of the difficult environmental issues the U.S. faces as it enters the 1990s.

It's not the number of women and minorities in high-ranking positions that has won P&G praise, but instead its programs allowing these groups access to top slots. Hence, the company was included in *The Best Companies for Women*, "The 60 Best Companies for Working Mothers," *Black Enterprise*'s survey of the 50 best workplaces for blacks, and *The 100 Best Companies to Work for in America*. *Black Enterprise* attributes the company's successful affirmative action program in part to CEO John Smale, who makes all managers responsible for putting EEO goals into action. The company ranked fourth out of 305 major companies in *Fortune*'s January 29, 1990, survey of corporate reputations.

P&G alone accounts for an estimated 1% of the nation's solid waste,[68] although it is taking steps to reduce this. In 1988 it unveiled a Spic & Span bottle made from recycled plastic, and in Europe it is test-marketing refill pouches of concentrated liquid detergent to cut down on bottles being discarded. Another sign of its commitment is its efforts to reduce the volume and weight of products and packaging; for example, its redesigned Crisco bottles require 28% less plastic and yet hold the same volume of oil as the original ones. P&G uses recycled paperboard in 70% of its paper packaging.

P&G is also a generous corporate contributor to charitable causes, earmarking 2–3% of annual pretax earnings for this.

In September 1989 P&G acquired consumer-products-maker Noxell, long a favorite of ethical investors.

FAST FACTS:
- A pick of Franklin's *insight* as of late 1989.
- Profit-sharing program.
- Received a 1988 Corporate Conscience award from the Council on Economic Priorities for seeking alternatives to animal testing; over the past five years, P&G says it has decreased animal use 30%.
- Some unionized workers.
- Received President's Citation for Volunteer Action Award in 1989.
- A preexisting licensing agreement in the divestiture of its former Richardson-Vicks subsidiary connects the company to South Africa until 1995.
- Of 41,100 U.S. employees, 13,000 are women and 6500 minorities.
- Two minority members but no women in the 58 slots designated VP or above; 24% of managers are women and 11% are minorities.
- 79,000 employees worldwide.
- In 1987–1988 P&G purchased $84 million in goods and services from minority-owned businesses, and $36 million from women-owned firms.
- Responded to questionnaire.
- Cincinnati, OH.

THE QUAKER OATS COMPANY

Quaker was on Working Assets', Franklin's, and Calvert's buy lists in 1989 for its equal employment opportunity practices and its generous matching gift program. Quaker will match employee donations of $25–$300 to higher education, the arts, education, health, youth and social service programs on an extremely generous three-for-one basis. Gifts to social service organizations are matched dollar for dollar. What's more, its Dollars for Doers program allows employees to apply for grants of up to $500, which are awarded to programs where they volunteer. The company paid out $96,300 in FY89 (June 30) through this program. Between the Quaker Foundation and the company's donations and food gifts, total contributions exceeded 4% of the company's FY89 pretax profits.

Roughly 21.7% of Quaker's 2444 employees considered upper management are women and 7% minorities. On its 15-person board of directors sit one woman and one minority. Quaker publishes a brochure entitled "A Message to Minority Suppliers," and it purchased

$18.1 million in goods and services from minority vendors and $14.7 million from women-owned businesses in 1988.

In 1989 the state of Texas leveled a lawsuit against Quaker, charging that advertisements for its oatmeal and oat bran falsely claim that eating these cereals as part of a low-fat, low-cholesterol diet helps reduce cholesterol and the possibility of a heart attack. Quaker has filed a countersuit against the Texas attorney general, asserting its ads are truthful and not misleading and are supported by 25 years of scientific research on links between oats and cholesterol. Although no decision has been reached, the Federal Trade Commission found in Quaker's favor a year earlier when a health advocacy group questioned the company's health claims.[69]

FAST FACTS:
- No South African ties.
- No weapons-related businesses.
- 70% unionized; unions in place for 20 years.
- Quaker owns and operates a paper and cardboard recycling facility.
- Solid-waste task force increases recycling at manufacturing plants; environmental professionals on staff.
- 17,151 employees.
- Responded to questionnaire.
- Chicago, IL.

REYNOLDS METALS

Reynolds Metals began recycling aluminum more than 20 years ago and now recycles more aluminum cans than it produces. In 1988 the company recycled over 433 million pounds of consumer-generated aluminum and paid out $173 million to recyclers. Reynolds has more than 750 consumer recycling locations nationwide. However, its commitment to recycling goes beyond aluminum—the packaging for Reynolds Wrap, Reynolds Freezer Paper, CUT-RITE wax paper, and Sure-Seal plastic bags is made from recycled paperboard, and the printing on almost all of its consumer products is done with low-solvent technology, dramatically reducing emissions. Reynolds' Pres-to Products subsidiary recycles plastics and is working on developing a biodegradable trash bag; it already offers photodegradable ones.

Fifty-five percent of Reynolds' workforce is unionized through unions organized over 50 years ago. In December 1988 the United Steelworkers of America (USWA) and the Aluminum, Brick and Glass Workers International Union (ABGWIU) as well as local unions signed a new 43-month labor agreement with Reynolds, featuring a profit-sharing program, wage increases, and pension improvements.

FAST FACTS:

- Reynolds was the second most admired of ten metals companies in the January 29, 1990, *Fortune* survey.
- The Reynolds Foundation made $727,707 in charitable contributions in 1988 (net income for that year was $482 million).
- Of 20,226 U.S. employees (excluding those at subsidiaries), 2935 were women and 4184 minorities.
- Reynolds purchased $24,301,038 from women-owned businesses and $4,812,329 from minority-owned businesses in 1988.
- Responded to questionnaire.
- Richmond, VA.

RIEDEL ENVIRONMENTAL

Who's cleaning up some of the toughest-to-tackle hazardous-waste sites in the country? Riedel. For this reason, the company was described as "inherently responsible" by *Clean Yield*, which rated the stock a buy as of July 1989. The company offers the full range of hazardous-waste cleanup products and services, from site assessment to off-site treatment and disposal. In 1988 it won two performance awards from the EPA totaling $847,000 for superior work and cost controls. Its other businesses are recycled rubber products and solid-waste management, both of which are environmentally useful. Its OMNI division turns recycled rubber into rubber railroad crossings. Meanwhile, the company has a new subsidiary, Riedel Environmental Engineering, which specializes in projects requiring extensive civil engineering and construction capabilities in addition to environmental and waste management expertise. Riedel has been designated hazardous-waste emergency response contractor in 23 Western states.

One social drawback to Riedel, the *Clean Yield* noted, is that it has few women in influential positions. Indeed, there are no women and no minorities on its six-person board of directors. However, Judith E. Ayres, Principal, William D. Ruckelshaus Associates, does sit on the company's five-person Environmental Advisory Board.

FAST FACTS:

- No exposure to South Africa.
- Does have military contracts to clean up waste sites, which *Clean Yield* calls a plus.

■ Responded with annual report.
■ Portland, OR.

ROYAL DUTCH/SHELL GROUP OF COMPANIES

Target of a visible boycott because of its operations in South Africa, the Royal Dutch/Shell Group of Companies is the result of a 1907 alliance to merge the interests of the two companies of the name on a 60:40 basis and yet maintain two separate identities. The Royal Dutch Petroleum Company is based in the Netherlands and the Shell Transport and Trading Company in the United Kingdom. When people say they are boycotting Shell Oil, the U.S. subsidiary, for its South African operations, they are incorrect—the parent, Royal Dutch/ Shell, owns the South African operations.

The boycott of Royal Dutch/Shell is international and has been supported by the World Council of Churches, the United Mine Workers of America, the Anti-Apartheid Movement of the U.K., and Anglican Bishop Desmond Tutu.[70] The company has widely been accused of breaking the oil embargo against South Africa, something it vigorously denies. Shell South Africa employs over 4300 people, and a further 4000 are employed in subsidiaries of which Shell South Africa owns more than 50%. The company complies with the European Community Code of Conduct for Companies with Interests in South Africa.

Shell Oil's reputation in the U.S. is mixed—it was listed among *The 100 Best Companies to Work for in America*. Yet it has been cited for environmental and OSHA violations. The company is partially responsible for 59 toxic waste sites designated by the EPA as in urgent need of attention.[71] Meanwhile OSHA proposed a $244,960 penalty for record-keeping violations at its Deer Park, Texas, operations in December 1986, and Royal Dutch finally paid $103,000. And yet Shell has taken some environmentally positive positions, such as working toward making the quantity of materials it recycles equal to that of what it disposes by the end of 1990. And it operates a coal gasification unit, designed to demonstrate that coal can be converted to a clean fuel.

On the plus side, Shell's Child Care Resource and Referral Service assists working parents, and it sponsored a day care unit for children with minor illnesses, called KIDS ON THE MEND. Since 1971 the company has purchased goods and services worth more than $900 million from minority- and women-owned businesses.

FAST FACTS:

- Company won the 1988 National Association for the Advancement of Colored People Corporate Membership for support and the President's Volunteer Action Award in 1987.
- Shell contracts with outside firms to conduct animal testing.
- Shell Oil made more than $17 million in donations in 1988.
- Responded to questionnaire.
- Houston, TX.

RUBBERMAID

Rubbermaid is considered by most to be a socially responsible company. Both Franklin's *insight* and Calvert recently counted it among their investment selections. And Rubbermaid ranked third most admired of 305 companies in *Fortune*'s January 29, 1990, survey.

Within the community of Wooster, Ohio, Rubbermaid has demonstrated that it is a good corporate neighbor. Around five years ago the company purchased an old school building, restored it, and turned it into a local art center and home for the county Head Start program for underprivileged children. It also razed a factory adjacent to the school and turned the land into a playground. In 1989 Rubbermaid designed and constructed a building for the United Way and other community service activities. The company would not divulge charitable giving numbers.

Rubbermaid is using recycled materials whenever possible. It recently teamed up with Amoco and McDonald's to manufacture food trays from used styrofoam.

Its Little Tikes toy factory has an on-site day care center available to employees and a limited number of community members. When asked if the company had any weapons-related businesses, a spokesperson answered "No, not even our toy company makes toy weapons."

Rubbermaid strives to maintain good employee relations. "According to a regional director of the United Rubber Workers, which represents about one quarter of Rubbermaid's workforce, union-management relations at Rubbermaid are exemplary. Additionally, more than one half of the employees own stock in the company," noted Calvert.

FAST FACTS:

- No South African operations.
- Two women but no minorities on the 12-person board of directors.

■ No live-animal testing.
■ Responded with information.
■ Wooster, OH.

RYDER SYSTEM

Ryder System, an international company engaged in both highway transportation and aviation services, passes most socially responsible investors' screens and was a selection of both Parnassus and Franklin's *insight* in 1989. In the early 1980s the company increased its benefits substantially, according to *The 100 Best Companies to Work for in America.* The company has an on-site gymnasium that prorates fees by income as well as a tuition reimbursal program.

In 1988 the company gave $2,437,120 through the Ryder System Charitable Foundation. While much of the giving is traditional, Ryder has made several innovative grants. For example, the company polled its Cincinnati employees to determine what charitable projects to support and then made donations to the Council on Child Abuse of Southwestern Ohio and the Bethany House of Hospitality to renovate a children's playroom at the shelter. Human needs, education, and cultural arts are the three areas Ryder funds.

CEO M. Anthony Burns, who was elected chairman of the National Urban League in 1987, is credited with the company's emphasis on equal employment issues. Ryder was listed among the 35 "best of the best" in *Black Enterprise*'s February 1990 survey. At year-end 1988 7% of Ryder's officers and managers were minorities and 13% women. There is one minority member and no women on its 14-person board. The Ryder Advisory Council, consisting of six senior managers, meets with Burns to discuss EEO goals, and the company has a black employee network. Five percent of purchasing contracts are directed to minority and women vendors. Affirmative action is part of managers' performance evaluations.[72]

FAST FACTS:
■ No South African operations or involvement.
■ No weapons contracting.
■ Recycles engine oil and computer paper.
■ Roughly 42,000 employees, 27% of whom are unionized.
■ Ryder's in-house PAC contributed $55,110 to campaigns in 1987 and 1988; it is recommended that employees make a 0.25% salary deduction to the PAC.

- Responded with information.
- Miami, FL.

SAFETY-KLEEN

As its name implies, Safety-Kleen performs an important environmental task—it recycles used motor oil and other hazardous waste solvents. Through its parts-cleaning business, Safety-Kleen provides customers a parts-washer machine and solvent, then on a scheduled basis replaces used solvent and recycles or reclaims the used fluids. Stricter EPA regulations in 1984 proved a boon since companies producing as few as 220 pounds of hazardous waste fluids a month were required to dispose of these liquids properly, a requirement that Safety-Kleen meets. Growing concern over used motor and industrial oils could result in their being classified as hazardous, which would hike demand for the company's services. That Safety-Kleen is equipped to deal with small businesses producing relatively little streams of hazardous waste is a unique niche.[73]

Safety-Kleen has branched out into related businesses. One example is its collecting hazardous fluids used on garments from dry cleaners; another is its training course on proper procedures for using solvents. The October 1989 issue of Franklin's *insight* called the company's environmental record above average, although it pointed out that the company is a potentially responsible party at ten Superfund sites.

Of around 4800 employees, roughly 800 are women and 300 minorities. There are neither minorities nor women on the eight-person board of directors; around 10% of the 400 employees considered upper management are women and roughly 4% minorities. Worker safety is emphasized at Safety-Kleen through formal training programs at all facilities.

The company gives around 1% of pretax income annually in charitable contributions.[74]

FAST FACTS:
- No South African operations or agreements.
- No arms-contracting.
- CEO Donald Brinckman was named CEO of the Decade by *Financial World* magazine in 1989.
- No unionized employees.
- No child care arrangements and no minority purchasing program.
- Responded to questionnaire.
- Elgin, IL.

SARA LEE CORP.

Corporate commitment is something Sara Lee takes seriously—in fact, the company goes so far as to look at employees' community records on their annual evaluations. John H. Bryan, Sara Lee's chairman and CEO, has spoken about community service in a variety of publications, including a 1988 opinion piece for *Business Week*.

Sara Lee publicly states its commitment to donating a generous 2% of domestic pretax earnings to charitable organizations, a goal it exceeded in FY89 (June) by donating $7.4 million in cash and more than $2 million worth of products. The Sara Lee Foundation, which gave more than $2.3 million in cash grants during FY89, is unusual because of the projects it funds: It earmarks half of its funds for the disadvantaged and 40% for the arts. Recent recipients included a one-stop, integrated food and nutrition-education facility in Chicago's Austin neighborhood, the Hispanic Women's Consultation project, and the Chicago Symphony Orchestra.

The company's Hanes subsidiary was targeted by OSHA in 1980 for violations allegedly causing tendonitis and other physical disabilities among factory workers. In 1981 the company piloted an ergonomics project, and since then has changed its chairs and lighting, trained plant nurses in upper-extremity disorders, and videotaped workers to identify problems. More recently, on August 30, 1989, Sara Lee signed an agreement with OSHA to reduce the occupational hazards of cumulative trauma disorders (CTDs) at 31 of its meat processing plants. The company agreed to employ ergonomic consultants to review processes that pose CTD hazards and eliminate these factors.

FAST FACTS:
- No South African ties.
- No unionized employees.
- There are two women and two minorities on its 19-person board of directors.
- Most admired of ten companies in Food category of *Fortune's* January 29, 1990, survey.
- In FY89 two-thirds of profits came from food, one-third from consumer goods.
- In September 1989 the company removed "light" claim from its 200-calorie-a-slice cheesecake in response to legal problems.
- Responded to questionnaire.
- Chicago, IL.

SCOTT PAPER

Scott's response to the environmental challenges that forest- and paper-product companies are confronted with has been mixed. Although the company was praised in the mid-1980s by *Rating America's Corporate Conscience* for having won numerous environmental awards, it is being boycotted by the Nova Scotia-based Scott Boycott Committee for "irresponsible and harmful forestry practices."[75] Boycotters contend that Scott used a highly destructive clear-cutting technique and dangerous herbicides in violation of spraying guidelines. The committee also charges that Scott's policy of replanting clear-cut areas with softwood forests is not sound given that these trees are highly susceptible to insect outbreaks. A Scott spokesperson explained that the company's use of herbicides is minimal given that it occurs during only one rotation of a crop that rotates every 60 years. The company also noted that hardwoods come back without being planted. And Scott has major investments in tree nurseries and does extended tree planting and work to improve forest species for the future.

In 1989 the Scott Paper Company Foundation donated $4,180,314 to charitable causes, 0.83% of pretax income. Its charitable focus is children in need. In addition, the company made roughly $2.1 million in cause-related marketing grants that year.

FAST FACTS:
- No South African operations.
- Around 40,000 employees.
- Ranked second most admired in Forest Products category of *Fortune's* January 29, 1990, survey.
- Two women on 14-person board of directors.
- Its Winslow, ME, facility was fined $813,000 for record-keeping violations of the Occupational Safety and Health Act in September 1987. The company corrected the problem and the final payment came to approximately $400,000.
- Responded with printed materials.
- Philadelphia, PA.

SNAP-ON TOOLS

Snap-on Tools, the world's largest manufacturer and distributor of mechanical tools, takes a community-based approach to corporate responsibility. Although the company would not reveal charitable contribution numbers, it says its giving is geared toward local need.

Snap-on has no large strikes against it in terms of social responsibility, and it was a *GOOD MONEY* pick as of early 1989.

The company has what it described as "one of the most elaborate" recycling facilities for plating in the country. Through a nonprofit agency it is beginning a paper-recycling program at its general office, the proceeds of which will fund community youth projects.

Snap-on Tools has neither women nor minorities at the VP level or above. No provisions are made for child care, although flextime is informally available. Just the same, the company belongs to the Wisconsin Minority Supplier Development Council.

Around 2–3% of its sales come from the DoD, which purchases mechanical tools from the company.

Around 28% of Snap-on's 7500 employees are affiliated with a union. In 1988 workers went on a six-week strike at the company's Natick, Massachusetts, air-tool plant. This was, however, the only work stoppage the company had experienced in nine years. Snap-on promotes employee wellness through restricted smoking, free cholesterol screening, on-premise aerobics classes, and an at-work Weight Watchers program.

A small number of former Snap-on dealers sued the company in 1988, claiming they were mistreated and Snap-on was responsible for the failure of their businesses. The company denies the merit of these claims and won the only case that had gone to trial by the end of 1988.

FAST FACTS:
- No South African operations.
- Responded with limited information.
- Kenosha, WI.

STUDENT LOAN MARKETING ASSOCIATION

The Student Loan Marketing Association, known as Sallie Mae, is an interesting option for socially responsible investors. Its business—purchasing student loans from banks, providing collateralized advances to banks making such loans, and providing software and servicing support for the administration of these loans—is socially useful, given that it increases the supply of capital available to support higher education. Four out of every ten Guaranteed Student Loans are financed directly or indirectly by Sallie Mae, and this frees up lenders to make new loans, which is important for financing post-secondary education. And of course, this business doesn't pollute and has no links to South Africa or to the Department of Defense.

Women are in the majority at Sallie Mae—1075 of 1649 total employees are women and 402 are minorities. There are two women and two minorities on Sallie Mae's board of directors. And in the D.C. area, the corporation contracts with a child care referral service as well as offering pretax child care reimbursement.

Of 1600 companies that Franklin follows, Sallie Mae is one of only 200 it recommended in 1989. It is also a pick of *Clean Yield* and Calvert.

The company would not reveal charitable contribution numbers; nevertheless its activities include educational programs, community service and arts organizations.

FAST FACTS:
- No unionized employees.
- Responded to questionnaire.
- Washington, DC.

SYNTEX

Instrumental in developing the birth control pill, Syntex, a pharmaceutical and medical diagnostics company with worldwide operations, has an excellent record on employment issues for women. It was recently hailed as one of the top ten companies for working mothers in *Working Mother* magazine. The company opened a near-site child care center that accommodates up to 150 children, the majority of whom belong to employees. Financial scholarships for The Children's Pre-School Center are awarded on a need basis, and pretax dollars can be put aside for paying fees. Slightly more than half of Syntex's roughly 10,000 employees worldwide are women. Women make up 30% of Syntex managers and 56% of professionals, according to the October 1989 issue of *Working Mother*. *The Best Companies for Women* praises Syntex for taking steps to rectify the historical pay inequities for women. The company notes that as an international company with major operations in the Bahamas, Mexico, Puerto Rico, the Continental U.S., and Asia, minority hiring statistics aren't meaningful.

Franklin's *insight* named Syntex as one of five companies with significant projects or charitable programs to combat AIDS.[76] In July 1989 the company introduced Cytovene (ganciclovir), an antiviral compound developed to treat cytomegalovirus (CMV) retinitis, which approximately 20% of AIDS patients develop and, if left untreated, often leads to blindness. Through a compassionate-use program, Syntex has made the drug available free of charge to more than 10,000 AIDS patients.

The company donates 0.8% of worldwide pretax earnings to charitable organizations each year. These funds are distributed to education (40%), health (20%), community welfare (20%), arts (5%), and other areas (15%).

Although Syntex has no South African operations, its prescription drugs and diagnostic systems are sold there through distributors. The company believes it is immoral to deny prescription drugs to any country.

FAST FACTS:
- No arms-related businesses.
- Performs live-animal testing.
- Has won awards for recycling programs in Palo Alto.
- Responded to questionnaire.
- Palo Alto, CA.

TANDEM COMPUTERS

Tandem is a company that takes its commitment to its employees and its community seriously, but in innovative ways. From the Friday afternoon get-togethers to its EAR employee assistance programs, Tandem demonstrates its commitment to its workforce. Terms like *values* and *ethics* pop up everywhere; they dot CEO James Treybig's speeches and are topics in Tandem's publications. Its town meetings, in which senior executives field employee questions and complaints, its articles on employee concerns such as workaholism, and its information on home recycling through its electronic mail system demonstrate how responsibility at the top can set the tone for the entire corporation.

One exceptional program is Tandem's public service sabbatical. Employees can extend their full paid, six-week leave to up to nine weeks to volunteer for a nonprofit project and Tandem will pick up part of the expenses. Projects undertaken have ranged from working with dyslexic children in Appalachia to tackling the problem of alcoholism on an Indian reservation. The focus of Tandem's charitable giving is human service and community work, and here, too, the company's approach is refreshing. Tandem has budgeted $600,000 worth of cash contributions and $2 million in equipment grants for

1990. Examples of projects it funds include programs for the homeless, a learning center for the undermotivated, and a fund for employees who lost homes in the San Francisco earthquake.

Tandem was included as one of *The 100 Best Companies to Work for in America*, and was a pick of Parnassus as of summer 1989.

Tandem has a comprehensive EEO statement and advertises career opportunities in minority-targeted publications. However, there are no women on its 12-person board of directors and the company did not release overall EEO statistics. Child care can be funded with up to $5000 annually in pretax salary dollars, and Tandem has CARE, which stands for Childcare Assistance Referral Program. When possible, flextime is available to ease hard-to-juggle schedules.

Tandem has had a full-time environmental and safety manager on staff since 1982. It has an active employee recycling program for office paper, aluminum cans, and cardboard, and the company's reproduction center is targeting 80% corporate use of recycled paper for 1990. In 1988 Tandem won the Mayor's Award of Excellence in Water Conservation out of a field of major Silicon Valley companies, and in 1989 received the Corporate Energy Management Award from the Silicon Valley Association of Energy Engineers for reducing its overall energy consumption. Tandem's safety performance for 1985–1986 was 49% below the average accident rate within the electronics industry.

FAST FACTS:
- No South African operations.
- No unionized employees.
- Tandem has a PAC, which makes small ($500–$1000) contributions to federal candidates.
- Over 9500 employees in FY89 (Sept.).
- Responded to questionnaire.
- Cupertino, CA.

TECO ENERGY

TECO Energy is predominantly an electric company with some diversified, energy-related businesses; it has no exposure to nuclear power. TECO has recently branched out into the development and production of natural gas from coalbeds, which is environmentally attractive because natural gas burns much more cleanly than most other fuels. TECO is generally regarded as a socially responsible company and in 1989 was a pick of Pax, *insight*, and *Clean Yield*.

TECO has taken several environmentally responsible steps including co-generation, recycling, and nature conservation. The company installed a scrubber to remove sulfur dioxide from boiler emissions at its Big Bend Station, but depending upon what acid rain legislation is passed, it might have to make considerable capital outlays to meet future regulations. In many of its processes it uses recycled water. And it sells off slag, a byproduct of coal combustion, for sandblasting, roofing, and road building. TECO's Waste Minimization Program works toward reducing the volume of overall waste. The company is involved in supporting artificial reefs, in relocating osprey nests to Tampa Electric nesting platforms, in saving the manatees, and in sponsoring environmental education programs.

Annually, TECO contributes between 0.4–0.6% of pretax earnings to charitable organizations.

FAST FACTS:
- No South African operations.
- No military-contracting work.
- One woman on 13-person board of directors.
- Around 50% of employees are unionized.
- No provisions for child care.
- No formal minority purchasing program.
- No PAC.
- 4500 employees.
- Responded to questionnaire.
- Tampa, FL.

TENNECO

Tenneco makes a difference through its Volunteers in Assistance program; established in 1978, it identifies community needs and furnishes corporate financial support for the projects its employees undertake. The company has an active communications program to promote volunteering and keep employees informed of its progress. This program won Ronald Reagan's Volunteer Action Award in the early 1980s. The company contributed an estimated $6.5 million to charitable programs in 1988, according to the *Taft Corporate Giving Directory*, or approximately 0.67% of that year's pretax earnings. Education is heavily emphasized; Tenneco has teamed up with other Houston agencies to offer scholarship initiatives for the Jefferson Davis High School.

And yet Tenneco, a diversified industrial conglomerate with chemical, natural gas, and agricultural interests, gets mixed reviews in other social departments. *The 100 Best Companies to Work for in America* praised it for building an $11-million fitness center in the early 1980s, which CEO James Ketelsen said would position the company to compete for the most talented employees. Just the same, *Everybody's Business* described Tenneco this way: "A company with an insatiable appetite for other companies and one that's in constant hot water with authorities."[77] The authors said Tenneco had been accused of thwarting union organization and of health and safety violations in the 1970s. The Tenneco of today has not known similar problems.

Tenneco sold off its South African J. I. Case farm and construction subsidiary in late 1988 and was in the process of selling off its passive stock ownership interest in two small South African specialty chemical companies, which employed around 85, as of December 1989. The interests are held by Tenneco's U.K.-based Albright & Wilson Ltd. subsidiary. Tenneco was a signatory of the June 1989 Statement of Principles and received the highest compliance rating, Making Good Progress.

The company has interests in natural gas pipelines, an environmentally attractive business since this fuel burns so cleanly. And Tenneco embarked on a cleanup program for PCB contamination, costing $20–30 million, because of low-level contamination on the company's property caused by materials it had used to lubricate equipment.

FAST FACTS:
■ One woman but no minorities on 12-person board of directors.
■ Around 90,000 employees.
■ Responded with limited information.
■ Houston, TX.

TEXACO

Texaco has several social strikes against it, and yet its record in some areas has improved. Its exposure to South Africa and its environmental problems are generally considered negatives, yet it has made gains in employee relations.

Texaco is one of the 11 largest emitters of potentially carcinogenic chemicals unregulated by the Clean Air Act for release of the chemical 1,3- Butadiene from its Port Neches, Texas, plant, according to the Natural Resources Defense Council. Modernization of this plant, slated for completion by the end of 1991, should reduce these emissions 90%. It also is partially responsible for 40 toxic waste sites designated by the EPA as in urgent need of attention.[78] And yet Texaco has established a public responsibility committee to review and report to the Board on environmental, health, and safety matters. One environmental positive is its clean coal technology, which converts coal mixed with water into a gas. Sulfur and nitrogen oxide are extracted before the gas is burned, making it a clean energy source.

Texaco and Chevron jointly own Caltex, the only major U.S. oil company currently operating in South Africa. The company does not prohibit sale to the South African government or military, something it says it is not legally capable of doing. Caltex is a signatory of the Statement of Principles, and received the highest rating, Making Good Progress, for the year ending June 1989. This is an improvement over its middle rating the year before. Caltex employed 2056 South Africans in mid-1989, 1013 of whom were nonwhite. The General Assembly of the Episcopal Church of the United States is boycotting Texaco for its South African involvement.[79]

Franklin's *insight* says that Texaco's employee relations have improved—especially in its Port Arthur, Texas, refinery, which had experienced years of "labor unrest." This refinery is now managed by Star Enterprise, a joint effort between Texaco and the Saudi Arabian Oil Company.

Overall, Texaco has made gains in hiring women and minorities. Between 1979 and 1989, despite a 33% decrease in its workforce, minority representation increased from 12.9% to 17.1%, and numbers of women rose from 12.1% to 20.6%. On the managerial and professional staff, minorities have increased from 5.4% to 10.6% and women from 9.0% to 19.3% for the same period.

FAST FACTS:
- According to Franklin, charitable contributions equalled only 0.24% of pretax earnings.
- Responded with information.
- White Plains, NY.

TEXAS AIR

Texas Air is known for a series of heated skirmishes between labor and management waged throughout the 1980s. Texas Air itself is a holding company that owns Continental Airlines, including former Frontier, People Express, and New York Air companies, as well as

Eastern Air Lines. In the past, CEO Frank Lorenzo has acquired a number of airlines, pushed for concessions that have often led to strikes, and then filed for bankruptcy and achieved cost cuts through bankruptcy proceedings. After Eastern's acquisition by Texas Air, new management demanded $150 million in wage and work-rule concessions. A company spokesperson asserted that Eastern's management had called for the same concessions prior to the sale, and that this was a better alternative than liquidation. This spurred a machinists' union strike, involving 8500 workers, which was honored by pilots and flight attendants and began on March 4, 1989. Five days later, Eastern sought protection under Chapter 11 of the bankruptcy code, and subsequently hired and trained new pilots and employees in order to resume operations. Eastern pilots and flight attendants ended their strike in late November 1989, after President Bush vetoed a panel of inquiry to investigate the dispute, but the machinists remained on strike.[80] Both Eastern and Continental were on the AFL–CIO's September/October 1989 "Don't Buy" list. And Parnassus includes Texas Air on its "worst company" list because of the company's treatment of its employees and the carrier's service problems. Texas Air was among the ten least admired out of 305 major companies in *Fortune*'s January 29, 1990, survey.

That these events paralleled Texas Air's acquisition of Continental has been particularly disturbing to organized labor. In the early 1980s, Texas Air created New York Air as a nonunion subsidiary and unions at other Texas Air subs viewed this as a way to evade their contracts and called for a boycott. When Texas Air acquired Continental in 1981, it moved quickly for wage concessions from employees, encountered resistance, went into bankruptcy, and managed thereby to cancel some of its union obligations. Lorenzo used bankruptcy as a way to make drastic wage cuts at Continental, and many view the current situation at Eastern as history repeating itself.[81] A company spokeswoman pointed out that bankruptcy was the only opportunity for the company to be revived.

FAST FACTS:

- No women on the 11-person Texas Air board of directors, although there is one woman among around a dozen corporate officers.
- Involved in several lawsuits over its acquisitions and bankruptcy proceedings.
- Responded with limited information.
- Houston, TX.

TIME WARNER

Time Warner, the 1989 megamerger of Time Inc. and Warner Communications, is a corporation in transition; however, if it holds onto some of Time's strengths—its good employee relations, fair treatment of women and minorities, and community literacy projects—it will be a socially responsible communications giant.

Time Warner is a challenge to evaluate because even within Time alone programs differed radically by division. *Working Mother*, which is 50% owned by Time, called HBO the standout division for women. However, the article notes that the magazine group was trying to reverse a history of male-dominance by initiating a work/family program, including workshops, support groups, and a senior management women's group.[82] Women constitute 56% of Time's workforce and minorities 23%. *Black Enterprise* also named Time as one of the 50 best places for blacks to work in its February 1989 survey. In 1988 Time purchased more than $51 million in goods and services from minority- and female-owned businesses. In a rare step, Time issued an explicit company statement protecting all employees with AIDS from discrimination. And HBO presented a documentary on AIDS as a public-service effort.

The company has confronted illiteracy in a variety of ways. Its reading improvement program for adults, Time to Read, had grown to a network of 800 volunteers (38% of them Time employees) by year-end 1988. The program was awarded the President's Volunteer Action Award in 1988. Employee donations to education are matched at a generous three-for-one clip.

Although Time has taken socially responsible steps on several fronts, similar initiatives could not be located for Warner. What this means for the new Time Warner remains to be seen.

FAST FACTS:

- Time was one of the ten best in *The 100 Best Companies to Work for in America*.
- Time Warner is an endorser of the Statement of Principles, which means that it has fewer than 25 employees in South Africa and gives an annual contribution to the program.
- Time publishes its social initiatives in its annual report.
- Responded with information.
- New York, NY.

USAIR GROUP

USAir Group has never had a strike—a particularly impressive fact given the bitter labor/management relations of many other major airlines. For this reason, Shearson Lehman Hutton's social investment division considered the stock attractive in 1989. Of USAir's roughly 50,000 employees, around half are unionized.

This airline is primarily a domestic carrier, and neither flies to South Africa nor has other ties there. Through the merger of Piedmont into USAir in August 1989, the airline's domestic routes have been greatly increased.

One woman sits on USAir's 14-person board. And among the top 40 corporate officers five are women, although none are minorities.

The company said contributions are made in every city the airline serves, generally to the local United Way chapter. USAir matches employee gifts to education and medical research dollar for dollar.

FAST FACTS:
■ No arms-related businesses.
■ Has a minority-purchasing program but would not release the size.
■ Responded with information.
■ Washington, DC.

UNION CARBIDE

Union Carbide is known for one of the worst industrial accidents in history—the Bhopal tragedy of December 3, 1984, in which methyl isocyanate was emitted from a plant owned and operated by Union Carbide India Ltd. The death toll was between 2000 and 5000, with many more injured. Although there have been roughly 464,500 injury claims filed, Union Carbide estimates there are only 7500 persons with total or partial, permanent or temporary disability from the disaster, based on early results of comprehensive medical examinations filed with the Supreme Court of India. Warren M. Anderson, chairman at the time of the disaster, was charged by the Indian government with homicide and was arrested as he stepped off a plane in Bhopal.[83] Union Carbide was counted among the ten worst corporations of 1988 by the *Multinational Monitor* because of evidence of corporate irresponsibility: The Bhopal plant was inadequately designed, the workforce was poorly trained, and operating materials were written only in English.[84] The company denied all of these charges and attributed the accident to employee sabotage.

Union Carbide has been accused of liquidating assets and making payouts to shareholders in order to avoid making a large settlement to the Bhopal victims.[85] The company denied this. Nonetheless, the final $470 million settlement fell far short of the Indian government's initial request for more than $3 billion and came nearly five years after the disaster had occurred.

Even prior to Bhopal, Union Carbide was involved in several controversies, primarily environmental ones. The company had released 2.4 million pounds of mercury into the ground, water, and air between 1950 and 1963 at the Y-12 plant. This was the U.S. government's main nuclear weapons factory, run by Union Carbide until 1984. UC disputed these figures, given in the *Multinational Monitor*, saying around 700,000 pounds of mercury were "lost" and another 1.3 million pounds unaccounted for (in part due to uncertainty as to the amount of mercury delivered to the plant). Although the Justice Department considered prosecuting Carbide officials responsible for the leak, no charges were brought against them. (The company operated Y-12 for the Department of Energy under DoE direction.)

In 1986 Carbide agreed to a $40- to $50-million cleanup plan for uranium dumping by its Umetco Minerals subsidiary in Uravan, Colorado.[86] Additionally, the company was handed down what was then the largest OSHA fine ever levied for alleged violations of federal health and safety laws at its Institute, West Virginia, plant in 1988; it ultimately paid around $240,000. Meanwhile, Union Carbide has been named a potentially responsible party for 75 toxic waste sites designated by the EPA as in urgent need of attention.[87] In the late 1980s the company took steps to reverse these negative trends, including reducing the annual amount of potentially harmful chemicals released into the air by 45% between 1985 and 1989. More than half of the hazardous solid waste its chemical plants generate is recycled or reused.

Union Carbide has two South African affiliates and has signed the Statement of Principles. Both received the highest compliance rating, Making Good Progress, in June 1989. These operations employ roughly 600 people.

FAST FACTS:
- Targets 0.5% of worldwide pretax income for charitable contributions, and expects to give $4.1 million in 1990.
- 18% unionized.
- Least admired of ten in Chemicals category of *Fortune*'s January 29, 1990, corporate survey.

- Full-service employee assistance program.
- Child care referral.
- No weapons-related businesses.
- Has a PAC, for which contributions are generally around $26,000 per cycle.
- Responded to questionnaire.
- Danbury, CT.

WANG LABORATORIES

This computer concern was part of *GOOD MONEY*'s recommendations as of early 1989. Although the company does not have any of the negatives that would scare away socially responsible investors, it has gone through a financially difficult period in the middle and late 1980s.

A unique aspect of the company is that following the death of Dr. An Wang on March 24, 1990, the company's board appointed a nonAsian to succeed him. It is the first time a nonAsian has held this position in the company's 41-year history. Board members include four Asians, one of whom is a woman.

The company has reduced its workforce to around 20,000 from 31,000 in mid-1988, and has taken steps to turn around some financial problems.

FAST FACTS:
- No South African operations.
- Not one of the top 500 DoD contractors.
- Among the ten least admired in *Fortune*'s January 29, 1990, survey of 305 major U.S. companies.
- Responded with limited information.
- Lowell, MA.

WARNER-LAMBERT

In the second half of the 1980s, Warner-Lambert, a health-care and consumer company, took to curing some of the inequities in the workforce. While women made up only 29% of total employees in 1984, that figure leapt to nearly 43% by late 1989, according to *Working Mother*'s October 1989 article, "The 60 Best Companies for Working Mothers." Warner-Lambert offers resource and referral services for child care and reserves slots for employees' children in child care centers near headquarters. Flextime has long been an option—employees must work the core hours of 9:30 A.M. to 3:15 P.M., however they may begin their day as early as 7:00 A.M. "Participating in a Diverse Workforce" is Warner-Lambert's mandatory program for management; issues tackled include women and minority concerns and working to integrate multilingual employees. Minorities make up 18% of Warner-Lambert's U.S. workforce, which includes 10,276 employees. There are one woman and one black on W-L's 16-person board.

Warner-Lambert has an employee assistance program, and as of June 1990 all offices are smoke-free, something the biannual surveys indicate employees want.

On average Warner-Lambert earmarks 1% of pretax earnings annually for charitable giving. Education is the largest program, followed by health care, social programs, community projects, and the arts. In 1988 W-L adopted the Dover, N.J., high school, near its headquarters city of Morris Plains, and around 100 employee volunteers tutor or make presentations at the school on company time. Employee donations to colleges, universities, or the United Negro College Fund are matched on a generous two-for-one basis.

Warner-Lambert does have a South African subsidiary, employing around 600, which accounts for less than 1% of the corporate assets. Over half of its South African employees are nonwhite. It is a signatory of the Statement of Principles, and received the highest compliance rating, Making Good Progress, for the three years through June 1989. Each top executive at a South African affiliate is expected to "adopt" a project that uses his or her specialized expertise, and this is part of the manager's annual performance appraisal.

The company expanded its operations in Puerto Rico "to further avail ourselves of Puerto Rico's tax benefits," the company wrote in its annual report.

FAST FACTS:
- In early 1990, W-L said it had developed the first biodegradable plastic, called "bio-plastic starch," which is made from starch derived from potatoes, corn, rice or wheat, according to *The Wall Street Journal* (January 24, 1990).
- Only a small percentage of employees are unionized.
- Live-animal testing.
- No weapons-related businesses.
- Responded with information.
- Morris Plains, NJ.

THE WASHINGTON POST COMPANY

CEO Katharine Graham is one of the few women to head a major U.S. corporation. The company she heads, The Washington Post Company, was part of Calvert's portfolio in 1989 because it meets basic standards of corporate responsibility and delivers a high-quality product that enriches the community. In addition to the D.C. paper of that name, most famous for having broken the Watergate story, The Washington Post Company owns *Newsweek*, Stanley H. Kaplan Educational Center, and four television stations.

Graham is a director of the American Women's Economic Development Corporation.

FAST FACTS:
- *Newsweek* maintains a news bureau in South Africa for reporting from there.
- Has a profit-sharing plan.
- Approximately 6300 full-time employees.
- More than 2700 employees are affiliated with unions.
- Responded with information.
- Washington, DC.

WASTE MANAGEMENT INC.

A national leader in the solid waste business, Waste Management is tackling some of the most significant environmental problems the U.S. faces, and yet the company has been criticized for toxic waste handling problems and allegations of antitrust violations. Its 79% ownership of Chemical Waste Management gives the company exposure to the hazardous-waste area, and its 22% stake in Wheelabrator Technologies links it to the waste-to-energy business. *Business Week* said Waste Management is "successfully diversifying into hazardous waste, asbestos, and medical-waste incineration."[88] At year-end 1988 the company operated 123 North American landfills. And its stock was one of the top ten holdings of the Fidelity Select Environmental Services Portfolio as of the fall of 1989.

Waste Management has several admirable programs. Its Recycle America service recovered an estimated 750,000 tons of recyclable materials from 1.2 million households during 1989. The company received the National Recycling Coalition's Outstanding Corporate Leader award in 1988. It has also joined forces with Baxter Healthcare to help U.S. hospitals reduce solid and medical waste and to meet state regulations. Not only is this environmentally necesary, but it is important for Waste Management workers who are endangered by the inappropriate disposal of medical waste. Meanwhile, in 1989 the company formed a joint venture with Du Pont called the Plastic Recycling Alliance, which plans to process 40 million pounds of plastic refreshment bottles and milk jugs a year.

The company has also taken the admirable stance of declaring no net loss of wetlands will result from its operations; therefore, beginning in 1988 it created wetlands equal to what was lost from developing sites. In 1988 it won an award from Stanford University for setting up a habitat for an endangered species of butterfly.

At the same time, Parnassus includes Waste Management on its "worst company" list because of its environmental problems and allegations of price-fixing.[89] A class action suit has been filed against Waste Management and Browning-Ferris Industries, alleging that these two competitors formed a nationwide conspiracy to fix prices for containerized waste services. The suit will likely be tried by the U.S. District Court in Philadelphia, although a trial date had yet to be set as of this writing. Waste Management points out that in four previous criminal cases for antitrust violations, for two of which the company pleaded no contest, the employees concerned were dismissed. Since the mid-1980s the company has held a training program for managers and sales people to inform them of their legal obligations.

Waste Management has recently attempted to take its business overseas. A *Business Week* article suggests its European image may be making this difficult. Ocean Combustion Service, a Waste Management subsidiary, has burned toxic waste on incineration boats in the North Seas about 100 miles off of the Netherlands since 1980. The company has been blasted by environmentalists, including Greenpeace International, for leaving toxic deposits there. Although the company stands by this practice, it will phase it out by 1992, before it is banned in 1994.[90]

FAST FACTS:
- No South African operations or ties.
- No women or minorities on 11-person board of directors.
- A dollar-for-dollar matching gifts program.
- 40,000 employees.
- Responded with information.
- Oak Brook, IL.

WELLMAN, INC.

Wellman's main businesses, recycling plastic and fiber waste into fiber and manufacturing specialty fibers and plastic resin products, are environmentally attractive. In 1988 the company used 70% of the returned plastic beverage bottles in the U.S. as raw materials for other products, and recycled more than 350 million pounds of plastic and fiber.[91] In November 1989, Wellman acquired Fiber Industries, which makes and markets polyester textile fibers under the Fortrel name.[92]

Given that it has no South African operations and is not involved in the defense business, Wellman is free of many of the don'ts that deter ethical investors. In 1989 it was a pick of New Alternatives, Franklin's *insight*, and a favorite of Shearson's ethical investment specialist.

FAST FACTS:

- Of 1950 U.S. employees, more than half—1058—are minority members, and 444 are women. Of 294 considered management, 38 are women and 41 minorities.
- Wellman contributed $1896 to the South Carolina Textile Manufacturers Association PAC in 1988.
- Responded to questionnaire.
- Shrewsbury, NJ.

WHEELABRATOR TECHNOLOGIES

Wheelabrator Technologies specializes in the method of burning trash and selling the energy given off to local utilities as a source of power known as waste-to-energy recycling. This technology is environmentally attractive because it reduces the volume of waste 75–90%, and at the same time generates a needed product: energy. Wheelabrator established the first successful waste-to-energy plant in 1975. The company has 11 plants operating in the U.S. and can burn more than 16,000 tons of waste per day. Moreover, it had three projects under construction and 15 under development as of mid 1990.

Wheelabrator has teamed up with Waste Management; the latter will own a 55% stake in Wheelabrator, and in exchange, Wheelabrator will be allowed to build waste-to-energy plants on Waste Management's landfills.[93]

In addition to waste-to-energy plants, Wheelabrator has developed wastewater treatment centers so efficient that the water is of drinkable quality. It also develops air pollution control equipment, specifically the scrubbers that reduce the acid rain-causing emissions given off in the incineration process. These are marketed directly to industry as well as used in its own waste-to-energy facilities.

Wheelabrator promotes recycling efforts through Recycle First, which helps communities start recycling programs. For every ton recycled, Wheelabrator reduces the price of waste-to-energy treatment, creating a financial incentive for neighborhoods to recycle. And it recently acquired technology to remove paper, cans, and other recyclables from refuse as it enters the waste-to-energy plant.

FAST FACTS:
- No South African operations.
- No women on the nine-person board of directors.
- 8,000–9,000 employees.
- Responded with information.
- Hampton, NH

ZENITH ELECTRONICS

Zenith, known for manufacturing televisions and VCRs, passes many social screens, and was a Parnassus pick as of the summer of 1989. The company agreed to sell its fast-growing computer unit late in 1989, and concentrate exclusively on its consumer electronics, cable products, and electronic components businesses.[94]

Once Zenith resumes profitability, it plans to participate again in a program to donate 2% of pretax income to charitable organizations. In 1988 it gave an estimated $300,000, according to the *Taft Corporate Giving Directory*.

The company won an award from the State of Missouri, where its Springfield color TV plant is located, for energy cost savings over the past two years.

This consumer electronics concern has a long-standing written Employee Code of Conduct and a toll-free Zenith EthicsLine, which all employees can call to discuss business ethics issues.

Since 1972 Zenith has had a minority business development program, which assists minority-owned businesses in becoming suppliers to the company. Each year Zenith now purchases "tens of millions of dollars" worth of goods and services from minority vendors. Managers are responsible for coming up with affirmative action goals. The program has had particular success in the Chicago area—of 6000 employees, 55% are minorities.

Zenith does sell electronics to the DoD, although this now accounts for under 2% of its overall revenues.

FAST FACTS:
■ No South African operations.
■ No women and no minorities on the ten-person board of directors.
■ A corporate wellness program, which varies by location, offers nutrition and aerobics classes.
■ Around 50% of domestic workforce is unionized, 75% unionized worldwide.
■ Responded with information.
■ Glenview, IL.

ZURN INDUSTRIES

Zurn, a provider of products and services principally to the waste-to-energy and water control markets, is attractive for its positive environmental stance. Zurn manufactures water-control products, delivers clean water, and constructs water and wastewater treatment plants. Waste-to-energy accounts for around 45% of its business and is the fastest growing segment. Zurn was selected as one of five environmental winners in a June 1989 *Money* article on the growing emphasis on the environment.

Zurn also manufactures mechanical drives, which accounts for less than 10% of its overall business. Although the majority of its sales are commercial, a small percentage of total company sales are to the DoD.

Although Zurn would not release charitable contribution numbers, it listed the United Way, food processing at local food banks, and community public broadcasting as activities it supports. In 1989, United Way contributions were up 10% from the previous year and equalled corporate pledges of roughly $40 per employee.

Zurn was a recent pick of *GOOD MONEY* and of Franklin's *insight*.

FAST FACTS:
■ No South African operations.
■ One woman, Juanita Kreps, former U.S. Secretary of Commerce, is on Zurn's eight-person board of directors, and two women out of 19 executive and staff officers.
■ Some unionized divisions.
■ Around 4250 employees.
■ Responded with information.
■ Erie, PA.

■ 10 ■
A DIRECTORY
OF
RESOURCES

General Information and Investment Services

- Council on Economic Priorities
  30 Irving Place
  New York, NY 10003
  212-420-1133
- Interfaith Center on Corporate Responsibility
  475 Riverside Dr.
  New York, NY 10115-0050
  212-870-2296
- Investor Responsibility Research Center
  Suite 600, 1755 Massachusetts Avenue N.W.
  Washington, DC 20036
  202-939-6500
- Peter D. Kinder & Company
  7 Dana Street
  Cambridge, MA 02138
  617-547-7479
  Performs social research on corporations.
- National Minority Supplier Development Council
  1412 Broadway, 11th Floor
  New York, NY 10018
  212-944-2430

- Social Investment Forum
  711 Atlantic Avenue
  Boston, MA 02111
  617-451-3252

Information on Issues

- Industry Support Unit Inc.
  Room 7E #1601
  150 E. 42nd Street
  New York, NY 10017-5666
  212-883-7464
  Copies of the Statement of Principles for South Africa can be obtained here.

- INFACT National Office
  256 Hanover Street
  Boston, MA 02113
  617-742-4583

- INFORM
  Environmental Research & Education
  381 Park Avenue South
  New York, NY 10016
  212-689-4040

- NAACP Fair Share Program
  586 Central Avenue
  Ste. 10-14
  East Orange, NJ 07019
- Nuclear Free America
  325 East 25th Street
  Baltimore, MD 21218
  301-235-3575

Publications

- Clean Yield Publications
  Box 1880
  Greensboro Bend, VT 05842
  802-533-7178
- Franklin's *insight*
  711 Atlantic Avenue
  5th Floor
  Boston, MA 02111
  617-423-6655
- GOOD MONEY Publications
  Box 363
  Worcester, VT 05682
  802-223-3911

Mutual Funds

- Calvert Social Investment Fund
  1700 Pennsylvania Avenue N.W.
  Washington, DC 20006
  301-951-4820
- Dreyfus Third Century Fund
  666 Old Country Road
  Garden City, NY 11530
  1-800-645-6561
- Fidelity SELECT Environmental Portfolio
  The Fidelity Building
  82 Devonshire Street
  Boston, MA 02109
  1-800-544-6666

- Freedom Environmental Fund
  One Beacon Street
  Boston, MA 02108
  1-800-225-6258
- New Alternatives Fund
  295 Northern Boulevard
  Great Neck, NY 11021
  516-466-0808
- The Parnassus Fund
  244 California Street
  San Francisco, CA 94111
  415-362-3505
- Pax World Fund
  224 State Street
  Portsmouth, NH 03801
  603-431-8022

Individual Account Managers

- Franklin Research & Development Corp.
  711 Atlantic Avenue
  Boston, MA 02111
  617-423-6655
- Progressive Asset Management
  1814 Franklin Street, Suite 600
  Oakland, CA 94612
  415-834-3722
- Shearson Lehman Hutton
  14 Wall Street, 9th Floor
  New York, NY 10005-2186
  212-306-0695
  Michael Moffitt manages socially responsible investment accounts for individuals. Minimum investment $100,000.

■ Smith Barney Harris Upham & Company
53 State Street
Boston, MA 02109
617-570-9519
1-800-235-1205
   Anne Greenwood and Amanda Coues manage individual accounts by socially responsible criteria. Minimum investment $25,000.

■ Social Responsibility Investment Group, Inc.
The Candler Building, Suite 622
127 Peachtree Street, N.E.
Atlanta, GA 30303
404-577-3635
   Contact Bruce Gunter, VP, or Hugh Kelley, President; minimum investment $200,000.

■ The United States Trust Company
40 Court Street
Boston, MA 02108
617-726-7250
   Minimum for individually managed accounts $10,000.

Other Vehicles

■ AI Group
129 South Street
Boston, MA 02111-2802
617-350-0250

■ Community Capital Bank
P.O. Box 404920
Brooklyn, NY 11240
718-768-9344

■ First Affirmative Financial Network
410 North 21st Street, Ste 203
P.O. Box 6419
Colorado Springs, CO 80934-6419
719-636-1045

■ South Shore Bank
71st and Jeffery Boulevard
Chicago, IL 60649-2096
312-288-1000

■ Vermont National Bank SRB Fund
P.O. Box 804
Brattleboro, VT 05301
1-800-544-7108

■ Working Assets Money Fund
230 California Street
San Francisco, CA 94111
1-800-533-3863

BIBLIOGRAPHY

Anzovin, Steven (ed.). *South Africa: Apartheid and Divestiture*. The Reference Shelf, Vol. 59, Number 1. New York: H. W. Wilson Co., 1987.

Brown, Lester, et. al. *State of the World, 1989*. New York: W. W. Norton & Co., 1989.

Bruyn, Severyn T. *The Field of Social Investment*. Cambridge, Eng.: Cambridge University Press, 1987.

Davey, Harold W., Mario F. Bognanno, and David L. Estenson, *Contemporary Collective Bargaining*. Englewood Cliffs, N.J.: Prentice-Hall, Inc., 1982.

DeBell, Garrett (ed.). *The New Environmental Handbook*. San Francisco: Friends of the Earth, 1980.

Domini, Amy L., and Peter D. Kinder. *Ethical Investing*. Reading, Mass.: Addison-Wesley Publishing Co., 1986.

Kanter, Rosabeth Moss. *The Change Masters: Innovation and Entrepreneurship in the American Corporation*. New York: Simon & Schuster, 1983.

Klott, Gary. *The New York Times Complete Guide to Personal Investing*. New York: Times Books, 1987.

Lesko, Matthew. *The Investor's Information Source Book*. New

York: Harper & Row, 1988.

Levering, Robert, Milton Moskowitz, and Michael Katz. *The 100 Best Companies to Work for in America.* New York: NAL Penguin, 1985.

Little, Arthur D., Inc. *Thirteenth Report on the Signatory Companies to the Statement of Principles for South Africa.* New York: Industry Support Unit Inc., 1989.

Love, Janice. *The U.S. Anti-Apartheid Movement: Local Activism in Global Politics.* New York: Praeger, 1985.

Lydenberg, Steven D., Alice Tepper Marlin, and Sean O'Brien Strub. *Rating America's Corporate Conscience.* Reading: Addison-Wesley Publishing Co., 1986.

Meeker-Lowry, Susan. *Economics as if the Earth Really Mattered.* Philadelphia: New Society Publishers, 1988.

Moskowitz, Milton, Michael Katz, and Robert Levering (eds.). *Everybody's Business: An Almanac: The Irreverent Guide to Corporate America.* New York: Harper & Row, 1980.

Nader, Ralph, and William Taylor. *The Big Boys: Power and Position in American Business.* New York: Pantheon Books, 1986.

Taft Group, Inc. *Taft Corporate Giving Directory: Comprehensive Profiles & Analyses of Major Philanthropic Programs,* rev. ed. Washington, DC: The Taft Group, Inc., 1989.

Will, Rosalyn, Alice Tepper Marlin, Benjamin Corson, Jonathan Schorsch, et. al. *Shopping for a Better World.* New York: Council on Economic Priorities, 1989.

Zeitz, Baila, and Lorraine Dusky. *The Best Companies for Women.* New York: Simon & Schuster, 1988.

NOTES

Introduction
1. Eric Eckholm, "River Blindness: Conquering an Ancient Scourge," *The New York Times Magazine*, January 8, 1989.

CHAPTER 1
1. "The Mommy Track," *Business Week*, March 20, 1989.

CHAPTER 2
1. "TV is Giving Star Status to Environment," *The Wall Street Journal*, October 3, 1989.
2. Joan Bavaria, "Business, Clean Up Your Environmental Act!," *Newsday*, September 7, 1989.
3. "A New Sales Pitch: The Environment," *Business Week* (July 24, 1989), p. 50.
4. William Ruckelshaus, "The Politics of Waste Disposal," *The Wall Street Journal*, September 5, 1989.
5. "Waste Not, Want Not? Not Necessarily," *Business Week*, July 17, 1989.
6. "A New Sales Pitch," p. 50.
7. Ibid.
8. "Save the Trees—And You May Save a Bundle," *Business Week*, September 4, 1989.

9. Lester Brown, et. al., *State of the World 1989* (New York: W. W. Norton & Co., 1989), p. 67.
10. "The Next Love Canal?" *Business Week*, August 7, 1989.
11. "Kodak Says Drums of Chemicals Leaked, Releasing Hazy Cloud," *The Wall Street Journal*, September 8, 1989.
12. *State of the World 1989*, p. 78.
13. "AT&T's Big Push," *Electronic Business*, September 18, 1989.
14. "Detroit's Big Worry for the 1990s: The Greenhouse Effect," *Business Week*, September 4, 1989.
15. "Arco to Offer New Blend of Low-Emission Gasoline," *The Wall Street Journal*, August 16, 1989.
16. Wayne Owens, "Turn the Valdez Cleanup Over to Mother Nature," *The Wall Street Journal*, July 27, 1989.
17. "Getting Ready for Exxon vs. Practically Everybody," *Business Week*, September 25, 1989.
18. "Troubled Waters," *Business Week*, October 12, 1987.

CHAPTER 3
1. Fred Rasheed, "Toward Economic Empowerment," *Minority Business Journal of Kansas City* (January/February 1989), p. 5.
2. Catalyst, Working Women Fact Sheet (New York, 1989).
3. "The New Civil Rights Movement," *Ebony*, August 1989.
4. "Investing: The Profits of Conscience," *Lear's*, November/December 1988.
5. Baila Zeitz and Lorraine Dusky, *The Best Companies for Women* (New York: Simon & Schuster, 1988), p. 374.
6. "The 50 Best Places for Blacks to Work," *Black Enterprise*, February 1989.
7. Dana Friedman, *Child Care Makes It Work* (Washington, D.C.: National Association for the Education of Young Children, 1986).
8. Catalyst, Parental Leave Fact Sheet (New York, 1989).
9. Catalyst, Working Women Fact Sheet (New York, 1989).
10. "Watch that leer, stifle that joke," *Forbes*, May 15, 1989.
11. *The Best Companies for Women*, p. 373.
12. "Flight Attendants at Pan Am Settle a Weighty Matter," *The Wall Street Journal*, September 1, 1989.
13. *National Boycott News* (Spring/Summer 1989), p. 157.
14. Ibid., p. 161.
15. "Unleashed Power: Activists Score a Victory on ddI," *Village Voice*, August 1, 1989.

CHAPTER 4

1. "Real Sanctions, Real Change," editorial by Diane K. Bartz, *Multinational Monitor*, September 1988.
2. "Tighter Sanctions Eyed by Congress," *Money Matters* (Working Assets' Newsletter), Summer 1989.
3. "Bishop Desmond Tutu," *Rolling Stone*, November 21, 1985.
4. Michael Maren, "Fortress South Africa," *African Report*, March - April 1989.
5. Russell Mokhiber and E. Virgil Falloon, "The 10 Worst Corporations of 1988," *Multinational Monitor*, December 1988.

CHAPTER 5

1. Robert Levering, Milton Moskowitz, and Michael Katz, *The 100 Best Companies to Work for in America* (New York: NAL Penguin, 1985), p. 137.
2. Ibid., p. 90.
3. Dick Youngblood, "Safety Pays Several Ways at H. B. Fuller," *Star Tribune* (Minneapolis, Minnesota), December 19, 1988.
4. "Companies Step in Where the Schools Fail," *New York Times*, September 26, 1989.
5. "Aetna Schools New Hires in Basic Workplace Skills," *The Wall Street Journal*, November 10, 1989.
6. *Label Letter* (Washington, D.C.: Union Label & Service Trades Department, AFL-CIO), September/October 1989.
7. "Challenging Concessions," *Multinational Monitor*, March 1989.
8. Franklin's *insight* (Boston: Franklin Insight, Inc.), September 15, 1989.
9. Rosalyn Will, Alice Tepper Marlin, Benjamin Corson, Jonathan Schorsch, et. al., *Shopping for a Better World* (New York: Council on Economic Priorities, 1989), p. 5.
10. Jim Donahue, "The Foundations of Apartheid and the Nuclear Industry," *Multinational Monitor* (December 1988), p. 7.

CHAPTER 6

1. Catherine Breslin, "Day of Reckoning," *Ms.*, June 1989.
2. "Blood on Their Shields," *Ms.*, June 1989.
3. Public Citizen Health Research Group, correspondence dated February 7, 1987, October 29, 1986 and October 31, 1984.
4. *INFACT Brings GE to Light* (Boston: INFACT, 1988).
5. "PACs a Menace to Democracy," *Boston Globe*, September 1, 1985.
6. Lester Brown, et. al., *State of the World 1989* (New York: W. W. Norton & Co., 1989), p. 176.

7. "Finding a Burial Place for Nuclear Wastes Grows More Difficult," *New York Times*, December 5, 1989.
8. "There's More Than One Way to Skin an Amoeba," *Business Week*, October 30, 1989.

CHAPTER 8

1. "AMP Brings Quality to the Countryside," *Electronic Business*, October 16, 1989.
2. "AT&T: All in the Family," *Newsweek*, June 12, 1989.
3. *National Boycott News* (Spring/Summer 1989), p. 40.
4. *The Wall Street Journal*, August 3, 1989.
5. "AT&T's Big Push," *Electronic Business*, September 18, 1989.
6. "AT&T's New Pact on Union Benefits," *Business Week*, June 12, 1989.
7. Franklin's *insight*, (Boston: Franklin Insight, Inc.), September 15, 1989.
8. Milton Moskowitz and Carol Townsend, "The 60 Best Companies for Working Mothers," *Working Mother*, October 1989.
9. "Arco to Offer New Blend of Low Emission Gasoline," *The Wall Street Journal*, August 16, 1989.
10. "Waste Not, Want Not? Not Necessarily," *Business Week*, July 17, 1989.
11. Jerry Edgerton, "Tanker from Hell," *Money*, June 1989.
12. "The 50 Best Places for Blacks to Work," *Black Enterprise*, February 1989.
13. Baila Zeitz and Lorraine Dusky, *The Best Companies for Women* (New York: Simon and Schuster, 1988).
14. "'We decided to show how things can work,'" *Forbes*, September 18, 1989.
15. "Bell Atlantic Units Get Pact Ending Strike," *The Wall Street Journal*, August 29, 1989.
16. "America's Most Admired Corporations," *Fortune*, January 29, 1990.
17. Franklin's *insight*, October 1989.
18. Steven D. Lydenberg, Alice Tepper Marlin, and Sean O'Brien Strub, *Rating America's Corporate Conscience* (Reading: Addison-Wesley Publishing Co., 1986), p. 349.
19. "The New Power in Black & Decker," *Fortune*, January 2, 1989.
20. "Boeing Is Said Ready to Accept Felony Charges," *The Wall Street Journal*, November 6, 1989.
21. "Businesses Are Signing up for Ethics 101," *Business Week*, February 15, 1989.

22. "Why Boeing's Hard Line Didn't Pay Off," *Business Week*, December 4, 1989.
23. Franklin's *insight*, August 15, 1989.
24. "Boeing Discovers Solar Cell Yielding Higher Efficiency," *The Wall Street Journal*, September 18, 1989.
25. "Boeing Co. to Pay Penalty of $200,000 for Safety Violations," *The Wall Street Journal*, September 14, 1989.
26. "OSHA Proposes Penalties, Citing 535 Violations at Mill," *The Wall Street Journal*, September 14, 1989.
27. Robert Massa, "Unleashed Power: Activists Score a Victory on ddI," *Village Voice*, August 1, 1989.
28. "Doctors Vow to Proscribe Infant-Formula Ad Plans," *The Wall Street Journal*, August 24, 1989.
29. "The 50 Best Places for Blacks to Work," *Black Enterprise*, February 1989.
30. Taft Group, Inc., *Taft Corporate Giving Directory: Comprehensive Profiles & Analyses of Major Philanthropic Programs*, revised edition (Washington, D.C.: The Taft Group, Inc., 1989).
31. "Businesses Are Signing up for Ethics 101," *Business Week*, February 15, 1989.
32. Susan Meeker-Lowry, *Economics as if the Earth Really Mattered* (Philadelphia: New Society Publishers, 1988), pp. 26-27.
33. "Citicorp and Brazil," *Multinational Monitor*, April 1989.
34. "America's Most Admired Corporations," *Fortune*, January 29, 1990.
35. "Coca-Cola Fund, RJR Nabisco Plan to Focus Their Giving on Education," *The Chronicle of Higher Education*, November 8, 1989.
36. *National Boycott News*, Spring/Summer 1989.
37. Ibid.
38. Ibid.
39. *The Best Companies for Women*, p. 312.
40. *GOOD MONEY*, November/December 1988.
41. Working Assets press release (San Francisco, Summer 1989).
42. "America's Most Admired Corporations," *Fortune*, January 29, 1990.
43. "Datapoint Suspends Preferred Dividend, Posts 1st Period Loss," *The Wall Street Journal*, December 11, 1989.
44. "A Raider Tries to Beat Asher Edelman at His Own Game," *Business Week*, September 25, 1989.
45. "At Digital Equipment, Slowdown Reflects Industry's Big Changes," *The Wall Street Journal*, September 15, 1989.

46. Robert Levering, Milton Moskowitz, and Michael Katz, *The 100 Best Companies to Work for in America* (New York: NAL Penguin, 1985), p. xi.
47. *GOOD MONEY*, November/December 1988.
48. Ruth Simon, "Deals That Smell Bad," *Forbes*, May 15, 1989.
49. Ibid., p. 52.
50. "Energy Dept. Says It Kept Secret Mishaps at Nuclear Weapons Plant," *New York Times*, October 4, 1988.
51. "Kodak Says Drums of Chemicals Leaked, Releasing Hazy Cloud," *The Wall Street Journal*, September 8, 1989.
52. "Companies Step in Where the Schools Fail," *New York Times*, September 26, 1989.
53. "U.S. Indicts Exxon Over Big Spill of Oil Last March in Alaska Bay," *The Wall Street Journal*, February 28, 1990.
54. "Getting Ready for Exxon vs. Practically Everybody," *Business Week*, September 25, 1989, p. 190.
55. Wayne Owens, "Turn the Valdez Cleanup Over to Mother Nature," *The Wall Street Journal*, July 27, 1989.
56. "Exxon, Alyeska Seek to Keep Spill Evidence Secret," *The Wall Street Journal*, December 29, 1989.
57. *The Best Companies for Women*, p. 107.
58. *Star Tribune* (Minneapolis, Minnesota), March 3, 1989.
59. "Federal Express Corp.'s Fliers Reject Affiliation with Air Line Pilots Union," *The Wall Street Journal*, October 27, 1989.
60. "Federal Express Faces Test of Pilots' Loyalty Since Purchasing Tiger," *The Wall Street Journal*, October 23, 1989.
61. "'Same Song, Second Verse,' At First Interstate?" *Business Week*, January 29, 1990.
62. *National Boycott News*, Spring/Summer 1989, pp. 19-20.
63. "Anders Is Set to Pilot General Dynamics," *The Wall Street Journal*, October 3, 1989.
64. "Sound Environmental Practices Add to Bottom Line," *Electronic Business*, September 18, 1989.
65. "GE Is Said to Agree to a Settlement in Pentagon Case," *The Wall Street Journal*, February 5, 1990.
66. "Plan to Release CFC Coolants Produces Heat," *The Wall Street Journal*, September 6, 1989.
67. "Deals That Smell Bad," *Forbes*, May 15, 1989.
68. "General Electric," *Multinational Monitor*, May 1988.
69. "The 50 Best Places for Blacks to Work," *Black Enterprise*, February 1989.

70. "GE Capital Corp. to Settle Discrimination Charges," *The Wall Street Journal*, October 4, 1989.
71. Milton Moskowitz, Michael Katz, and Robert Levering, ed., *Everybody's Business: An Almanac: The Irreverent Guide to Corporate America* (New York: Harper and Row, 1980).
72. "GM Bias Settlement Approved," *Detroit News*, September 6, 1989.
73. "Deals That Smell Bad," *Forbes*, May 15, 1989.
74. "How the UAW Is Doing Its Part for GM's Parts," *Business Week*, February 13, 1989.
75. "GM, Reversing Stance, Recalls 1.7 Million Cars," *The Wall Street Journal*, July 14, 1989.
76. *The 100 Best Companies to Work for in America*, p. 173.
77. *National Boycott News*, Spring/Summer 1989, pp. 104-106.
78. *Taft Corporate Giving Directory 1989*.
79. "Labor Letter," *The Wall Street Journal*, October 3, 1989.
80. "AT&T's Big Push," *Electronic Business*, September 18, 1989.
81. Anthony Sampson, *The Sovereign State of ITT* (New York: Stein & Day, 1973).
82. "International Flavors Smells like Money Again," *Business Week*, April 18, 1989.
83. *Label Letter*, September-October 1989.
84. "Businesses Are Signing up for Ethics 101," *Business Week*, February 15, 1989.
85. Ralph Nader and William Taylor, *The Big Boys: Power and Position in American Business* (New York: Pantheon Books, 1986), p. 439.
86. Karen Stults, "Tarnish on the Golden Arches," *Business and Society Review*, Fall 1987.
87. Brian Bremner, "A New Sales Pitch: The Environment," *Business Week*, July 24, 1989.
88. "McDonald's Acts to Recycle Plastic," *New York Times*, October 27, 1989
89. "McDonald's Battles Ban on Burger Boxes," *USA Today*, February 5, 1990.
90. *Multinational Monitor*, December 1989, p. 16.
91. *National Boycott News*, Spring/Summer 1989.
92. "The 50 Best Places for Blacks to Work," *Black Enterprise*, February 1989.
93. *The 100 Best Companies to Work for in America*, p. 470.

94. "Look Where Joan Kroc Is Throwing Her McNuggets," *Business Week*, September 5, 1988.

95. "Lumbering in the Concrete Forest," Franklin's *insight*, September 1989.

96. "The 60 Best Companies for Working Mothers," *Working Mother*, October 1989.

97. "Merrill Lynch Cuts Its Links to South Africa," *The Wall Street Journal*, November 16, 1989.

98. "Lumbering in the Concrete Forest," Franklin's *insight*, September 1989.

99. *Rating America's Corporate Conscience*, pp. 425-427.

100. "The 60 Best Companies for Working Mothers," *Working Mother*, October 1989.

101. "Firms Heed Women Employees' Needs," *The Wall Street Journal*, November 22, 1989.

102. "Deals That Smell Bad," *Forbes*, May 15, 1989, p. 52.

103. Franklin's *insight*, September 1989.

104. *Chicago Tribune*, May 30, 1989.

105. "Deals That Smell Bad," p. 52.

106. "What Hooker Told Whom, When, About Love Canal," *The Wall Street Journal*, June 19, 1980.

107. Stuart Gold, "Occidental Petroleum: Politics, Pollution and Profit," *Multinational Monitor*, July/August 1989.

108. "The Next Love Canal?," *Business Week*, August 7, 1989.

109. Franklin's *insight*, August 15, 1989.

110. "Hammer's Wasteland," *Multinational Monitor*, July/August 1989.

111. "Exxon Puts Cost of Cleanup at $1.28 Billion," *New York Times*, July 25, 1989.

112. "How OSHA Helped Organize the Meatpackers," *Business Week*, August 29, 1989.

113. *The Best Companies for Women*, p. 280.

114. *Everybody's Business*, p. 414.

115. *The Community Relations Report*, October 1986.

116. "Companies Step in Where the Schools Fail," *New York Times*, September 26, 1989.

117. "Ralston Purina to Buy Beech-Nut Baby Food," *New York Times*, September 16, 1989.

118. *Rating America's Corporate Conscience*, p. 367.

119. "Rockwell Touts Non-Aerospace Business," *The Wall Street Journal*, December 27, 1989.

120. "Rockwell on the Defensive," *Business Week*, February 8, 1988.

121. "Rockwell Bomb Plant Is Repeatedly Accused of Poor Safety Record," *The Wall Street Journal*, August 30, 1989.
122. Ibid.
123. "Rockwell Threatens to Close Nuclear Weapons Plant," *New York Times*, September 16, 1989.
124. *The 100 Best Companies to Work for in America*, p. 433.
125. "Tektronix, Atten-Hut!," *Business Week*, April 18, 1988, p. 33.
126. "Tektronix on Toxics: Looking Good by Using Less," *Electronic Business*, September 18, 1989, pp. 40-41.
127. "Junkins Cites Rule No. 1: Compete Worldwide," *Dallas Morning News*, July 30, 1987.
128. "Will the Carrot and Stick Work at United?," *Business Week*, February 6, 1989.
129. "Crisis and Credibility," *Defense News*, August 1, 1988.
130. "Getting with the Cleanup," *Newsweek*, September 25, 1989.

CHAPTER 9
1. "Abbott Labs Drug Plant Is Cited by FDA for Alleged Quality Control Violations," *The Wall Street Journal*, December 8, 1989.
2. "The 50 Best Places for Blacks to Work," *Black Enterprise*, February 1989.
3. "Aetna Schools New Hires in Basic Workplace Skills," *The Wall Street Journal*, November 10, 1989.
4. Russell Mokhiber and E. Virgil Falloon, "The 10 Worst Corporations of 1988," *Multinational Monitor*, December 1988.
5. "Supreme Court Refuses to Hear Challenges in A. H. Robins Case," *The Wall Street Journal*, November 7, 1989.
6. Steven D. Lydenberg, Alice Tepper Marlin, and Sean O'Brien Strub, *Rating America's Corporate Conscience* (Reading: Addison-Wesley Publishing Co., 1986); Milton Moskowitz, Michael Katz, and Robert Levering, ed., *Everybody's Business: An Almanac: The Irreverent Guide to Corporate America* (New York: Harper and Row, 1980).
7. "The 10 Worst Corporations of 1988," *Multinational Monitor*, December 1988.
8. Franklin's *insight* (Boston: Franklin Insight, Inc.), October 15, 1989.
9. "Supreme Court Refuses to Hear Challenges in A. H. Robins Case," *The Wall Street Journal*, November 7, 1989.
10. Statement of August A. Busch III/Rev. Jesse L. Jackson, Press release from Anheuser-Busch, September 8, 1983.
11. "The 50 Best Places for Blacks to Work," *Black Enterprise*, February 1989.

12. "Doing Well by Doing Good," *Newsweek*, July 10, 1989.
13. *Clean Yield*, August 1989.
14. "Asbestos Dilemma," *Real Estate*, January 9, 1987.
15. "The 60 Best Companies for Working Mothers," *Working Mother*, October 1989.
16. "Campbell Soup's McGovern Forced Out; Baum, Harper Will Run Firm as Team," *The Wall Street Journal*, November 2, 1989.
17. "We're Not Running the Company for the Stock Price," *Forbes*, September 19, 1989.
18. *Rating America's Corporate Conscience*, pp. 123-124.
19. "Snap, Crackle, Stop," *Business Week*, September 25, 1989.
20. "Cleaning up on the Coming Cleanup," *Business Week*, October 16, 1989.
21. *Rating America's Corporate Conscience*, p. 312.
22. "The 50 Best Places for Blacks to Work," *Black Enterprise*, February 1989.
23. Ruth Simon, "Deals That Smell Bad," *Forbes*, May 15, 1989.
24. "We Don't Advertise," *Forbes*, June 12, 1989.
25. *National Boycott News*, Spring/Summer 1989, pp. 157-165.
26. "AFL-CIO Ends 10-Year Boycott of Coors," *National Boycott News* (Spring/Summer 1989), pp. 157-158.
27. Ibid., p. 161.
28. "Coors May Take a Gulp of a Rival Brew," *Business Week*, August 21, 1989, p. 70.
29. "One Firm's Bid to Keep Blacks, Women," *The Wall Street Journal*, February 16, 1989.
30. *Chicago Tribune*, May 30, 1989.
31. "With Its Spirit Shaken But Unbent, Cummins Shows Decade's Scars," *The Wall Street Journal*, December 13, 1989.
32. "Dayton Hudson Says: 'Play Nice,'" *Business Week*, November 20, 1989.
33. "Dun's Credit Reports, Vital Tool of Business, Can Be Off the Mark," *The Wall Street Journal*, October 5, 1989.
34. "Famed Credit Checker Dun & Bradstreet Gets a Few High Marks Itself as a Stock Purchase," *The Wall Street Journal*, November 9, 1989.
35. Tony Andersen (interview), *The Non-Profit Times*, June 1989.
36. Baila Zeitz and Lorraine Dusky, *The Best Companies for Women*, (New York: Simon and Schuster, 1988), p. 374.
37. "Cereal Makers Using Psyllium Face Scrutiny by FDA," *The Wall Street Journal*, September 1, 1989.

38. *Everybody's Business*, p. 576.
39. Franklin's *insight*, "Lumbering in the Concrete Forest," September 1989.
40. "Doctors Vow to Proscribe Infant-Formula Ad Plans," *The Wall Street Journal*, August 24, 1989.
41. "Gillette Closes Controversial Lab," *National Boycott News*, Spring/Summer 1989.
42. *Everybody's Business*, p. 297.
43. "Goodyear's Bribes," *Multinational Monitor*, June 1989.
44. Eloise Salholz, "The Next Love Canal?," *Newsweek*, August 7, 1989.
45. "The 60 Best Companies for Working Mothers," *Working Mother*, October 1989.
46. *Clean Yield*, July 1989.
47. Robert Levering, Milton Moskowitz, and Michael Katz, *The 100 Best Companies to Work for in America* (New York: NAL Penguin, 1985), p. 192.
48. "Fighting Back: The Resurgence of Social Activism," *Business Week*, May 22, 1989, p. 34.
49. "Kimmins Environmental Is Ready to Play with the Big Boys," *The Investment Reporter*, November-December 1989.
50. "Small Tots, Big Biz," *The New York Times Magazine*, January 29, 1989.
51. *The Best Companies for Women*.
52. *Everybody's Business*, p. 726.
53. Standard & Poor's *Stock Reports*, August 1989.
54. Franklin's *insight*, October 1989.
55. "The Mary Kay of the Herb Industry," *Business Week*, May 22, 1989.
56. "Nynex Reaches Accord with Striking Unions," *The Wall Street Journal*, November 14, 1989.
57. *GOOD MONEY*, November-December 1988.
58. "It Ain't Glamorous, but the Money Sure Is Good," *Business Week*, August 28, 1989.
59. "Flight Attendants at Pan Am Settle a Weighty Matter," *The Wall Street Journal*, September 1, 1989.
60. "U.S. to Continue Probing Pfizer's Troubled Valve," *The Wall Street Journal*, February 27, 1990.
61. Ibid.
62. "The 50 Best Places for Blacks to Work," *Black Enterprise*, February 1989.

63. Russell Mokhiber and E. Virgil Falloon, "The 10 Worst Corporations of 1988," *Multinational Monitor*, December 1988, pp. 18-19.
64. "Philip Morris to Launch Image Ads," *The Wall Street Journal*, November 1, 1989.
65. *Everybody's Business*, p. 525.
66. *The Best Companies for Women*, p. 284.
67. "In a Fast-paced World, Procter & Gamble Sets Its Store in Old Values," *The Wall Street Journal*, September 21, 1989.
68. "A New Sales Pitch: The Environment," *Business Week*, July 24, 1989.
69. "Quaker Oats Is Sued by Texas Over Ads That Claim Cereal Reduces Health Risk," *The Wall Street Journal*, September 8, 1989.
70. "Churches Join Shell Boycott," *Multinational Monitor*, December 1988; "Shell Meeting Ends in Uproar," *Financial Times*, May 12, 1989.
71. "Deals That Smell Bad," *Forbes*, May 15, 1989.
72. "The 50 Best Places for Blacks to Work," *Black Enterprise*, February 1989.
73. "Safety-Kleen Tidies up After the Little Guys," *Business Week*, October 5, 1987.
74. Franklin's *insight*, October 1989.
75. *National Boycott News*, Spring/Summer 1989.
76. Franklin's *insight*, September 15, 1989.
77. *Everybody's Business*, p. 849.
78. "Deals That Smell Bad," *Forbes*, May 15, 1989.
79. *Multinational Monitor*, December 1988.
80. "Eastern Pilots, Attendants End 264-Day Strike," *The Wall Street Journal*, November 24, 1989.
81. Editorial, "Challenging Concessions," *Multinational Monitor*, March 1989.
82. "The 60 Best Companies to Work for in America," *Working Mother*, October 1989.
83. "Good Times Again for Carbide?" *New York Times*, August 13, 1989.
84. "The 10 Worst Corporations of 1988," *Multinational Monitor*, December 1988.
85. "While Bhopal Waits, Union Carbide Cuts Its Losses," *Multinational Monitor*, March 1988.
86. "Union Carbide," *Multinational Monitor*, October 1988.
87. "Deals That Smell Bad," *Forbes*, May 15, 1989.

88. "Cleaning up on the Coming Cleanup," *Business Week*, October 16, 1989.
89. *Chicago Tribune*, May 30, 1989.
90. "Europe's Garbage Smells Sweet to Waste Management," *Business Week*, May 29, 1989.
91. "Cleaning up on the Coming Cleanup," *Business Week*, October 16, 1989.
92. "Recycling Concern Agrees to Acquire Marketing of Fortrel," *The Wall Street Journal*, August 24, 1989.
93. "Boosters of Impending Wheelabrator Merger See Gold in Nation's Mounting Garbage Piles," *The Wall Street Journal*, July 18, 1989.
94. "Zenith Electronics to Sell Computer Unit to France's Bull for up to $65 Million," *The Wall Street Journal*, October 3, 1989.

Pharos Books are available at special discounts on bulk purchases for sales promotions, premiums, fundraising or educational use. For details, contact the Special Sales Department, Pharos Books, 200 Park Avenue, New York, NY 10166